Democracy at Risk

CHICAGO STUDIES IN AMERICAN POLITICS

A series edited by Benjamin I. Page, Susan Herbst, Lawrence R. Jacobs, and James Druckman

Democracy at Risk

How Terrorist Threats Affect the Public

Jennifer L. Merolla and
Elizabeth J. Zechmeister

The University of Chicago Press | Chicago and London

Jennifer L. Merolla is associate professor in the Department of Politics and Policy at Claremont Graduate University. Elizabeth J. Zechmeister is assistant professor of political science at Vanderbilt University.

The University of Chicago Press, Chicago 60637
The University of Chicago Press, Ltd., London
© 2009 by The University of Chicago
All rights reserved. Published 2009
Printed in the United States of America

18 17 16 15 14 13 12 11 10 09   1 2 3 4 5

ISBN-13: 978-0-226-52054-4   (cloth)
ISBN-13: 978-0-226-52055-1   (paper)
ISBN-10: 0-226-52054-4   (cloth)
ISBN-10: 0-226-52055-2   (paper)

Library of Congress Cataloging-in-Publication Data

Merolla, Jennifer Lee, 1975–
    Democracy at risk : how terrorist threats affect the public / Jennifer L. Merolla and Elizabeth J. Zechmeister.
        p.   cm.
    Includes bibliographical references and index.
    ISBN-13: 978-0-226-52054-4 (cloth : alk. paper)
    ISBN-13: 978-0-226-52055-1 (pbk. : alk. paper)
    ISBN-10: 0-226-52054-4 (cloth : alk. paper)
    ISBN-10: 0-226-52055-2 (pbk. : alk. paper)
    1. Terrorism—Prevention—Government policy—United States—Public opinion. 2. Terrorism—United States—Prevention. 3. Voting—United States. 4. Political psychology. I. Zechmeister, Elizabeth J., 1972– II. Title.
    HV6432.M47 2009
    363.325'12—dc22

                                                        2009010523

Contents

For Web Supplements A, B, and C, see http://www.press.uchicago.edu/books/merolla.

Figures

Acknowledgments

This project had two starting points. The first dates back to our days as graduate students at Duke University, when the foundation of a strong friendship and collaborative relationship was formed. The second dates to a spring day in northern California when, over a glass of Napa Valley wine and as freshly minted PhDs, we began a long conversation about the ways in which context influences political behavior. What you will be reading was originally meant to be a book about the conditions under which different candidate traits carry more or less weight in the voting booth. We may still write that book one day and, in fact, the current book does devote some attention to this question. Our choice, however, to begin with a look at the effects of terrorist threat on candidate traits led us down a path that ultimately is centered on the former more than the latter.

As we implemented and then analyzed the data from this project's first experiment, we became increasingly interested in the many different ways in which the attacks of September 11 and the threat of future attacks have affected and continue to affect citizens around the globe. Rare as it might be for a couple of academics to agree with Dick Cheney, we nonetheless agree that the attacks led to a fundamental shift in how citizens engage in the political world. More specifically, the specter of terrorist threat affects how citizens interact with each other, how they evaluate their political leaders and make decisions in the voting booth, as well as their preferences over interaction with other nations.

Despite the somber topic, we thoroughly enjoyed the process of developing this book project. Academia, at its core, is a social phenomenon in which researchers independently, in pairs, or in larger groups, seek to make contributions that are grounded in previous research, speak to current research, and (ideally) influence future research. In the case of this particular project, the synergy produced by our own collaboration, by our work with graduate students, and by the process of soliciting feedback from others along the way was energizing, productive, and enjoyable. For graduate students in the middle of their studies, or undergraduates contemplating a career in academia, we would like to say unequivocally, yes, this is a great job.

This project would not have been possible without the support, advice, and feedback of countless individuals, and the support of various institutions. We attempt to identify and thank the support of those key people and organizations in what follows. To the extent that we accidentally omit someone from this list, we apologize for this. Such omissions and, of course, any errors or weaknesses that remain in the manuscript itself are our responsibility alone.

Funding from a variety of sources helped to make this project possible. We are grateful for support received from the political science departments at the University of California–Davis and Claremont Graduate University. We also benefited from several small grants internal to both universities, including several awards from the Institute for Governmental Affairs (IGA) at UC–Davis and two Fletcher Jones grants from CGU. We further thank IGA for assistance with outside funding applications. A grant from the University of California Institute on Global Conflict and Cooperation helped to cover the costs of our experimental work in Mexico and allowed us to expand the scope of the project to consider foreign policy preferences.

The vast majority of data we use in this project comes from experiments conducted within the Department of Political Science at UC–Davis. We are eternally grateful to Bob Huckfeldt for so generously sharing his research lab and related resources. We also thank John Daniels and the Social Science Data Service (SSDS) for technical help with the UC–Davis lab studies. We thank Cindy Kam, Bob Huckfeldt, and Walt Stone for helping to create The Omnibus Project (TOP), an organization that facilitates the collaborative collection of experimental data in the political science department at UC–Davis. We ran five experiments via TOP from the fall of 2004 to the spring of 2007 (one with a nonstudent subject pool), and therefore our debt to this resource and these people is significant. We also owe thanks to various members of TOP for their contributions to the shared data collection processes, to the faculty who contributed to the subject pool, and to the undergraduate and graduate research assistants who staffed the lab on those five occasions.

We also use data from an experimental study we conducted in Mexico, at the Instituto Tecnológico Autónomo de México (ITAM). The political science department at ITAM has welcomed us on a number of occasions, as we have undertaken investigations on their campus. We thank the department and, in particular, Eric Magar and Jeff Weldon for hosting our research and helping us to find research assistants. Finally, we are grateful to Ulises Beltrán for generously allowing us to place questions on the CSES-CIDE national survey in Mexico, sharing the entire dataset expeditiously, and for bringing us to Mexico City to present and receive feedback on our results.

One of the most enjoyable aspects of this project was our work with graduate students. We have many individuals to thank who assisted on this project while pursuing their graduate studies. First and foremost, we would like to thank Travis Coan and Jennifer Ramos for coauthoring chapter 6 of this book. Their hard work, great ideas, and expertise in international relations helped to complete our story of how citizens cope with conditions of terror threat. Jennifer was also a collaborator on several projects related to the book, including a study of charisma and evaluations of George W. Bush in the 2004 presidential election, as well as two experimental studies on authoritarian attitudes. We draw from our collaborative work with Jennifer on the subject of charisma in chapters 1 and 5, which are influenced by and contain some original elements of an article that was published by the *Journal of Politics* (Merolla, Ramos, and Zechmeister 2007). Some ideas about authoritarianism presented in chapter 1 first appeared in a conference paper on which Jennifer collaborated (Merolla, Ramos, and Zechmeister 2006); this conference paper also contained some of our original analyses of two experimental studies focused on authoritarianism, and we present an updated subset of those analyses alongside other work in chapter 3. Travis's imprint is likewise discernable in other parts of the manuscript; for example, he assisted with some research for the introduction. We owe thanks to Carl Palmer, who programmed all of our experimental studies at UC–Davis, transformed the data into Stata format, and helped oversee various aspects related to managing the lab. Jen Wilking played a role, in her work on the UC–Davis nonstudent study, as she oversaw recruitment efforts and the implementation of the lab study, as part of her collaborative work with Zechmeister on a different project with Cindy Kam. Other graduate students at UC–Davis played smaller but helpful roles working in the lab. At Claremont Graduate University, Caryn Peiffer provided research assistance for the introduction and read through several drafts of the chapters as we were preparing the manuscript for submission, while Katie Bryant, Lindsay Eberhardt, Zhidong Fang, Evis Mezini, Saúl Sandoval Perea, and Maja Primorac helped with general research assistance. We would like to thank our undergraduate research assistants at ITAM, Manuel Cabal, Humberto Pedro Moreno, and Patrick Signoret, who helped with translating the study materials, setting up the logistics of the study, running the study, and entering the data. Finally, we also acknowledge some very helpful assistance by undergraduates at UC–Davis, including those who worked in the lab during the course of the studies and Melina Casillas, who helped us to prepare the study instruments for Mexico.

The project also benefited from presentations we delivered at various stages of the project. We received constructive feedback from participants in the Political Psychology working group at the University of Chicago, the Dartmouth College American Politics Seminar, the UC–Davis Micro Politics Group, and the political science departments at UC–Riverside, Stanford, Claremont Graduate University, and Vanderbilt. We are especially grateful to John Aldrich, Mike Munger, and Emerson Niou for sponsoring a two-day workshop at Duke on the first draft of the book. We received valuable feedback from the faculty and graduate students who took the time and effort to attend, and who represented several subfields within the discipline. We also thank Renan Levine and Laura Stephenson for serving as discussants during this two-day workshop, and for the helpful feedback they provided in those sessions and beyond.

It is a next to impossible task for us to list and thank all of the individual people who provided feedback on aspects of the project along the way. We would like to offer our sincere thanks to everyone who provided comments, encouragement, advice and, support with respect to different components of the project. This list includes John Aldrich, Allyson Benton, Michelle Bligh, Shaun Bowler, John Brehm, Darren Davis, John Geer, Paul Gronke, Kirk Hawkins, Marc Hetherington, Michael Hogg, Vincent Hutchings, Bob Jackman, Joe Klesner, Claire Kramer, Joy Langston, Rick Lau, Chap Lawson, Milton Lodge, Michael Parkin, Jason Reifler, Don Rothchild, Andreas Schedler, Jean Schroedel, Matt Singer, John Transue, Nicholas Valentino, and Carole Wilson. We owe a special debt of gratitude to Cindy Kam, who provided extensive feedback on our early conference papers and articles, read several draft chapters, and was also a collaborator on some of the omnibus data collection processes. We are especially grateful to Ted Brader for his careful reading of several versions of the manuscript and thoughtful comments. We also want to thank other individuals who read several chapters and/or working papers and provided constructive comments, including Adam Berinsky, Bob Huckfeldt, Renan Levine, and Laura Stephenson. Andy Apodaca and Andy Tardibuono also read full chapters and provided critical feedback. We must also thank Bob Huckfeldt, again, this time for helping put us in contact with the University of Chicago Press.

It has been truly a pleasure to work with the University of Chicago Press. We thank John Tryneski, Susan Herbst, and Jamie Druckman for so enthusiastically supporting the project early on. John and Rodney Powell made the whole process smooth and seamless. We especially thank Susan and John for pushing us to write in a more accessible and digestible way! The manuscript was also greatly strengthened by the two reviewers, and we are grateful for their frank, clear, and thoughtful reactions.

We now come to the section in which we want to thank our family and friends. We want to first thank John Aldrich, whom we still to this day feel honored to call a friend. We owe a special thanks to John for his mentorship, friendship, and advice throughout the years. It was through working on projects with him at Duke that we began to collaborate and, through this and other collaborations at Duke, learned how rewarding collaborative research can be. As we indicated above, John also worked to help organize a two-day workshop for this project. His influence, in short, is present in this project at the start and the end, and in many ways in between.

We would like to thank the wonderful friends and colleagues we have met in our short time as academics. These people have influenced our approach to political science and the project itself in numerous small ways, by the role models they are and the support, encouragement, and advice they've given to us as we have worked on this project.

We would like to thank Andy Apodaca for his voiceover work and Andy Tardibuono for his editing work. We are especially grateful for getting the spousal-discounted rate for these tasks!

Jenn would like to thank her family and friends for all of their love, encouragement, and support. To my parents, thank you for always encouraging me to follow my goals even when that meant living further away. To Andy, thank you for all of your help and enthusiasm throughout this project, from editing our treatments, to reading drafts, to our countless conversations about it, to making me take breaks from time to time.

Liz would like to thank her family and friends for all the influence they have had on the type of person and academic she has become; all errors remain her own. To Andy, from the bottom of my heart, thank you for your unfaltering support, from graduate school applications, to graduate school itself, to junior faculty status, with each step getting just a bit crazier along the way. The introduction of a wonderful, bright, funny, and occasionally rambunctious baby girl along the way didn't make our life more sane, but I wouldn't trade it for the world.

Introduction

[T]hey're doing everything they can to find ways to strike us.
And they are actively . . . trying to get their hands on deadlier
weapons than anything they've ever used before—specifically
chemical, biological agent, or even a nuclear weapon, if they can.
And you can imagine what would happen if we had an Al Qaeda
cell loose in the middle of one of our own cities with a nuclear
weapon. The devastation that that would bring down on hun-
dreds of thousands, maybe millions of Americans.

Vice President Dick Cheney, August 6, 2004

The attacks on September 11, 2001, jarringly awoke the average
American to the grim reality that even a major power like the United
States is susceptible to international terrorism. Prior to 9/11, the
United States had not experienced a significant foreign attack on
its shores since Pearl Harbor and, in that case, the attack was by an
easily identified enemy who targeted a military base. Since 9/11,
the *threat* of another terrorist attack continues to loom large in the
minds of U.S. citizens, in particular during election years or when
the terror threat level is raised.

This is not only a U.S. phenomenon. In recent years, Al Qaeda,
groups affiliated with Al Qaeda, and other extremist groups have
waged their war against the West and Western interests by carrying out deliberate, violent, and lethal attacks in countries such
as Egypt, India, Indonesia, Kenya, Morocco, Saudi Arabia, Spain,

Turkey, and the United Kingdom. This list is not close to exhaustive, nor does it include other countries in which plots by international terrorists have been foiled. These attacks and plots have resulted in frequent reports by the media on the danger posed by international terrorism. Thus, even in the absence of a particular incident, the threat of future attacks often weighs heavily on the minds of individuals around the globe. These concerns affect people as they go about their everyday lives, including as they interact with the political world.

Our principal argument is the following: Politics proceeds under the shadow of terrorist threat, but *not* "as usual." Looking at the last several years, it is easy to find examples of cases in which concerns about terrorism have intersected with politics. In 2004 voters in Spain went to the polls just days after devastating train bombings in Madrid. In the summer of 2007 the new British prime minister's first week in office was occasioned by attempted terrorist attacks in London and Glasgow. And, as we already mentioned, it seems quite clear that even several years out from 9/11, the issues of terrorism and homeland security are still salient in the United States. Yet, while it appears that individuals are increasingly making political assessments, developing political attitudes, and expressing these under conditions of terrorist threats, we know little about how such crisis conditions affect citizens' preferences over domestic and foreign policies, their evaluations of leaders and the political system, and their political behavior.

In this book, we examine how the threat of terrorist attacks affects individuals across these numerous domains. Using data from both surveys and experiments, we compare citizens experiencing conditions of national security crisis (brought on by the threat of terrorism) to those experiencing other conditions, primarily times of well-being and prosperity or times of economic crisis. Our principal message and findings can be simply stated: the specter of terrorist threat results in attitudinal, evaluative, and behavioral shifts, some of which can potentially endanger democracy.

The arguments that we will make briefly here, and more fully in the next chapter, are meant to be general in scope. We expect that citizens in democratic nations around the globe will react similarly to the threat of international terrorism. That being said, many of our examples, and the majority of our data, come from the U.S. case. One reason for drawing many examples from the U.S. case is that the terrorist attacks that took place on 9/11 were lethal to an unprecedented degree. Second, there is more survey data related to terror threat and political behavior available in the U.S. context. Finally, as scholars located in the United States, we found it relatively easier to collect experimental data in this country. However, as a point of comparison, we also use data from Mexico, which differs from the United States in terms of its relatively weaker military strength, lower level of economic development, shorter history of party competition, and other factors. In particular, Mexico has been threatened by, but not hit by, an international terrorist attack. Where relevant, we insert discussion and examples from other countries into the text. In the book's conclusion, we return to a discussion of how general our results likely are to residents of other democratic nations threatened by international terrorism.

In the remainder of this introduction, we first set the stage, so to speak, by showing evidence that the scope and degree of threat posed by international terrorist activities have increased over time. We then present some initial theory and evidence concerning the ways in which citizens cope with this threat. That section is followed by a discussion of whether these methods of coping might actually threaten democracy. Finally, we conclude with a brief overview of the structure of the book.

Setting the Stage: The Terrorist Threat

While there is no universally agreed upon definition of terrorism, the U.S. Code defines terrorism as "premeditated, politically motivated violence perpetrated against noncombatant targets by sub-national groups or clandestine agents, usually intended to influence an audience."[1] Since terrorism is generally carried out by nonstate actors, it is similar in kind to other criminal acts. However, a few components of this definition distinguish terrorism from general criminal acts and, as well, from acts of war by a country. Unlike a criminal act, terrorist violence is generally connected to political goals and is intended to strike fear into the hearts of the public in the hope that the government will have little choice but to cede to the group's demands. In order to attain such influence, terrorist groups often claim credit for incidents, unlike more general criminals. Unlike state actors, terrorists often directly and openly target civilians in violation of international norms with respect to rules of war. While comprehensive in many ways, one factor missing from the U.S. Code definition of terrorism is the *threat* of violent actions. We will show that even the threat of a substantial attack can effectively terrorize a civilian population.

It is also worth distinguishing between domestic and international terrorism. Domestic terrorism is contained within one country, and typically propagated by residents of that territory, while international terrorism involves individuals and/or territory from more than one country.

Unless otherwise stated, throughout this book, we focus on the *threat posed by international terrorism*: the credible threat by foreign, nonstate actors to carry out violent and destructive acts against residents of a particular country.

The threat of international terrorism has become a permanent and growing fixture of modern times. In the last half of the twentieth century and into the new century, attacks and plots generated by international terrorist groups have grown in number, size, and geographic scope. The Memorial Institute for the Prevention of Terrorism tracked the number of international terrorist incidents from 1968 to 2006.[2] At the beginning of the series, in 1968, there were 97 incidents of international terrorism. A decade later, that number more than doubled to 220 annual incidents. International terrorist incidents continued to rise, reaching a peak in 1985 at 433 incidents. These numbers then declined to a low point of just over 100 incidents in 2000. The years since have seen a sharp increase, peaking again around 2004 with 395 incidents. The regions with the biggest increases in incidents over the last decade are the Middle East and Asia.

In addition to the mere number of events, the fatalities and injuries associated with terrorist incidents have climbed dramatically in recent years. In fact, a hallmark of the modern era of terrorism is the increasing size and magnitude of new plots and attacks, often aimed at highly visible targets (Laquer 1999). Earlier incidents of this type of attack include the 1993 World Trade Center bombings, which killed six people and injured more than 1,000 others.[3] Pre-2000, the number of terrorist-induced fatalities due to international terror incidents hovered between 0 and 500 (see fig. I.1). A huge spike in the number of fatalities occurred in 2001, as a result of 9/11. Excluding the nineteen hijackers, 2,974 people were killed in those attacks, the first time that so many civilians had been killed by a foreign attack on U.S. soil. Annual fatalities from international terrorist attacks declined again following 2001, but still remain mostly higher than they were pre-9/11. As an example of one post-9/11 incident, the 2004 Madrid train bombings resulted in 191 deaths. As the figure documents, the number of civilian injuries has increased significantly over time from the 1990s through the 2000s. Thus, the number of attacks is at historically high levels *and* these attacks are increasingly consequential with respect to the harm inflicted on innocent civilians. While Western nations have not witnessed the greatest increase in the number of incidents (as indicated above), they are among those experiencing the highest numbers of fatalities. Europe and the United States, along with the Middle East, top the list of regions most affected by high fatalities over the last decade.

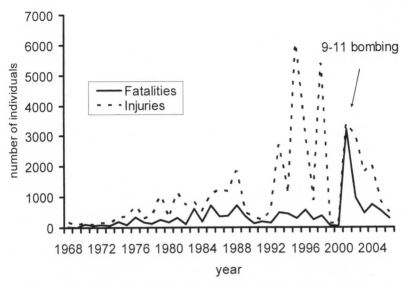

Figure I.1. Fatalities and injuries associated with international terror incidents, 1968–2006
Source: MIPT Terrorism Knowledge Database.

Given the spread and lethality of international terrorism in recent years, it is not surprising to find that individuals are worried about future attacks. The aftermath of 9/11 revealed numerous expressions of this concern by the public. Following the attacks, the *Washington Post* reported an increase in gas-mask sales, with one supplier indicating that he sold more than "1,000 gas masks in September, up from the usual 100 a year." High levels of anxiety were further evident in relatively low birth weights among children born in New York City immediately following 9/11. In interviews with reporters, citizens also expressed high levels of concern. One New Yorker decided to relocate to New Jersey within a month after the attack, but remarked, "I don't think that will make much of a difference. I don't think I will ever feel safe again." Two months after the attacks, a courier from New York admitted, "I still am a bit leery when jumbo jets fly by. I look up, and if I spot it, I keep an eye on its course and altitude." While these sentiments were registered soon after the attacks, five years later, many U.S. citizens still felt the same. In a survey interview, a receptionist from Brooklyn indicated, "I don't feel safe. I don't know when there will be another attack." Such feelings extended across the country. Interviewed around the same time, a woman living in San Jose, California, remarked, "I think that from now on, we're living under the fear of being attacked. They're planning things all the time."[4]

We can get a more general sense of worry in the United States by looking at data from the Gallup organization. Since 9/11, this polling organization has asked individuals: "How worried are you that you, or someone in your family, will be a victim of a terrorist attack?" Responses have indicated a relatively high and constant level of concern among a majority, or near majority, of the U.S. population. Between September 2001 and July 2007 the percent of individuals who indicated that they were "very worried" hovered around 10 percent, with minor fluctuations (see fig. I.2). As expected, these elevated worry levels were highest in September of 2001 (about 15%), then dipped down a bit, and spiked again after the Madrid train bombings in March of 2004 and after the London bombings in July of 2005. This portrait of concern about terrorism expands significantly if we look at those who said they were "somewhat worried." A full 35 percent indicated that they were somewhat worried about being the victim of a terrorist attack in the month that 9/11 occurred. The pattern of responses parallels, though at greater levels, the data on "very worried" dropping following September 2001 and spiking following attacks on other Western nations. In figure I.2, the line marked "combined worry" shows the combined percent of individuals indicating some or significant worry. The series begins and ends with over 45 percent of individuals worried that they will be personally affected by a terrorist attack. Data not shown here reveals a similar pattern (though even slightly more elevated on average) in response to questions asking about worry over the possibility of another terrorist attack on U.S. soil.[5]

Worry about terrorism is not confined to the U.S. public alone. The Pew Research Center for People and the Press conducted surveys in 2002 and 2007 across a range of countries and asked people to indicate whether terrorism was a very big problem, a moderately big problem, a small problem, or not a problem at all. In table I.1 we show the percent who responded that terrorism is a "very big problem." As we would expect, this number was high in the United States in 2002 (50%), but it is also high across many countries. For example, in 2002, significant numbers of people identified terrorism as a significant problem in many of the major industrialized countries in Europe, such as France (65%), Germany (45%), and Italy (71%). These numbers were similarly high in Mexico (69%) and in many other countries south of the United States, such as Argentina (65%), Brazil (56%), Peru (70%), and Venezuela (62%). Substantial portions of the civilian population in Asia and throughout the Middle East, such as in Pakistan (78%), Lebanon (40%), and South Korea (68%), also indicated that terrorism is a very big problem. Looking across time, we see that most of these

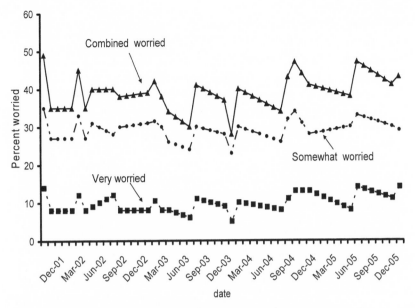

Figure I.2. Worry over being a "victim" of a terrorist attack, 2001–2007
Question: How worried are you that you or someone in your family will become a victim of terrorism: very worried, somewhat worried, not too worried, or not worried at all? "Worried" shows the total percent of individuals expressing either level of worry (very and somewhat).
Source: Gallup Poll; Pew Research Center

percentages decreased somewhat by 2007, but nonetheless remained fairly high. Exceptions to this pattern include Canada, in which the table shows a shift from 19 to 24 percent, and Britain, which went from 23 to 30 percent, between 2002 and 2007. What likely explains these atypical shifts across time is the fact that, in the intervening years, the United Kingdom was hit by a terrorist attack (in 2005) and Canada faced credible terrorist threats. We also see a high percentage in Spain, 66 percent, another country targeted by terrorist attacks (Spain was not included in the survey in 2002). In short, concern about terrorism has afflicted and presumably continues to afflict citizens around the globe.

There is simply no denying the fact that we live in a changed world. As the data show, international terrorist attacks worldwide are at historically high levels, and a new feature of these attacks is that they are more dangerous. Given these statistics, combined with high levels of media coverage and elite rhetoric, it seems natural that worry about terrorism is high among citizens living in a range of countries with different positions on the world stage and who have and have not been victims of international

Table I.1 Percent of individuals who think terrorism is a "very big problem"

Country	2002	2007	Country	2002	2007
Argentina	65	42	Kuwait	—	37
Bangladesh	92	77	Lebanon	40	76
Bolivia	58	42	Malaysia	—	10
Brazil	56	44	Mali	42	15
Britain	23	30	Mexico	69	50
Bulgaria	21	24	Morocco	—	81
Canada	19	24	Nigeria	—	40
Chile	—	46	Pakistan	78	76
China	—	11	Peru	70	70
Czech Republic	31	16	Poland	45	35
Egypt	—	53	Russia	65	48
Ethiopia	15	23	Senegal	66	22
France	65	54	Slovakia	28	17
Ghana	—	20	South Africa	34	20
Germany	45	31	South Korea	68	12
India	95	72	Spain	—	66
Indonesia	46	48	Sweden	—	3
Italy	71	73	Tanzania	27	19
Israel	—	70	Turkey	57	72
Ivory Coast	26	57	Uganda	52	34
Japan	—	59	Ukraine	33	23
Jordan	15	42	United States	50	44
Kenya	63	24	Venezuela	62	41

Source: Pew Global Attitudes Project

terrorism. This brings us to the heart of this book: How do citizens cope with anxiety over the threat posed by international terrorism, and what consequences might these reactions have for politics? We turn to exactly these questions in the next section.

How Citizens Cope with Terrorist Threats: Theory and Preliminary Evidence

Terrorist threats endanger individuals' physical, psychological, and even financial security. By their very nature they are collective crises and, therefore, create conditions in which solutions lie beyond individuals' particular decisions or actions. The argument that we develop and support in this book is the following. In reaction to conditions of terror threat, people adopt any combination of several coping strategies, which affect how they perceive and treat other individuals, their political leaders, and other nations.[6] One technique is designed to restore feelings of control and order by changing how one relates to other individuals. Expressions of this coping strategy are centered around increased distrust, hostility, intolerance, and punitiveness toward other individuals. A second technique is to find and turn over control to an external actor, such as a political figure whom one deems capable of solving or handling the crisis. Expressions of this coping strategy include the projection of unique leadership capabilities onto certain political leaders, an increased likelihood of voting for someone based on assessments of his or her leadership qualities, and an increased tendency to protect and assist the selected leader. A third strategy is used when considering how to treat other nation states (as well as people coming from other nation states). The expression of this third coping technique is increased preferences for the dual objectives of protecting the homeland while engaging on the terror front abroad.

A logical question that may arise with respect to these different coping strategies is whether they reflect purely instrumental reactions or whether they signal deeper psychological processes. By instrumental, we mean whether the strategies to cope with terrorist threat are things that one could easily and rationally determine are needed to resolve or mitigate the crisis. For example, a solid argument could be made that decisive and strong leaders are needed in times of threat. In fact, if we think of U.S. presidents who are typically considered great leaders, such as Abraham Lincoln and Franklin Delano Roosevelt, their tenure was characterized by conditions of grave threat. Preferring and seeking out strong leaders could conceivably lead to a quicker resolution to the crisis condition. Developing a preference for stronger domestic security and an activist foreign policy may also be considered an effective, instrumental response to an external threat. In each of these cases, we might applaud individuals for reacting in reasonable and beneficial ways in response to the given threat. Some aspects of the three coping strategies we identify can in fact be instrumental along similar lines.

However, some of these coping strategies reflect psychological processes that lie outside the realm of overt and rational calculations. While it may be instrumental to trade civil liberties for more security, is it instrumental to target certain groups for more punitive public policies, even those who are not at all related to the particular threat environment? We argue that the tendency to become less tolerant of different groups in society reflects a more psychological response to times of threat. Furthermore, while it may be instrumental to select decisive leaders in times of terror threat, *projecting* leadership qualities onto certain leaders arguably reflects a psychological desire to find a savior deemed capable of rescuing individuals from the crisis situation. Rather than merely making a rational calculation to elevate to office the most competent of leaders, we will show that individuals come to perceive selected leaders differently in times of crisis than they would otherwise. At the extreme, this process could negatively affect instrumental attempts to resolve the crisis, if individuals blindly pin their hopes on a relatively unqualified leader.

In the next chapter, we discuss each of these coping strategies in depth. Our particular focus is on the expressed manifestations of these coping strategies, though we will return to the question of whether these are grounded in purely instrumental, psychological, or both types of processes. For now, we present some preliminary evidence suggesting the use of these three coping strategies within the United States and abroad. Our intention here is to draw on existing data and scholarship to provide some initial support for the notion that, in times of terrorist threat, attitudes, evaluations, and behaviors with respect to other individuals, political leaders, and other nation states shift. And, moreover, they shift in ways that may place democracy at risk.

As noted above, one coping strategy in response to terrorist threat is to become more distrustful, hostile, intolerant, and punitive. Another way to state this is that some individuals may react to threat by becoming more authoritarian. An authoritarian individual is one who is relatively more morally absolute, more likely to obey authority, and more likely to conform to norms. In response to threatening conditions, authoritarian-inclined individuals may become more reverent with respect to symbols of authority and in-groups and, at the same time, less tolerant of societal out-groups. Such feelings likely underlie two attitudinal shifts that survey evidence, news stories, and scholarship have related to 9/11 and its aftermath: increased patriotism and hostility toward Arabs and Muslims.[7]

Survey evidence has documented these attitude shifts in the United States. In November of 2001, *Newsweek* asked citizens if they felt more patriotic since September 11. A whopping 78 percent said yes. Other surveys have shown that Americans have become more suspicious and less trusting of Arab and/or Muslim Americans in the post-9/11 world. In a CBS/*New York Times* poll in September of 2001, 28 percent of the public indicated that they thought that Arab Americans were more sympathetic to terrorists than were other American citizens. Years out from 9/11, 32 percent of the public thought U.S. Muslims are more loyal to Islam than the United States, 19 percent thought U.S. Muslims condone violence, and 54 percent were worried about radicals within the U.S. Muslim community.[8] Not only has the U.S. public expressed less trust in U.S. Muslims, they have also supported policies that single out those who likely belong to this group. In a 2001 Gallup Poll, 49 percent of the sample favored requiring Arabs, even U.S. citizens, to carry a special ID card. That number dipped slightly to 46 percent in a 2005 Gallup study and was even lower, at 39 percent, in a 2006 *USA Today*/Gallup poll. Meanwhile, 53 percent supported requiring Arabs, even U.S. citizens, to undergo more intensive security checks before boarding U.S. planes.[9]

Even more alarming is the fact that some citizens have not simply stated such beliefs but have acted on them with hostility. Soon after the calamitous events of September 11, 2001, the media around the world reported numerous incidents involving attacks on individuals perceived to be of Middle East origin and/or of Muslim faith. On September 14 *The Times* reported attacks on and threats against Islamic mosques and schools in London, Manchester, and Birmingham. On September 24 the *Sydney Morning Herald* described a "fourth major assault" on Muslims in the state of Queensland; in one of these incidents a "bus carrying Muslim children . . . had rocks, bottles, and other missiles hurled at it."[10] In the United States, anti-Islamic hate-crime incidents recorded by the FBI catapulted from 28 in 2000 to 481 in 2001.[11]

While the above data is suggestive of an increased sense of patriotism and intolerance of out-groups, scholars have conducted more detailed analysis of this topic. After 9/11, citizens came to have greater levels of identification with the country (Moskalenko, McCauley, and Rozin 2006). Those with high levels of worry about future attacks were more willing to increase surveillance on Arabs and Arab Americans, increase security checks on Arab visitors, and decrease visas to Arab countries (Huddy, Feldman, Taber, and Lahav 2005). This evidence is consistent with our first proposed coping mechanism, but it is also limited in some key ways. For example, explorations into intolerant attitudes and behaviors have typically been limited to a focus on Arab- and/or Muslim-appearing individuals. Does the range of authoritarian attitudinal shifts end there? We believe it does not. In addition, there is a tendency in much of this scholarship to assume that individuals respond similarly to worry about terrorist threats. Later in this book, we take up the task of establishing a more nuanced set of relationships among certain types of individuals, terror threat, and general authoritarian attitudes using both survey and experimental data. However, one thing should be clear from this brief introductory discussion: such attitudes and behaviors *may* threaten the very fabric of democracy by singling out particular groups as second-class citizens, which may lead to treatment and policies that deny equal rights and equal protection.

We now turn to some very preliminary evidence of the second strategy of coping, which entails looking for a leader capable of resolving the crisis situation. At a minimum, does available data suggest that people project leadership capabilities onto selected leaders in times of terror threat? Anecdotally, mentions of President George W. Bush and former New York mayor Rudy Giuliani as being strong leaders became ubiquitous after 9/11. In a LexisNexis database search of all U.S. newspapers and wires between March of 2001 and 2002, we found that the number of articles that mentioned Bush or Giuliani as a strong leader tripled after 9/11. The only survey-based indicators available for us to look at over time with respect to projections of leadership were approval ratings for these two leaders, pre- and post-9/11. During this time period, we were also able to look at approval ratings for another leader, Tony Blair of Great Britain. The approval ratings for all three political leaders are presented in figure I.3.

Bush began his presidency in the shadow of the controversy surrounding the 2000 election, in which he lost the popular vote but gathered enough Electoral College votes (and Supreme Court support) to win the election. Before the attacks of 9/11, his approval ratings hovered around 50 percent. Immediately following the attacks, his approval ratings spiked to over 80 percent and stayed high for a while before starting a gradual decline mostly due to disappointment with the war in Iraq. This huge rally behind Bush is at least consistent with our claim that individuals project leadership qualities onto select leaders during times of terror threat.

A similar pattern emerges for Giuliani. While pre-9/11 he had earned a positive reputation among some New Yorkers for improving the city (e.g., lowering crime rates), other citizens did not approve of his tactics. Furthermore, his image was scathed by various personal and professional scandals. Thus, Giuliani's approval level hovered around 40 to 50 percent for all of 1999, 2000, and most of 2001. His 42 percent approval rating on September 5, 2001, shot up to an 89 percent approval rating on November 7, 2001. We again witness a dramatic rally in the shadow of a terrorist attack, this time around the mayor of New York City. Giuliani became a household name following the attacks of 9/11. He went on to become *Time* magazine's Person of the Year for 2001, was a featured speaker at the 2004 Republican National Convention, and ran for the Republican presidential nomination (2008) on a national security platform.

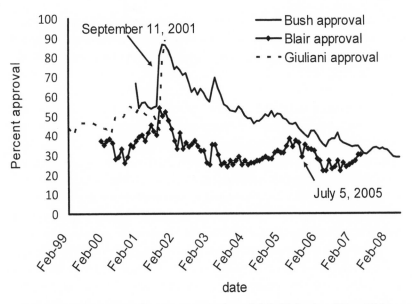

Figure I.3. Approval ratings for George W. Bush, Rudolph Giuliani, and Tony Blair, 2001–2008

Questions: Do you approve or disapprove of the way George W. Bush is handling his job as president?

Do you approve or disapprove of the way Rudolph Giuliani is handling his job as Mayor?

Are you satisfied or dissatisfied with the way Mr. Blair is doing his job as Prime Minister?

Sources: Multiple sources, accessed through Roper Polls Online Database (Bush); Quinnipiac University Poll, directed by Douglas Schwartz, Ph.D. (Giuliani); Ipsos MORI (Blair).

If we turn to Tony Blair, pre-9/11, his approval rating fluctuated greatly and ranged between about 27 and 42 percent. Even though the attacks of 9/11 occurred on U.S. soil, Tony Blair also experienced over a 10-percentage-point increase in approval from UK citizens following the event. After that point, his approval ratings declined likely due to British involvement in the Iraq war (which the public did not support). It is hard to tell if he received any boost in approval ratings immediately after the bombings in London on July 7, 2005, since our first available survey after that point was not until August 5. Overall, his approval ratings continued to slide as the unpopularity of the war in Iraq continued to mount with the British public.

Thus, across all three leaders, we find instances where terrorist attacks were followed by increases in approval ratings. Scholars have examined some of these rallies and have established a direct link between the attack and increased approval ratings (Kam and Ramos 2008; Hetherington and Nelson 2003). Put simply, individuals evaluated leaders differently under crisis conditions than they might otherwise. It could be argued that approval ratings soared in each of these cases because the leaders "earned it" by way of competent leadership in the aftermath of the attacks. While this is a possibility, we believe these reactions were based at least in part in deeper psychological processes by which individuals sought to restore their own sense of calm and hope by projecting greater evaluations onto these figures. This is, of course, difficult to substantiate with the approval ratings data alone, which do not capture the specific concepts in which we are most interested: perceptions of leadership abilities and the public's expressed willingness to protect and assist the given leader. Using both experimental and some survey evidence, we will explore such manifestations of the use of our second proposed coping strategy. While spikes in approval ratings may reflect more psychological processes, some of the other aspects of this coping mechanism that we assess in subsequent chapters likely also reflect instrumental motivations. Regardless, we will also provide reason to suspect that, to at least some degree, the specific expressions of this coping mechanism carry the potential to place democracy at risk.

Finally, we turn to the third strategy of coping, which concerns preferences over relations with other countries, individuals coming from other countries, and the general security of one's own country. To refresh, we expect that during times of terrorist threat people will support policies that protect the homeland within, while at the same time they will prefer greater engagement abroad. For example, with respect to protecting within, they will support policies that make it more difficult to enter and exit the country, as well as policies that enhance security (often at the expense of civil liberties). Engaging abroad can include militant actions such as attacking terrorist training camps as well as nonmilitant actions such as sharing intelligence with other nations. Support for these policies may reflect instrumental motivations on the part of citizens, though again they may also reflect more psychological processes. Surveys have included a wide range of questions related to these dual objectives; here we will just highlight a few bits of survey evidence that relate to this coping strategy.

Turning first to policies meant to secure the homeland, the post-9/11 U.S. public has been very supportive, even with respect to policies that might threaten civil liberties. For example, in surveys since 2002, the Gallup organization has asked respondents: "Which comes closer to your view? The government should take all steps necessary to prevent additional acts of terrorism in the U.S., even if it means your basic civil liberties would be violated. OR, The government should take steps to prevent additional acts of terrorism, but not if those steps would violate your basic civil liberties."

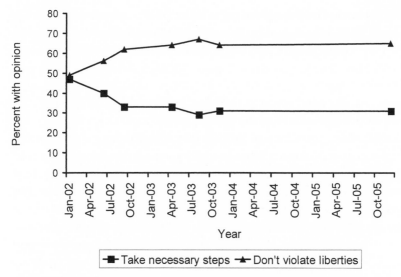

Figure I.4. Support for policies restricting civil liberties, 2002–2005
Question: Which comes closer to your view? The government should take all steps
necessary to prevent additional acts of terrorism in the U.S., even if it means your basic
civil liberties would be violated. OR, The government should take steps to prevent additional acts of terrorism, but not if those steps would violate your basic civil liberties."
Options rotated. Form B (N = 522, MoE ± 5).
Source: CNN/*USA Today*/Gallup Polls.

Responses to this question over time are presented in Figure I.4. In the poll
closest to 9/11 (January 2002), 47 percent of respondents chose the first
option. Thus, a high proportion of Americans was willing to have basic civil
liberties violated (one of the central tenets of democracy) in order to prevent additional acts of terrorism. While this support has waned over time,
as of December 2005, 31 percent of respondents still chose that option.
With respect to more specific types of policies, data from Gallup surveys
in 2005 and 2006 indicated that a majority of Americans supported the
PATRIOT Act and thought the Bush administration was right to engage in
wiretapping without a warrant.[12] On the other hand, and to provide some
balance to this discussion, a somewhat different trend is found in citizen
perceptions of whether the Bush administration went too far in restricting
people's civil liberties in order to fight terrorism. In June 2002 only 11
percent expressed this opinion (according to Gallup data), while in May
of 2006 41 percent expressed this opinion.

We see a similar willingness to restrict civil liberties in light of the terrorist threat in the case of the United Kingdom. In a survey conducted just

after the attacks in 2005, a You Gov/Mirror/GMTV survey found that 75 percent of the public supported a provision in the proposed new terror bill that would allow the government to hold terror suspects without trial. In a study by the same organization a year later, 69 percent of the public still supported holding terror suspects without trial (though the question now said for up to ninety days). In this study, 55 percent also supported the introduction of passenger profiling in airports.

If we turn to preferences for engaging abroad, there is evidence of support for this foreign policy orientation in both the United States and the United Kingdom. A vast majority of Americans supported the Bush administration's decision to send military forces into Afghanistan. For example, in a CNN/*USA Today*/Gallup poll in November of 2001, when asked whether the United States made a mistake by sending forces into Afghanistan, 89 percent of the public said no. When asked the same question in a poll conducted in July of 2004, the percentage of people saying no was exactly the same. Support for the Iraq war was also quite high early on, 71 percent in May 2003, according to the same polling organization. At the same time it is worth noting that support has waned over time as the United States has been unable to help the new government maintain stability and as the number of troops being killed has increased. In the 2006 survey of UK citizens discussed above, 53 percent thought that the United Kingdom needed to change its foreign policy to be tougher and more aggressive in response to the terrorist threat.

Of the three coping strategies we assess and examine, there has been more scholarly work that examines preferences over homeland security policies and international engagement (though it is not framed with respect to dual foreign policy preferences). Using survey data, scholars have found that citizens who were more worried about terrorism were more willing to trade civil liberties for more security (Davis and Silver 2004a; Davis 2007; Huddy et al. 2005). With respect to international engagement, as individuals' anger over the terrorist attacks increased, they became more supportive of the United States being active in the world, the campaign against terrorism, and military action in Afghanistan (Huddy et al. 2005). While these findings are consistent with our arguments, in subsequent chapters we consider additional types of homeland security policies as well as international engagement policies that are more cooperative in nature. Furthermore, we ask whether citizens in countries other than the United States, principally Mexico, might adopt similar preferences of protecting at home and engaging abroad.

The picture that emerges from our brief review is that there is some preliminary support for each of the coping mechanisms that we identified. In times of crisis, individuals' attitudes, evaluations, and behaviors shift. And they do so at three levels: with respect to other individuals, with respect to political leaders, and with respect to other nations. In the next section we take a step back and consider the general relationship between conditions of threat, the use of these coping strategies, and the quality of democracy.

Do Conditions of Threat Place Democracy at Risk?

> They that can give up essential liberty to obtain a little temporary safety deserve neither liberty nor safety.
>
> Benjamin Franklin (1759)

Benjamin Franklin's quote has historically been embraced by defenders of civil liberties, especially in times of threat. For many, it suggests that democratic citizens, if they are to be considered as such, have a duty to defend their liberties even in the face of security crises. The quote has been employed in various protests and even served as inspiration for the Benjamin Franklin True Patriot Act (HR 1131), a bill sponsored and introduced by Dennis Kucinich (D-Ohio) and Ron Paul (R-Texas) in the U.S. House of Representatives close to the end of the 108th Congress. The bill represented a joint effort by those on the left and Libertarians to challenge, unsuccessfully, some provisions in the PATRIOT Act, such as roving wiretaps, secret record searches, and detention of noncitizens.

However, there are some qualifiers in the quote, which might point to a more measured interpretation of what it means to be a good citizen in times of threat. First, the quote does not merely say liberty, but essential liberty. There can certainly be a reasoned debate about which liberties are essential. Second, the quote discusses "a little temporary safety," not unqualified safety. One could make an argument that times of security crisis, such as terrorist threat, are those in which the objective is the survival of the nation itself. President Lincoln brought up exactly this point in his order to suspend the writ of habeas corpus in April of 1861: "Are all the laws but one to go unexecuted and the Government itself go to pieces lest that one be violated?"[13] Later in time, Justice Robert H. Jackson echoed these sentiments in a dissenting opinion in *Terminiello v. City of Chicago* (1949): "There is danger that, if the [Supreme Court] does not temper its doctrinaire logic with a little practical wisdom, it will convert the constitutional Bill of Rights into a suicide pact." The argument is, simply put, that it may be necessary to give up some liberties to preserve the nation. The pertinent question then may be whether those liberties are restored when the threat recedes.

We have outlined three coping strategies that citizens may employ in times of terror threat. In this section, we explore what implications the use of these coping mechanisms has for the quality of democracy. As we consider these implications, we will keep in mind some of the complexities discussed above. First, we briefly review some of the more general literature on what it means to be a good citizen and how citizens live up to this ideal in times of well-being and times of crisis.

While conceptions of what it means to be a good citizen have shifted throughout U.S. history, the Progressive era shaped the notion of a good citizen as being an informed, rational individual who participates in political life (Schudson 1998). Not only are these qualities desirable, they are often considered *necessary* for a healthy democracy. But how well do individuals live up to this ideal in general? For decades, scholars depicted the average (U.S.) voter as someone who cared little, knew little, and thought little about the political world. These assessments were seemingly validated by low turnout levels, (often dismally) low levels of political information, and an absence of coherent opinions on the major issues of the day (see, e.g., Campbell, Converse, Miller, and Stokes 1960; Converse 1964; Delli Carpini and Keeter 1996). Incentives to become politically engaged and to acquire information about politics vary by electoral laws and party systems, and thus are often higher outside the U.S. context (e.g., Gordon and Segura 1997; Jackman 1987; Jackman and Miller 1995; Powell 1986). Nonetheless, even taking into consideration the importance of institutions in shaping citizens' incentives, few would argue that the average individual in any context meets the demanding criteria of being copiously informed and constantly active with respect to politics.

The exogenous shock of a crisis, however, can launch the average individual out of political complacency and into action. This may seem counterintuitive in that the conventional wisdom is that when people become more anxious or "emotional," they tend to become less coherent and withdraw from the world around them. However, new research crossing disciplinary boundaries suggests that, under times of anxiety, processes triggered within the brain motivate individuals to seek out information relevant to reducing anxiety (see Marcus, Neuman, and MacKuen 2000). In addition, individuals are more likely to use that new information when making decisions. Applying this logic and basic understanding of neurological responses to the political world, Marcus, Neuman and MacKuen (2000) have found that individuals who feel anxious (with respect to politics) are more interested in politics, more likely to seek out information on candidates, more likely to base voting decisions on issue opinions and candidate traits, and less likely to base voting decisions on long-standing dispositions such as partisanship. Brader (2005) has demonstrated a similar set of results among individuals who were exposed to a negative political advertisement with fear cues. Furthermore, there is some evidence that anxious individuals are more likely to engage in a variety of participatory activities (Marcus, Neuman, and MacKuen 2000, Radcliff 1992; but see Brader 2005 and Valentino et al. 2006).[14] Thus, certain negative emotional responses may, at first glance at least, lead citizens to behave more in line with normative theories about what constitutes a good political citizen.

While we agree that crises lead to shifts in attitudes, evaluations, and behavior compared to normal times, our principal assertion is that this process under certain conditions may subject democracy to stress. Specifically, the threat of terrorism may in some ways lead to shifts in behavior that are healthy for democracy and, at the same time, in other ways lead to shifts that are less desirable for the quality of democracy. Collective crises, such as terrorist threat, typically elicit anxiety, distress, and a host of related negative emotional responses. The studies noted above suggest that such responses can cause individuals to become more attentive and informed about the political world and potentially more engaged. However, what are the implications for democracy when citizens use the three coping strategies that we have outlined?

Turning to the first coping strategy, consider the threat to the quality of democracy if an anxiety-producing situation causes individuals to become both more authoritarian in their attitudes *and* more engaged in the political system. Such a response can threaten the very fabric of democracy by singling out particular groups as second-class citizens, which may lead to policies that deny equal rights and equal protection. Certainly the quality of democracy in such a situation would suffer, at least in the short term. The question then becomes whether those attitudes and responses recede after the threat is gone. Several factors suggest that these attitudinal shifts may have long-lasting implications. In the first place, one potential problem with respect to the war on terrorism is that there is not a clear end in sight. Furthermore, to the extent that this process is largely psychological, it is not clear that citizens recognize that they are in fact shifting their attitudes in ways that threaten the democratic value of tolerance. Finally, the effect of these shifts may be long-lasting if they are translated into actual legislation, which is frequently difficult to remove once in place. Overall, such a response may not threaten the regime type itself, but it arguably has negative implications for the quality of democracy. Thus, the regime remains a procedural democracy but one with a diminished social fabric and, potentially, one that fails to grant full rights to all citizens.[15]

With respect to the second strategy of coping with terror threat, is any threat to democracy posed simply by weighting leadership qualities more heavily in the voting booth? If we lived in the founding period, we might argue that this is in fact the way one should select leaders (Schudson 1998). Today we may also consider it a sign of a healthy democracy to the extent that citizens are choosing leaders they deem capable of finding a resolution to the crisis. As we indicated earlier, many great leaders came to power during times of crisis, such as FDR, Lincoln, and Churchill. We would likely be hard pressed to find anyone who considered the weighting of strong leadership in these elections as a reflection of an unhealthy democracy. However, the intersection of trait projection *and* voting on leadership gives us pause for thought. If individuals are expressing biased evaluations and making decisions based on these, then is it at least possible that the outcomes are not ideal from the perspective of the functioning and quality of democracy?

We may find cause to be even more concerned about the implications of threat for democratic quality and processes if individuals are also willing to cede more power to the selected leader. In the U.S. context, citizens have historically been willing to cede more authority and power to the executive office in times of threat. Some presidential scholars contend that the expansion of executive power during these contexts has significantly shifted the balance of power between the branches (Fisher 1995); however, others argue that the executive has always had such authority under the Constitution (Nichols 1994). Even if there have been shifts in the balance of power between the branches, the democratic regime in the United States has not been seriously threatened since the Civil War. And yet, we may be concerned if individuals are willing to cede more power to the selected leader in a context without a time horizon, such as a terror threat. In this case, standard checks and balances may be indefinitely diminished and the executive granted wide latitude to pursue policies with potentially little oversight. That being said, it is worth noting that the U.S. Congress and Supreme Court are pushing back a bit on presidential powers in the war on terror seven years out from the attacks.

For the most part we assume that it is democratic quality that suffers (e.g., via diminished civil liberties) in the face of such increased executive power. At least, this is the likely scope of such effects for established democratic systems. However, there have been cases in which the combination of crisis and a strong, charismatic executive was followed by the dissolution of democracy, such as occurred in Nazi Germany. The potential for more dramatic shifts in regime type is greater in newer democracies with more fragile systems. One example of terrorist activity influencing a shift away from democracy as a regime type is that of Peru in the 1990s. The brutal domestic terrorist activities of the Sendero Luminoso, a Maoist revolutionary group active in the 1980s and 1990s, compelled many Peruvians to throw their support behind Alberto Fujimori's election in 1990 and—more important to our case—his *auto golpe* (closure of congress and other governmental institutions) in 1992. Fujimori was widely perceived as a charismatic leader and, in part due to the terrorist threat (alongside other factors), was granted such centralization of authority by the public that the once-democratic state could no longer be considered as such. International outcry forced Fujimori's hand, and the system reverted back to a somewhat more democratic state in 1995 (with a new round of elections) and subsequently returned to competitive party politics following Fujimori's flight into exile in 2000. Overall, the use of this second coping strategy presents a mixed bag with respect to its implications for democracy, ranging from actions illustrative of a healthy citizenry to those that might destroy (under certain conditions) the very regime type itself.

We have already touched on the tension between security and civil liberties that is related to the homeland security component of our third coping mechanism. While civil libertarians contend that any reduction in civil liberties poses a threat to liberal democracy, others can make a convincing case for the necessity of such measures in times of threat. The question then, as we have noted already, hinges on whether civil liberties are restored in full when the threat recedes. Again, one potential issue with terror threat is the extended time horizon; another is the degree to which these practices are put into enduring legislative policies. In contrast, it is more difficult (but perhaps not impossible) to determine clear threats posed to liberal democracy through the practice of an activist foreign policy. As we proceed through the book, we will carry this general theme with us. To what extent, if any, does the terrorist threat pose a threat to the quality and, potentially in some cases, the very existence of democracy?

Looking Ahead

In the next chapter, we further delineate our conception of conditions of terror threat and how this particular crisis condition affects the public. We also discuss, to a much greater extent, the three coping strategies that we have outlined briefly in this introduction, which we argue affect how citizens perceive and treat other individuals, political leaders, and other nations. The theory and arguments we assert in chapter 1 draw on scholarship across several disciplines (political science, sociology, psychology, and organizational science) and across subfields within political science (international relations, comparative, and U.S. politics).

Chapter 2 presents the data and methods we use to demonstrate support for the arguments identified in chapter 1. We employ unique experiment-based data, existing survey data, and specially developed survey data. The majority of our data come from experiments using student and nonstudent subjects, in both the United States and Mexico. In all of our experimental studies, subjects were randomly assigned to one of at least two conditions: one that sought to increase concerns of a terrorist attack and one that sought to diminish such concerns. In addition to the data generated from the experiments, we test select arguments through the use of survey data in the United States and Mexico. This "triangulation" of research methods allows us to demonstrate the robustness of our findings to different research instruments and samples of people.

In chapter 3 we examine the conditions under which and the types of individuals who might employ the first coping mechanism, related to how citizens perceive and treat other individuals. We argue that one manifestation of this coping strategy lies in the expression of increased distrust, dislike, intolerance, and punitiveness toward certain groups in society. We first demonstrate a basic relationship between terrorist threat and authoritarian attitudes using U.S. survey data. However, we also argue that not all individuals will necessarily employ this coping strategy. Rather, those high in authoritarian predispositions are more likely to exhibit authoritarian attitudes during times of national security crisis. In order to examine this type of conditional relationship, and better assess our causal claim, we turn to evidence from three experiments conducted in the U.S. and Mexico.

Chapter 4 is the first of two chapters focused on the second strategy of coping, which entails looking for and delegating leadership to those who appear capable of resolving the crisis. We begin by arguing that in contexts of national security crisis, individuals project leadership traits onto select individuals; that is, they perceive certain leaders as more qualified than they otherwise would. Furthermore, individuals then weight leadership qualities more heavily in their voting decisions. We demonstrate support for these arguments using data from experiments held during two U.S. elections.

In chapter 5 we explore the relationships among terror threat, perceptions of charisma, and behavioral and evaluative consequences. We argue that terror threats cause individuals to project charisma onto likely leaders. Individuals also then become willing to protect and assist the selected leader. More specifically, individuals are less likely to blame charismatic leaders, are more likely to sacrifice their own personal resources for a leader they deem charismatic, and are (sometimes) more likely to give that leader additional institutional powers to resolve the crisis situation. We demonstrate support for these relationships across several experimental studies conducted in the United States and in Mexico.

In the next chapter (chapter 6), we investigate the third coping strategy by looking at how foreign policy preferences over a range of issues are affected by conditions of terror threat. Here we demonstrate quite clearly that citizens in both major- and minor-power countries come to have similar foreign policy preferences under times of terror threat, supporting the dual objectives of protecting at home and engaging abroad. In this chapter, we employ data from experiments conducted in the United States and Mexico, and compare these results to surveys from both countries conducted by the Chicago Council on Foreign Relations (CCFR).

In our conclusion, we summarize our findings, discuss their implications, and discuss potential avenues for future research on the topic. Most important, in this final chapter we draw out and comment further on the thread that visibly ties together the preceding chapters: conditions of terror threat have effects on political attitudes, evaluations, and behaviors that put democratic quality, and possibly democratic durability, at risk.

Coping with the Threat of Terrorism

During times of collective crisis — in particular, terrorist threat — individuals may experience heightened distress, anxiety, hopelessness, loss of control, worry, fear, and anger. By their very nature, collective crises create conditions in which solutions remain out of the reach of individual decisions or actions. Reacting to conditions of terrorist threat, people may adopt one or more coping strategies that affect how they perceive and treat fellow individuals, their political leaders, and other nations. We argue that of the three main strategies, one is aimed at imposing order on the world nearest an individual, especially with respect to one's relations with other people. Expressions of this coping technique are increased distrust, punitiveness, dislike, and intolerance in particular with respect to societal outgroups. A second coping strategy is to find and turn over control to an external actor, such as a political figure whom one deems capable of solving or handling the crisis. Examples of this coping strategy include the projection of unique leadership capabilities onto a selected individual, increased weight accorded to strong leadership qualities in voting decisions, and an increased tendency to protect and assist the selected leader. A third strategy is to assert increased preferences for dual objectives in foreign policy whereby the homeland is secured while select efforts are pursued abroad.

To develop this multipart argument, we journeyed back and forth across an academic landscape built by political scientists, sociologists, psychologists, and even scholars of business organization theory. We collected relevant insights from these different fields of study and never failed to marvel at how well they fit together. In this chapter, we begin by clarifying our conception of the phenomena that lie at the very core of this book: crisis and, in particular, terrorist threat. We then identify the logic that we believe connects times of terrorist threat to each of the general coping strategies we have identified. We conclude the chapter by returning to a central theme: the ways in which conditions of terrorist threat may (or may not) place democracy at risk.

Conceptualizing Crisis and Threat

Our primary goal is to better understand how individuals respond to a particular type of crisis: terrorist threat. We do so principally by comparing citizens' evaluations, attitudes, and behaviors across conditions marked by greater international terrorist threat and those marked by times of relatively more calm and well-being. At times we extend our comparisons to other cases of crisis (and their relationships to those "good times"). An obvious starting point for this investigation, then, is to offer definitions of crisis and threat.

Crises are moments in time characterized by the potential and/or realization of significant change away from some status quo point. Thus, Webster's first definition of the term *crisis* considers an act that has occurred and describes a crisis as a "turning point," "a paroxysmal attack," or an "emotionally significant event or radical change of status." Webster's third definition considers forthcoming events, describing crisis as "an unstable or crucial time or state of affairs in which a decisive change is impending."[1] While dictionaries tend to offer valence-neutral definitions of crisis, we assume that the anticipated and/or realized change associated with a crisis is most often negative in character. We consider conditions of crisis to be *threats* if they carry the potential, not yet realized, to inflict harm. Conditions of terrorist threat thus are situations in which a hostile and destructive attack by a terrorist group appears imminent.

What matters most to us, in terms of understanding citizens' attitudes, evaluations, and behavior, is the *perception* of threat, which arguably may be higher than the actual threat level.[2] Obvious factors such as the scope of or one's proximity to a past event or future threat might affect the perceived magnitude of the crisis. For example, we can quite reasonably assume that residents of New York City experienced higher levels of anxiety post-9/11 compared to those living in other parts of the United States.[3] Existing research further tells us that individuals tend to overestimate the likelihood of certain extreme events, especially if the event is considered to be intentional and morally offensive and/or if elites highlight (or even exaggerate) the threat.[4] Terrorist threats appear to have both of these characteristics, though the latter characteristic does vary across political systems.

Generally speaking, crises can occur at the individual or collective level. For example, rising inflation tends to affect the whole population, while the firing of a single individual does not typically have effects beyond that household. Individual-level responses to household crises are common and, ideally, productive. Thus, an individual who has lost a job could hit the pavement (cement or cyber) to search for new employment, enroll in a job retraining program or other education-oriented activity, and/or possibly secure unemployment assistance. Collective crises tend to have solutions that lie beyond the control of any given individual or household. Individuals might take certain measures in order to mitigate the personal damage that occurs in the face of a collective crisis (e.g., stocking the house with gas masks in the face of a terrorist threat) but these individual measures are unlikely to forestall or resolve the crisis condition entirely. It is these types of crises—collective crises—with which we are concerned. By their very nature, such crises highlight individuals' limitations with respect to controlling external circumstances that threaten their financial, psychological, and/or physical well-being.

It is because of the potential to inflict an array of harms, and the fact that remedies mostly lie beyond an individual's control, that we believe citizens facing a collective threat will tend to adopt one or more politically relevant coping strategies. In the next section we turn to a discussion of several means by which individuals might cope with the threat of future terrorist attacks in their interactions with the political world.

Coping with Crisis and Threat

In general, large-scale collective crises evoke a range of emotions. By highlighting an individual's lack of control over environmental conditions, such crises tend to arouse feelings of concern and distress. Central to these feelings is a cognitively based and emotionally laden perception of a loss of control and a sense of hopelessness. That is, an individual is likely to perceive the situation as beyond her immediate influence, and this recognition is likely to elicit feelings of anxiety.[5] Such crises tend also to induce worry and fear with respect to the harm that might be (or continues to be) inflicted on an individual or a group's financial, physical, and/or psychological well-being. Collective crises may also evoke feelings of anger and disgust, in particular when one's worldview or core values are threatened and/or when one identifies and assigns intentional motivations to the crisis provoker.[6] So individuals made aware of the threat of a terrorist attack may feel anxious about such a possibility, fearful for their own safety (and/or the safety of others around them), and possibly also harbor feelings of anger toward terrorist leaders and groups.

Perceptions of terror threat combined with negative emotions should cause individuals to employ coping strategies. These strategies are likely to vary, to some extent at least, from coping techniques employed during individual-level crisis conditions.[7] The key difference between collective and individual threats is control, and thus we expect that some of the most prominent coping techniques directed at collective threats will be aimed at restoring feelings of control, efficacy, and security. Further, we posit that the coping mechanisms employed during times of terrorist threat (which we occasionally also refer to as security crisis) will be expressed with respect to three objects: other individuals, leaders and institutions, and other collective entities (e.g., other nation-states and citizens of those countries). Some of the coping strategies may also be relevant in the face of other types of collective crisis, such as an economic or political crisis, while others may be more specific to the issue of terror threat. In the following three subsections, we describe the three coping strategies that are the focus of our project: coping via authoritarian and related attitudes, via strong leadership and charisma, and via dual objectives in foreign policy.

Coping via Authoritarian and Related Attitudes

One way individuals may cope with threat is by changing their perceptions of and attitudes toward other individuals. By inserting rigidity and resoluteness into this realm, individuals may increase their overall feelings of control and security. They may do so for some instrumental reasons, but we suspect that the employment of such a coping strategy is motivated less by rational calculations and more by a desire to mitigate general feelings of anxiety and helplessness. It seems plausible that individuals would rationally select to be less trusting of others in the age of terrorism, given how difficult it may be to recognize a terrorist in advance of an attack. However, to the extent that these perceptual and attitudinal shifts seem overly extensive, we suggest this is evidence of deeper, noninstrumental mental processes. Two basic types of general assessments that might conceivably be affected by terrorist threat are interpersonal trust and authoritarian attitudes.

Levi and Stoker provide a concise definition of trust: "Trust is relational; it involves an individual making herself vulnerable to another individual, group, or institution that has the capacity to do her harm or to betray her. Trust is seldom unconditional; it is given to specific individuals or institutions over specific domains" (2000, 476). Since we are looking at relations among individuals, we focus on trust among individuals in society, often called interpersonal or social trust. In line with the above definition, we hold that interpersonal trust is subject to fluctuation, especially across contexts of threat. The first part of our argument, then, is that individuals, in times of terrorist threat, become increasingly suspicious of those around them. We recognize that this assertion flies in the face of some of the assumptions and findings about societal and governmental relations following 9/11. After the terrorist attacks, numerous media stories documented substantial efforts by individuals to help each other, both in the aftermath of the crisis specifically and in terms of general volunteer work and giving to charities (Skocpol 2002). Caution is advised in drawing conclusions from these reports. Some research shows that levels of civic volunteerism did not increase substantially in the aftermath of 9/11 (Putnam 2002; Traugott et al. 2002). Scholars have found that trust in the national government nearly doubled in response to the terrorist attacks (Chanley 2002). Nonetheless, just because individuals came to trust more in the national government and give to 9/11-related charities does not necessarily mean that they also became more trusting of others. In a panel study, Putnam found huge increases, about 44 percent, in trust of the national government from 2000 to post-9/11, but much more modest increases, 6 percent, in trust in neighbors (2002). Thus it appears that existing data points to little or maybe no significant shift in interpersonal trust in response to the events of 9/11.

Seemingly in contrast to Putnam's findings, we argue that individuals may actually become less trusting of others, including their neighbors, in times of terror threat. We know from existing research that collective-level experiences can influence the degree of interpersonal trust in a society. Hard economic times lead to scarcity, which may cause individuals to view others more skeptically and as potential competitors. Being a victim of crime also leads to lower levels of interpersonal trust (Brehm and Rahn 1997). In apparent contrast to the effects of terrorist threat, poor economic performance and increasing worry about domestic crime tend to decrease trust in government (Chanley 2002; Citrin and Green 1986; Hetherington 1998). Nonetheless, despite becoming more trusting of national government in response to worry about terrorism, it may be instrumentally rational as well as psychologically calming to decrease trust in other individuals. Citizen vigilance is arguably an effective strategy with which to counter or reduce the terrorist threat. After all, how can citizens be both vigilant in observing others, yet trusting at the same time? Such a strategy of scrutinizing others is in fact what President Bush recommended to the U.S. public: "A terrorism alert is not a signal to stop your life. It is a call to be vigilant—to know that your government is on high alert, and to add your eyes and ears to our efforts to find and stop those who want to do us harm."[8] Becoming less trusting is psychologically calming to the extent that one believes such vigilance, expressed in increased distrust, is indeed effective. By increasing their suspicion of those around them, individuals can feel efficacious and more secure at the same time, even if their efforts are largely irrelevant to the actual resolution of the crisis.[9]

While increased social distrust may be a relatively benign reaction to terrorist threat, this is only the tip of the iceberg. In addition to becoming less trusting, individuals will become relatively more hostile toward out-groups, intolerant, and punitive under the security crisis condition. In other words, individuals will become more authoritarian in times of crisis, though, as we will note below, not all individuals may react in this manner.

While scholars debate the origins and measurement of authoritarianism, there is general agreement on what it looks like. *Authoritarianism* can be understood as a set of tendencies that include the following: "obedience to authority, moral absolutism and conformity, intolerance and punitiveness toward dissidents and deviants, animosity and aggression against racial and ethnic out groups" (Stenner 2005, 3). [10] Authoritarianism can be expressed in attitudes and/or behaviors. Authoritarian attitudes will be closely connected to preferences for order and security as well as expressed intolerance of out-groups, while authoritarian behaviors may encompass the punishment of out-groups (recall the increased hate crimes against Arab Americans post-9/11 discussed in the previous chapter). Treatments of authoritarianism in the literature suggest that this is a psychological process by which individuals allay feelings of anxiety. We suspect most citizens would not argue that they elect to become instrumentally more intolerant in the face of a threat.

Historical evidence suggests a general tendency for individuals who feel physically, psychologically, and/or economically insecure to become less tolerant of difference and more willing to follow leaders and movements that espouse similar attitudes. Perhaps the most tragic phenomenon exemplifying this shift in public mood is the rise of Nazi Germany. Reflecting on conditions leading to World War II, Fromm (1941) argues that lower-middle-class German workers were drawn to fascism due to the isolation, uncertainty, and insecurity caused by monopolistic capitalism and the decline of old social symbols of authority, such as the monarchy.[11]

In fact, ample evidence exists at the aggregate and individual levels documenting a relationship between environmental threat and various indicators of authoritarianism.[12] For example, membership in authoritarian churches tends to increase in times of high threat compared to low threat (Sales 1972). As another example, Altemeyer (1988) conducted experiments in which subjects were given a future scenario representing a status quo condition, a right-wing threat condition, or a left-wing threat condition. He finds that subjects in the two threatening conditions were more inclined to adopt authoritarian attitudes in response to the hypothetical situation.

While these early, field-defining works test for a direct effect of threat on authoritarian attitudes and behaviors, there is reason to suspect that the relationships are more nuanced. This coping technique may only, or mostly, be used by a subset of individuals, those who are already predisposed toward authoritarianism. In order to further understand this argument, we need to clearly distinguish between authoritarian predispositions and authoritarian attitudes (chapter 3 will deal with issues of measurement for these two concepts). Authoritarian predispositions are related to one's views of the "appropriate balance between group authority and uniformity, on the one hand, and individual autonomy and diversity, on the other" (Stenner 2005, 14). Thus, individuals who lean more toward the group authority and uniformity end are more disposed toward authoritarianism. Authoritarian attitudes and behaviors, in contrast, are revealed preferences expressed by way of opinion statements or behavior.[13] The expression of authoritarian attitudes and behavior is likely to remain at relatively lower levels during times of nonthreat, since things are going well. However, when the need to exert control, calm anxiety, and act out anger surfaces in times of threat, an individual's authoritarian predispositions may be activated and thus lead to the increased expression of authoritarian attitudes and behaviors (Feldman and Stenner 1997; Lavine et al. 1996, 2002; Lavine, Lodge, and Freitas 2005; Stenner 2005).

A handful of studies analyzing individual-level survey data find support for this conditional relationship among authoritarian predispositions, threat, and consequent authoritarian attitudes and behavior (e.g., Feldman and Stenner 1997; Rickert 1998; Stenner 2005).[14] Numerous experimental studies also find that threats activate the effect of authoritarian predispositions on intolerant attitudes and behavior. For example, when subjects are asked to think about and write down their thoughts about their own death, authoritarian predispositions are activated (Greenburg et al. 1990; Lavine et al. 1996, 2002; Lavine, Lodge, and Freitas 2005). Similar support is found in Stenner (2005) across a wider range of different experimental conditions (five threatening and five reassuring conditions), with threats to one's social environment inducing the strongest effects.

In chapter 3 we will return to a consideration of the relationships among terror threat conditions, distrust, authoritarian predispositions, and authoritarian attitudes. As we have indicated throughout the text, we believe the adoption and expression of this coping mechanism is grounded more in psychological than instrumental motivations; we return as well to this discussion. Figure 1.1 depicts the relationships that we investigate, and substantiate, in chapter 3. The top portion of the figure captures the link between conditions of terrorist threat and increased feelings of distrust; we will show these effects hold with respect to others in general and with respect to one's neighbors. Second, we will provide evidence of a direct link between terrorist threat and certain authoritarian attitudes (specifically, dislike of out-groups and punitiveness). Third, using experimental data from both the United States and Mexico, we will document a conditional relationship among terrorist threat, authoritarian predispositions, and authoritarian attitudes.

Coping via Strong Leadership and Charisma

Another way that individuals may restore feelings of control and security is to select, protect, and assist strong and charismatic leadership. Thus, under conditions of crisis, individuals may become focused on finding a leader with the requisite traits and skills to rescue them from the crisis situation. We understand this search to be emotionally calming but also pragmatic, given the collective nature of the crisis. We further expect it to have a variety of manifestations, which we will eventually divide into two parts: first, a focus on perceptions of strong leadership and related voting behavior; second, a focus on perceptions of charisma and related nonelectoral evaluations and behavior. Because both parts are rooted in a tendency to evaluate selected leaders differently in times of crisis, we begin this discussion with a consideration of the effects of terror threat on perceptions of leaders' strength and charisma.

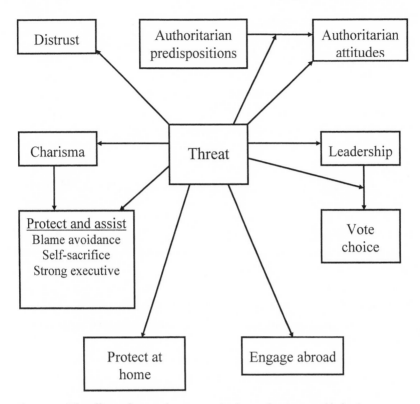

Figure 1.1. The effects of terror threat on attitudes, evaluations, and behavior

Looking for Leaders in All the Right Places

The presence of a collective threat causes individuals to focus increasingly on questions of leadership. Such an assertion seems uncontroversial and, perhaps, even intuitive. During these times, individuals may look for strong leaders whom they deem capable of resolving the given crisis situation. A more controversial assertion, which we make here, is that individuals not only look for such characteristics in times of crisis but they project *additional* leadership capabilities onto selected individuals during such times. That is, they perceive such individuals as stronger and more charismatic than they would during times of relative calm or prosperity. Why would they do so? The short answer is that such perceptions help individuals cope with the threat. By identifying a single heroic leader, individuals are able to reduce the negative emotions brought on by the crisis. We illustrate the relationship between threat, on the one hand, and charisma and leadership, on the other, in the middle portion of figure 1.1.

A range of theoretical perspectives supports our assertion that individuals project *additional* leadership capabilities onto selected individuals during times of terror threat relative to times of calm and well-being. Weber (1922, 1947) was one of the first scholars to recognize a relationship between times of crisis and the rise of charismatic leaders. In his classic work on charisma, Weber argues that charismatic leaders arise during times of crisis because they are perceived to possess the extraordinary ability to rescue individuals from that critical situation. Weber's conception assumes that charisma—rare qualities that elevate an individual above others in terms of perceived wisdom and competence—is essentially innate. However, later scholars draw on Weber to argue that the intersection of a crisis and certain leadership traits can result in a "charismatic bond," where individuals project charisma onto a leader whom they believe is capable of restoring feelings of efficacy undermined by the crisis (Madsen and Snow 1991). As we will discuss in more detail later (in chapter 5), conceptions of charisma have also shifted over time, toward more concrete definitions in which charisma consists of a bundle of perceived traits including optimism, confidence, empathy, and enthusiasm. In work that shares some similarities to research on the charismatic bond, some scholars posit that in times of security crisis people experience a heightened awareness of mortality, which causes them to turn to strong leaders who appear capable of providing protection (for a discussion see Landau et al. 2004). While the mechanisms across these studies differ (a desire to restore feelings of efficacy in the former and a desire to feel protected in the latter), both avenues of research suggest that during times of terror threat, the strong desire for a savior compels individuals to see, through rose-colored glasses, a stronger and more charismatic leader than they would otherwise perceive. We believe these reactions are based in deep psychological processes by which individuals seek to restore their own sense of calm and hope by projecting greater leadership evaluations onto likely leaders.

Existing studies provide empirical support for the argument that crises cause individuals to focus on and project charisma and leadership qualities onto selected leaders. If we look at the case of Latin America, we find that the rise of populist and charismatic political leaders often coincides with conditions of crisis (Willner 1984). For example, Juan Perón in Argentina, Hugo Chávez in Venezuela, and Alberto Fujimori in Peru all rose to power during times of national crisis (Madsen and Snow 1991; Roberts 1995; Weyland 2003). Evidence from experiments supports the connection between crises and projections of charisma and leadership. During the

2003 California recall election, the state economic crisis led citizens to rate challengers to Gray Davis as more charismatic (Bligh, Kohles, and Pillai 2005). With respect to terror threat, individuals in one study who were led to think about 9/11 perceived Bush as a stronger leader than those in a control group (Landau et al. 2004). In addition, a survey of students has shown that those who thought the United States was still facing a terrorist threat, and who thought Bush was handling it well, gave him higher values on a charisma scale (Pillai, Kohles, and Bligh 2007).

While existing theory and evidence take us a long way, they do not touch on two related issues. First, how do crises affect perceptions of rival candidates or leaders? A crisis condition causes individuals to evaluate leaders through a different lens, one determined to find a unique personality with, at the extreme, messianic qualities. We assert that this desire to single out a savior is likely to lead individuals to downgrade evaluations of alternate leaders. Thus, under conditions of collective crisis, we expect that individuals will not only project additional charisma and strong leadership onto a selected leader but they will simultaneously downgrade evaluations of other leaders on this dimension. Such a process confirms the special nature of the selected leader by placing her leagues ahead of her rival in this domain. Second, in any democratic political system, there are many candidates competing for office. To whom will individuals turn when a crisis strikes? We assert that it depends on the intersection of the type of crisis and three factors: the extent to which the leader is responsible for having caused the crisis; the party's reputation with respect to that issue area; and, finally, the leader's reputation with respect to that issue area.

In the case of an externally provoked crisis, such as a terrorist attack, the most likely recipient of this leadership boost is the incumbent. A vast array of evidence shows that sitting presidents receive a boost in approval, across many issue domains, when there is a dramatic foreign policy event (e.g., Bowen 1989; Brody 1991; MacKuen 1983; Mueller 1970, 1973). To the contrary, if the situation is such that the incumbent administration is perceived as the cause of the given crisis, or is otherwise discredited for handling the crisis, then citizens will likely look to challengers for help and project strong leadership traits onto them. For example, a typical economic crisis is likely to be blamed on the current administration and, consequently, likely to lead individuals to look to challengers who might be able to better manage the economy (see the vast literature on retrospective voting).

Second, the leader's party may play a role in determining the extent to which individuals turn to that leader for help. In general, parties have an incentive to develop long-term reputations in different issue areas, which voters can then use to guide their decisions in the voting booth (Downs 1957; Petrocik 1996). According to issue ownership theory, this reputation is based in citizens' perceptions that a given party is better able to handle a particular issue (Petrocik 1996). In times of threat, individuals may find an individual whose party "owns" the relevant issue to be more appealing. Petrocik (1996) finds that Republicans have traditionally owned the issue of national security. Thus, individuals, in general, should perceive candidates from this party as better able to handle terrorist threats, an issue clearly in the domain of national security. This is what we find in responses to the American National Election Study (ANES) in 2004. About 41 percent of the sample indicates that the Republican Party is better able to handle the war on terrorism, compared to only 26 percent who say the Democratic Party (33% said they were both capable).

Finally, the individual's own reputation and past experiences may matter in much the same way as party reputation. For example, individuals may find those leaders with backgrounds in the military or with experience in the ministry of defense or homeland security particularly appealing in times of security crisis. In sum, we expect that, given a slate of political leaders, which leader receives a boost in perceptions of leadership and charisma will depend on the intersection of the three factors above. As we have noted, it is also likely that—as individuals attempt to distinguish among leaders and select out that particular leader capable of resolving the crisis—they will come to evaluate other leaders more negatively. In order to make predictions concerning how exactly leaders will be affected by crises we need to consider case-specific details, a point we will return to in chapters 4 and 5.

Selecting Strong Leaders

The second part of our argument is that individuals place greater weight on strong leadership in the voting booth in times of terror threat compared to times of relative prosperity and well-being. This response can reflect both instrumental and deeper psychological processes. Some citizens may purposefully think that the most important quality to consider during times of security crisis is whether the candidate is a strong leader. Other citizens might not be aware that they are weighting leadership more heavily, in much the same way that they may also blindly project leadership qualities onto certain individuals.

A long line of scholarship on voting behavior shows that people typically select candidates on the basis of three factors: individuals' party identification, their opinions on issues, and/or their assessments of the candidates' traits. Scholars of the classic work *The American Voter* (Campbell et al. 1960) find strong support for party identification being the primary determinant of the vote, some support for candidate traits playing a role, and little evidence of issue voting. The weak findings for issue voting in *The American Voter* led to a large literature challenging those results. Broadly speaking, most scholars since argue that how much weight voters give to each of these three factors in their decisions varies across individuals and across contexts.

Much research focuses on the conditions under which people are more likely to bring their opinions on issues to bear on their voting decisions.[15] Less light has been shed on factors that condition the importance assigned to evaluations of candidates' traits, despite their central role in media coverage of U.S. electoral contests. Clearly, candidates' traits do matter. A number of studies find a direct and strong relationship between voters' appraisals of candidates' traits and their voting decisions, both within and outside the United States (e.g., Bean and Mughan 1989; Kinder 1986; Markus 1982; McCurley and Mondak 1995; Miller and Miller 1976; Miller and Shanks 1996; Miller, Wattenberg, and Malanchuk 1986; Stewart and Clarke 1992). Yet, little work looks at the conditions under which citizens place more or less weight on candidate trait considerations in the voting booth. Of the few studies that exist, some show how people use traits differently depending on how much information they have about politics,[16] while others look at how the media and campaigns sometimes cause people to focus more on candidate traits in their voting decisions (Funk 1999; Mendelsohn 1996). Existing work does not examine how the importance voters place on traits might shift in contexts of threat.

Our expectation is that for two principal reasons people will weight strong leadership more heavily in their voting decisions in times of terror threat than in better times. First, times of anxiety may lead to distinct decision-processes compared to situations of relative calm. Drawing from research in neurobiology, Marcus, Neuman, and MacKuen (2000) argue that anxiety-producing conditions trigger a surveillance system in which individuals stop and seek information, while during times of ease the disposition system governs behavior and individuals rely on standing decisions. What does this mean for voting decisions? Using data from the ANES, the authors demonstrate that under times of ease, individuals rely on longer-standing predispositions, such as one's partisan identification, in deciding for whom to vote. Under times of anxiety, individuals weight factors more proximate to the election, such as candidate qualities and issues, more heavily in their voting decisions. Brader (2005, 2006) extends this work using an experimental design and finds that subjects exposed to a negatively framed political advertisement with fear cues rely more on candidate traits and issues relative to those who do not receive the fear cues. Given that extreme collective crises are likely to elevate individual anxiety, we posit that terror threats should cause similar tendencies to focus on factors proximate to the campaign.

Second, and related, a characteristic of many crisis contexts is that the key issues are valence issues. That is, candidates are inclined to focus on ends (the valence) rather than means (policy stances). Valence issues are those for which candidates all take similar stances, for example "restoring economic growth" and "providing security." In situations where candidates are believed to take similar stances on salient issues, citizens should be inclined to look to other factors (Downs 1957) such as the traits of the candidates. Moreover, in times of crisis, candidates' rhetoric and campaign strategies will often make traits more salient than issues and this should further lead to voters placing a heavy weight on candidate traits. The 2004 U.S. election was exactly such a situation: The theme of terror threat was salient. Bush and Kerry both pledged their commitment to the same goal— making America safer. The focus then shifted to which candidate had the traits and experience necessary to accomplish this end.

Given our discussion in the previous section, the single trait that we think is most relevant during times of terror threat is strong leadership. Thus, conditions of terror threat are likely to compel voters to place a greater weight on strong leadership compared to times of well-being, and this could reflect either an instrumental or deeper psychological process.[17] There is some initial empirical support to our arguments. Berinsky (2009) examines our arguments using data from the ANES panel study and demonstrates that individuals weighted leadership more heavily in their feelings toward Bush in 2002 and 2004 compared to 2000. We provide further evidence for these arguments in chapter 4. Since our principal concern is the weight placed on leadership traits, we later examine but do not state specific expectations with respect to how the effect of issues and partisan identification vary across settings. Thus, the second part of chapter 4 concerns the links identified on the right side of figure 1.1, which shows a relationship between strong leadership and vote choice that is conditional upon terrorist threat.

Protecting and Assisting Leaders

The final part of our argument for this coping strategy is that there are several rewards for being perceived as charismatic. First, the combination of crisis and charisma causes individuals to become more willing to overlook poor performance by the selected leader. Second, the combination of crisis and charisma causes individuals to become more willing to sacrifice their own resources on behalf of the leader and, in some cases, to cede additional institutional power to that leader.

The first reward we consider is blame reduction. Existing theoretical perspectives suggest that in times of crisis individuals will seek to protect a selected charismatic leader and his or her image by diverting blame for policy or other mistakes made by that individual. By projecting charismatic qualities onto a selected leader, individuals form a "charismatic bond," that is, a sense of oneness with the leader. Their self-esteem, feelings of efficacy, and sense of security become intricately tied to the leader. As a result, individuals become relatively less willing to place blame on the leader for poor performance.

Scholarship on charisma supports this argument. The charisma factor, which is amplified in times of crisis, encourages citizens to look to place blame anywhere but on the leader's shoulders. For example, a crisis must be the result of "inherited" problems from previous administrations, the fault of the global situation, or the result of nefarious plotting by the opposition. In the case of Argentina, Perón was an expert at maintaining his following, despite sustained economic crises (Madsen and Snow 1991). In Bangladesh, the charismatic Sheikh Mujibur Rahman was able initially to avert blame during a crisis (Khan 1976). As time goes on, and expectations of the leader rise, charisma may not be sufficient to sustain support for the leader (Khan 1976); alternatively, the resolution of the crisis may, somewhat ironically, diminish perceptions of charisma.[18] Yet, at least in the near term, the intersection of crisis and charisma should provide a Teflon-like shield, allowing certain leaders to evade negative performance evaluations to a greater degree than would otherwise occur. Thus, crisis can affect blame reduction directly and indirectly, via perceptions of charisma. This could reflect a deeper psychological process in that individuals may feel a bond with a given leader, or it could the instrumental response of giving the leader more leeway to resolve the crisis.

Individuals facing threatening conditions are often motivated not only to protect the leader but to assist in resolving the crisis. The motivation may stem from psychological needs and/or from a practical realization that extra effort is required in order to mitigate the threat. With respect to the former, existing research shows that if people perceive oneness with a leader, then they are more likely to engage in self-sacrificial behavior (Cialdini et al. 1997). Feelings of oneness may be fostered by perceptions of empathy, a central component of charisma.[19] With respect to the latter, individuals may also be motivated out of a sheer desire to help facilitate the resolution of the crisis. In short, for one or more reasons, the intersection of threat and charisma is likely to cause individuals to sacrifice their personal resources (e.g., time, efforts, goods) on behalf of a selected leader.[20]

Finally, we suggest that perceptions of charisma and conditions of crisis cause citizens to prefer a stronger executive. Here we are admittedly on less solid ground, in that there exist no individual-level studies that examine relationships among crisis, charisma, and preferences over the consolidation of power in the executive office. Yet, ample anecdotal evidence suggests that these links exist. In the aftermath of 9/11, the U.S. public became highly supportive of the administration in general and of particular policies such as the Bush administration's unilateral foreign policy approach and limitations to civil liberties to increase domestic security (Davis and Silver 2004a; Huddy et al. 2005). Furthermore, a majority of Americans supported Bush's "terrorist surveillance" program, which entailed wiretapping without approval from the FISA court, and a majority thought the PATRIOT Act was a good thing for America.[21] In short, in the post-9/11 era, the U.S. public has often been a complicit partner—if not an active supporter—of programs and activities pursued by the Bush White House. This pattern of support for the executive is also characteristic of past wartime situations such as the Civil War and World War II.[22] This anecdotal evidence provides at least preliminary grounds for assuming relationships among conditions of terror threat, perceptions of charisma, and preferences over increased executive power.

Recent populist episodes in Latin America, among other regions, further support the notion that the combination of crisis and charisma may lead to preferences for a stronger executive. The rise of populist and charismatic leaders in times of crisis has been associated with the weakening of parties and of checks and balances (i.e., horizontal accountability; see O'Donnell 1998). Thus, Alberto Fujimori in Peru, Carlos Menem in Argentina, and Hugo Chávez in Venezuela all came to power under conditions of crisis and received citizen support while advocating antipolitics platforms aimed at dismantling and/or undermining traditional political institutions. For example, Fujimori's clear antiparty stance and refusal to cement his leadership in a new party left little to no room for political parties until such vehicles for democratic politics returned to the scene following Fujimori's removal from office. In Argentina, one of several ways Menem undermined checks and balances was by stacking the judicial system with his hand-picked appointees and increasing the number of Supreme Court justices in order to help tilt the balance of that branch in his favor. More direct attacks pursued by charismatic leaders include rewriting the constitution in order to shift power explicitly in favor of the executive. Thus, for example, the agenda of Chávez's constituent assembly included these tasks: "purge the judiciary, write a new constitution, shut down congress" (Roberts 2000, 15). While painted within the frame of direct democracy, such moves clearly strengthened the executive office at the expense of a system of checks and balances.[23]

Not only do these examples exist, but it seems highly reasonable to presume that individuals will select to cede greater authority to selected leaders in times of security crisis. In the first place, the elevated status acquired by charismatic leaders in times of crisis may seem to warrant their acquisition of greater power. To the extent that a charismatic leader is selected in times of crisis in order to restore feelings of efficacy, individuals may feel more efficacious the more power the leader has. In the second place, individuals may simply feel that a leader who is not only strong in traits but also in terms of institutional abilities is required for a swift, decisive resolution of the crisis condition. With respect to the specific issue of terror threat, individuals may therefore seek to cede increased power to the executive since that office is already vested with the authority to deal with issues related to the protection of national security. This could reflect instrumental calculations concerning what is deemed necessary to resolve the crisis. It could also be indicative of a more psychological response, especially if citizens are not fully reasoning through the potential long-term consequences of shifts in institutional power.

One reasonable reaction to the above set of arguments is that charisma is simply a code word for positive affect and, presumably, individuals are more motivated to assist and protect those whom they like compared to those they do not. However, charisma implies more than simply positive affect. In fact, the literature on charisma suggests that there is something "special" about charisma that leads to these evaluative and behavioral tendencies. Among the many possible types of leader and follower relationships (e.g., Avolio, Waldman, and Einstein 1988; Bass 1985; Hunt, Boal, and Dodge 1999), it is the transformational leader who, by means of his or her charismatic qualities, is able to elicit relatively more trust and loyalty from his or her followers (Bass 1985; Pillai and Williams 1998). That said, it is beyond the scope of our project to place general positive affect and perceptions of charisma in a horse race. We will instead show that, in times of terrorist threat compared to better times, individuals are less likely to blame and more likely to engage in self-sacrifice and cede institutional authority for the sake of the charismatic leader.

We illustrate the expected relationships among terror threat, charisma, protection, and assistance in the middle, left-side portion of figure 1.1. First, we expect that terror threats work indirectly on propensities to blame and assist the selected leader, via increased perceptions of charisma. Second, we also allow for a direct effect of terror threats on protection and assistance. In chapter 5 we provide evidence in support of this mediating argument. Specifically, we use experimental and survey data from both the United States and Mexico to document a relationship between terrorist threat and tendencies to avoid blame, self-sacrifice, and prefer a stronger executive, a relationship that works via perceptions of charisma.

Coping via Dual Objectives in Foreign Policy

Our third general coping strategy concerns foreign policy preferences. We assert that individuals are likely to cope with conditions of terrorist threat not only by shifting attitudes toward other individuals, collective leaders, and institutions, but also by shifting their preferences with respect to their country's relationship to the global community. The principal crisis condition we examine, threat from international terrorists, is unique in a number of ways, which has implications for the type of foreign policy preferences that elites and the public adopt. First, while terrorists might be part of a group, they often lack a hierarchical structure and clear political goals (Lesser 1999). Thus, it is often difficult to identify one coherent enemy, which may make attempts at negotiation impossible. Second, terrorists are spread out across different countries, with or without the knowledge of the states in which they reside. This identification problem makes it difficult to act against a terrorist target. Third, threats of attack are constant from terrorist groups, and yet it is more difficult to obtain accurate intelligence on the potential of future attacks. Finally, losses incurred from these attacks often affect more than one state. For example, death and material asset losses related to the 9/11 attacks on the World Trade Center involved more than eighty countries (Sandler 2005).

In the face of such a threat, we might expect leaders, regardless of the strategic power position of their country, to pursue the following foreign policy objectives: protect within and engage abroad.[24] In the first place, in order to prevent terrorists from infiltrating the country, elites may want to increase defensive measures related to protecting domestic populations (Sandler 2003, 2005; Sandler and Lapan 1988). These measures would entail policies such as increasing restrictions on entry and exit, improving technology such as metal detectors at airports, and creating terrorist alerts.

Second, policymakers will have incentives to prefer engagement abroad, which may include militant and nonmilitant behavior. With respect to the former, a nation may choose to retaliate against a terrorist organization with the support of a broad coalition, or work with a particular country to engage in limited strikes against terrorist targets. With respect to the latter, incentives may develop to cooperate on nonmilitant issues in order to preempt future attacks. For example, to gain a better sense of future behavior by terrorists and disrupt current plots and training camps, nations may want to share intelligence and freeze terrorist assets. Some studies suggest that international cooperation is a more effective strategy than unilateralism on issues of terrorism (e.g., Brophy-Baermann and Conybeare 1994; Charters 1994; Enders, Sandler, and Cauley 1990). Of course, countries may face collective action or other challenges that make cooperation difficult, especially in regard to military-related measures. For example, in response to shifting public opinion, Spain pulled out of Iraq following the 2004 Madrid train bombings. Nonetheless, in general, incentives for cooperation increase as the threat of terrorism escalates (Sandler 2005).

While the above reasons justify expecting dual objectives of protection at home and engagement abroad to be advocated by political elites, should we really expect citizens to come to similar conclusions regarding their foreign policy preferences in times of terrorist threat? We believe the answer is yes, for a number of reasons. The most obvious way that citizens might come to support dual objectives is by following elite framing. Studies of public opinion suggest that elite messages and framing influence the opinions of citizens, especially if consensus exists among elites (e.g., Druckman 2004; Zaller 1992; see also Huddy, Feldman, and Marcus 2007). A look at the Bush administration's antiterror policies shows a dual objective of protecting within and engaging abroad, and broad consensus on those objectives, especially early in the war on terror. With respect to protecting within, the Department of Homeland Security was created in 2002 in direct response to 9/11. The goal of the department is to lead a unified effort to secure the U.S. homeland. As travelers know, the department created a color-coded terrorist alert program and overhauled security at airports. At the same time, the administration also sought to engage other nations in the fight against terrorism. For example, NATO troops as well as Afghans were involved in the war in Afghanistan. The administration cobbled together a "coalition of the willing" for the war in Iraq, among other cooperative efforts pursued in the "war against terror."[25] Given such consensus, we might expect that citizen preferences (especially in the United States) also reflect these dual objectives (especially the closer we are to 2001).

What might happen if elite framing is absent or not as consensual? According to early research, individuals do not hold well-developed or firm opinions on matters of foreign policy (Almond 1950), thus we might not witness support for dual objectives in the absence of elite framing. However, more recent studies suggest that citizens have opinions on foreign policy that are available and cognitively accessible (e.g., Aldrich, Sullivan, and Borgida 1989). Scholars of the post-Vietnam era show that cleavages in foreign policy opinions among the public are represented by well-defined and internally consistent belief systems (Holsti 1979; Holsti and Rosenau 1984; Nincic 1992). Thus, citizens' predispositions influence their opinions on foreign policy (Nyhan and Reifler 2006). Furthermore, citizens also use information on relative power and security threats when making decisions on foreign policy positions (Herrmann and Tetlock 1999; Herrmann et al. 1997). A great deal of empirical research shows that when faced with a security threat the public becomes more inclined to support militant international behavior.[26] With respect to World War II, Page and Shapiro (1992) find substantial shifts in opinion from isolationist to internationalist after Pearl Harbor. In the aftermath of September 11, as perceived threat increased, individuals became more supportive of the United States being active in the world, the campaign against terrorism, and military action in Afghanistan (Huddy et al. 2005; Huddy, Khatib, and Capelos 2002). In the absence of significant elite framing, the adoption of such policies may be particularly appealing if they help individuals feel efficacious and secure in the face of a terrorist threat.

Of course, alternative solutions are theoretically plausible. In particular, a country and its citizens could conceivably shift toward a more isolationalist approach in light of a terrorist threat. One reason might be that it is believed that the country lacks the resources to fight the threat at both levels. Another may be that the threat induces more anxiety than anger among the public (Huddy et al. 2005). The example of Spain in 2004, which we will discuss in more detail in the book's conclusion, is worth mentioning here. In this case, citizens responded to terrorist bombings by demanding that the administration reduce its commitments to the global "war on terror" by withdrawing troops from Iraq. While one could assert that individuals are more likely to prefer flight rather than engagement in response to terrorist threat, we believe that such responses are more the exception than the norm. In chapter 6 we document substantial support for this assertion; more specifically, we provide evidence in support of the links illustrated in the lower portion of figure 1.1. First, conditions of terror threat (when compared to times of well-being) increase support for international engagement in general (and cooperation in particular) and with respect to issues related to security and terrorism. Second, conditions of terror threat cause citizens to be more supportive of policies related to protecting homeland security. Again, preferences for many of these policies might be deemed instrumental in resolving the given crisis context. During times of war, citizens (and elites) are often willing to cede civil liberties and close off borders in order to have more security (Rehnquist 1998). It also may be deemed necessary to engage more actively in the international arena. However, the speed with which individuals are willing to cede civil liberties to protect the homefront suggests that something more psychological may also be occurring. We use both survey and experimental data to show that these relationships hold across citizens of two countries (the United States and Mexico) that vary with respect to power, resources, and experience.

Comparing Crises

The above arguments are intended to apply to conditions of crisis but, in particular, to the threat of terrorism. That said, much (but not all) of the theory and many of the hypotheses could be relevant to other types of collective crises. In the empirical chapters that follow, where possible, we analyze citizens' political attitudes, evaluations, and behaviors in response to other collective threats, primarily economic decline. We compare the differences that individuals exhibit in times of economic threat relative to conditions of well-being and prosperity to those differences individuals exhibit in times of terrorist threat relative to those same "good times." We do not enter this process with overwhelmingly strong expectations concerning which of these two collective threats—one primarily security-related and one primarily financial—will have a greater impact. However, we do note below some literature and factors that might be relevant in thinking about this question.

Some scholarship suggests that terrorist threats should carry more weight than economic threats. In particular, while both conditions of crisis highlight individuals' lack of control via the collective nature of the threat, terrorism is more likely to increase the salience of one's mortality. Scholars of Terror Management Theory (TMT) show that mortality salience has a significant impact on individuals' evaluations and behaviors, and they have applied these findings to the realm of terrorism. In these studies the stimuli are either simple reminders of one's mortality (achieved, for example, by asking a subject to write down thoughts concerning her death) or reminders of 9/11 (see, for example, Landau et al. 2004). TMT research typically finds that these stimuli do not systematically affect negative or positive emotions; thus, it is only the salience of one's mortality that drives the attitudes and behaviors they look at (Landau et al. 2004; Pyszczynski, Solomon, and Greenberg 2002). Our project differs, then, from TMT in at least three important ways. First, we examine the *threat* of a terrorist attack. Second, we examine conditions of collective crisis rather than simply concerns about one's own mortality. Third, we posit (and demonstrate in later chapters) that this threat context (as well as an economic threat context) elicits a significant emotional response. In particular this third point means that threats other than those related to physical security may also elicit shifts in attitudes and behavior.[27] However, given that fears of mortality (and possibly certain other negative emotions) could be much higher in times of terror threat, it is plausible to expect stronger effects for this crisis context.

The perceived magnitude of terrorist threat or any other type of threat for that matter may, though, depend in part on the recency and vividness of the threat in a given country context. At the time our data were collected, in the United States at least, the effects of a severe terrorist attack likely seemed more vivid (given the country's experiences) compared to the effects of a severe economic recession. Thus, if crises compel individuals to seek coping mechanisms as a means of allaying negative feelings and if these negative feelings are more intense in the case of a terrorist threat, then it may be the case that the threat of terrorism (at least in the U.S. context we describe here) has a relatively stronger impact on citizens' political evaluations, attitudes, and behaviors than the threat of economic recession. As we are writing, the United States is now in the middle of a significant economic downturn that is repeatedly being compared to the Great Depression. This situation has likely made the threat of a severe economic recession more vivid than it was a few years ago.

While we have not (yet) analyzed data on how U.S. citizens react to economic threat in this changed context, we do have access to a case in which citizens may be similarly more prone to react to an economic threat: Mexico. Individuals in Mexico have experienced several economic downturns in recent years, most notably severe crises in the mid-1980s and the mid-1990s. In this context, then, economic recessions may appear relatively more vivid. We therefore have reason to expect to find differences in the effects of these two crisis scenarios, and their relationships to one another, across these two contexts. For the U.S. case, we should find stronger effects for the terror threat relative to the economic threat, given that the former threat was more salient during our study and it is related to fears of mortality. For Mexico, we should find that both threats influence individual attitudes, evaluations, and behavior. We do not have strong expectations for which of these threats will prove more consequential given that the two factors of fear of mortality and salience point in different directions. We consider this an open question that, where possible, we take up in the forthcoming empirical chapters.

Conclusion

In this chapter, we developed a theory of citizens' reactions to *collective* crises, namely terrorist threats, whose remedies lie beyond any one individual's control. Fundamental to our arguments is the notion that, in order to allay feelings of anxiety, fear, and/or anger, citizens experiencing such crises are likely to adopt one of several coping strategies.[28] We specified arguments and hypotheses with respect to coping strategies oriented at the individual, national, and international levels. The first coping strategy is the expression of increased distrust and authoritarianism in one's assessments of other individuals. Such tendencies allow a person to impose order and control with respect to those nearest him or her. The second strategy is the search for a heroic political leader, whose status is elevated and protected in order to increase one's feelings of efficacy and/or safety. The third strategy is an increased preference for dual foreign policy objectives whereby individuals seek to "lock down" the homeland while at the same time engage abroad.

What do these coping strategies have in common? We argue that the three are united in their potential to place democracy—its core values, procedures, and institutions—at risk. By this we mean that the application of these coping techniques has potentially troubling implications for the quality of democracy with respect to its social fabric, its administration, and its practices. More specifically, to the extent that increased authoritarian attitudes indicate less tolerance for "out-groups" (as we will show in chapter 3) and to the extent that these attitudes have actual policy implications, we raise the concern that under conditions of terrorist threat it may become more acceptable to deny rights and privileges to selected groups. To the extent that the public wills itself to perceive selected leaders as stronger and more charismatic than they would otherwise, focuses more on leadership traits in selecting political leaders, and actively seeks to protect and assist a leader's image and actions (as we will show in chapters 4 and 5), we raise the concern that, under conditions of terrorist threat, individuals may become less interested in monitoring the *means* by which a strong personality seeks certain agreed-upon ends. And, finally, to the extent that the public seeks to protect the homeland through restrictive, security-oriented policies and simultaneously seeks to cooperate with other nations to act against the perceived threat (as we will show in chapter 6), we raise the concern that, under times of terrorist threat, the value (and protections) placed on civil liberties and human rights both at home and abroad may decline.

We return to a more detailed discussion of terrorist threat and its potential to threaten democracy in chapter conclusions and, ultimately, in the concluding chapter of this book. We also, within these sections, acknowledge a counterargument, which is that these attitudinal shifts are either entirely harmless or even possibly helpful to the resolution of the crisis and/or the quality of democracy. Either way, we must first substantiate that these links between conditions of crisis, namely terrorist threat, and citizens' attitudes, evaluations, and behaviors do in fact exist. Thus, in the following chapters we draw on a variety of data to document the use of these three coping strategies in times of terror threat. We begin by first (in chapter 2) identifying our research approach and the data that we have assembled in order to pursue it.

2

Crisis Creation: A Methodological Tour

In this chapter we introduce the approach that we use to assess the effects of the threat of terrorist attacks (and other threats) on public opinion and behavior. We give a brief overview of the evidence we rely on in subsequent chapters, which includes both experiments and survey data. We discuss the merits of using experiments, then describe our experimental designs, and then present evidence that our experiments were effective in changing people's perceptions of the world around them. We close with a brief discussion of the survey data that we use to complement these studies.

Research Approaches, Approached

Central to our theoretical expectations is that people develop attitudes, register evaluations, make decisions, and behave *differently* in times of threat compared to times of relative calm and well-being. Evaluating our arguments entails making comparisons across these different types of environments, while holding constant as many noncontextual features as possible. Meeting this research need clearly poses some difficulty, given that contexts of threat are generally constant at single points in time and tend to lie beyond the control of an individual set of researchers. Nonetheless, researchers could use several potential types of evidence to test our arguments.

One way in which we might obtain leverage over our research questions would be to survey individuals during times of well-being and then survey them again during times of threat. Scholars call this a *panel design*, since one would survey the same set of individuals at several points in time. Such a design would allow us to hold many features associated with individual attributes constant (such as income, education, and race) across time. This would allow us to control for relevant individual characteristics while discerning the effect that shifts in the political environment have on the attitudes, evaluations, decisions, and behaviors that interest us. While not intended as a study of the effects of terrorist threat compared to better times, the ANES conducted a panel study in which respondents were interviewed in 2000, 2002, and 2004. Scholars have begun to use these data to examine how terrorism changed attitudes pre- and post-9/11 (e.g., Kam and Kinder 2007). Darren Davis and Brian Silver also conducted a panel study of attitudes toward civil liberties, with waves in 2001, 2003, and 2004 (for details see Davis 2007; Davis and Silver 2004a, 2004b). Our project seeks to complement, but also extend in some ways, the types of analyses and conclusions researched by scholars using such panel survey data.

Another possible way to assess some of our research questions is to hold the threat context constant, but make use of variation in individuals' perceptions of threat. This would mean looking at survey data from one point in time. We could then compare how opinions, evaluations, and behavior vary depending on how worried someone is about future terrorist attacks. Several scholars have employed this type of approach to study the effects of worry about terrorist attacks (Davis 2007; Davis and Silver 2004a, 2004b; Huddy et al. 2005) and, again, these studies make clear contributions to some of the questions at the center of our project.

However, exclusive reliance on panel and/or simple cross-sectional survey data has some important limitations. First, surveys conducted in the "age of terrorism" (post-9/11) tend to be characterized by higher than average levels of concern about such threats than we would find under conditions of true well-being and prosperity. This prevents researchers using a cross-sectional survey from obtaining maximal leverage on comparisons across times of threat and nonthreat. Second, it is notoriously difficult to assert cause-and-effect relationships between threat and political behavior with survey data since it is difficult to determine whether concerns about terrorism were formed prior to the attitudes and evaluations of interest. Panel studies (if timed correctly) at least allow the possibility of looking at public opinion before and after the increase in threat level; however, because other aspects of the information environment also change between interview dates, it is difficult to isolate the effect of threat alone. Further, because researchers often fail to anticipate crisis conditions and so long as time travel continues to elude researchers (with even above-average budgets), it is nearly impossible to acquire the ideal panel study for understanding the effects of a particular threat. Third, as many researchers have no doubt lamented, surveys tend not always to ask the "right" questions, where "right" is defined as "of interest to me and my research agenda." Thus, existing surveys only allow us to analyze a subset of the questions we raised in the preceding chapter.

A third method is to experimentally assign individuals to conditions of threat *or* to conditions of well-being and then compare opinions, evaluations, and behavior across these two environments. That is, we can bring people to a lab at the same point in time but expose them to different stimuli, with the intention of heightening concerns of a terrorist attack in one group and diminishing them in another group. Unlike survey data analyses, this method provides a clean test of cause-and-effect relationships by virtue of random assignment, which we will elaborate on in the next section. In fact, since the experimental treatment is only a small representation of what one would find in times of real crisis, one of the few sins the researcher might commit is to underestimate the true effects of these contexts. That said, experiment-based approaches are not necessarily a panacea for context-centered research; we return below to a more detailed discussion of the strengths and weaknesses of experiments.

In line with conventional wisdom on best research practices, we attempt to achieve the "best of all worlds" by relying on data from all three methods, which we combine—where possible—to evaluate our arguments. Given our concern with establishing a causal connection between features of one's political environment (specifically, the presence or absence of a threat) and political behavior, the vast majority of our data comes from experiments. These experiments were conducted over a three-year period beginning in 2004. Specifically, we conducted five U.S.-based experimental studies, some of which took place during the course of elections (fall 2004 and fall 2006) and one of which included nonstudent subjects. We also conducted a similar experimental study in the fall of 2006 in Mexico City.

We further provide evidence for select arguments through the use of survey data. This "triangulation" of research methods allows us to demonstrate the robustness of our findings to different types of data and to different types of individuals. We draw on three sources of survey data. First, we had the good fortune to place relevant questions on a national survey conducted in 2006 in Mexico, the Centro de Investigación y Doncencia Económicas (CIDE)–Comparative Study of Electoral Systems (CSES) survey. Second, we also employ survey data collected at the national level within both the United States and Mexico through a joint project by the Chicago Council on Foreign Relations (CCFR), CIDE, and Consejo Mexicano de Asuntos Internacionales (COMEXI). Finally, we make use of data from the 2000/2002/2004 ANES panel study.

Given its central place in our project and given that the use of experimentation to evaluate the types of questions we raise here is not common practice, in the next section we take up this question: *Why* is this method appropriate to study the effects of terrorist attacks on individual opinions, evaluations, and behavior? Having, we hope, convinced the reader of the usefulness of an experiment-based approach for this project, we then turn attention to the next obvious question: *How* do we employ this approach?

Why Use Experiments to Study the Effects of Terrorist Attacks?

Before discussing why experiments are appropriate in the context of our study, we first briefly identify some of the general advantages and disadvantages of using experimental methods. We then turn to why this method is appropriate for our research questions. We invite readers who need not be convinced to skip this section and apply their energies to the subsequent discussion of our specific experimental designs.

The experimental approach has several key benefits, including the ability to investigate cause-and-effect relationships, to break down complex relationships by isolating one variable at a time, and, finally, to measure precisely.[1] These three benefits all relate to the overarching and crucial strength of experimental methods: internal validity. Combining the first and second benefits, Kinder and Palfrey put it best: "by assigning subjects to treatments randomly, the experimenter can be confident (within the limitations established by statistical inference) that any differences observed between subjects assigned to different treatment conditions *must* be caused by differences in the treatments themselves" (1993, 11). In terms of measurement precision, experiments give researchers control over numerous aspects of the study, including subject recruitment, location of the study, and the design and implementation of the treatments (McDermott 2002). This control is vital to allowing researchers to address questions that often elude those using more standard methods (Babbie and Benaquisto 2002). For example, in the experimental lab, we know for certain whether a subject was exposed to campaign information; while, in survey research, measures that ask citizens to recall campaign information are often less accurate, due to guessing and errors in memory (Ansolabehere, Iyengar, and Simon 1999).

While experimental methods are high in internal validity, this feature often poses a different threat to scientific research: external validity (Campbell and Stanley 1963). By external validity, we mean how much the results can be generalized beyond the select sample of study participants. Typically, researchers using experiment-based methods face concerns that the effects detected in the lab (or similar controlled setting) may not necessarily be applied to the entire population of interest.[2] One of the more serious and common of these critiques focuses on the use of undergraduate students as research subjects, who are frequently used in political science studies and in other fields due to greater ease in compensation and recruitment. Because lab experiments are conducted in necessarily artificial settings and often use subjects who are not sampled from the national population, it is valid to question the extent to which conclusions drawn from experiments are limited in their generality. It is also worth noting that, depending on the nature of the study, at times certain characteristics of the student population may present a more difficult test case for researchers.

While acknowledging their strengths and their limitations, we believe experiments provide the best available method to compare attitudes, evaluations, and behavior of individuals in times of terror threat versus times of relative calm and well-being. To maximize internal validity, we want to isolate the effect of one factor: the threat (vs. nonthreat) context. An experiment allows us to do just that by bringing people to a lab at the same point in time and then randomly assigning them to be exposed to selected information. Our novel treatments are intended to heighten concerns of a terrorist attack in one group and diminish those concerns in another group. The approach successfully enables us to conclude that any changes in outcomes are attributable to the treatment, rather than to factors that might exist beyond the lab's walls.

We recognize—and attempt to overcome—potential drawbacks to experiment-based research: our samples are not representative of all individuals; our treatments approximate but cannot actually consist of true crisis situations; and the studies took place well after 9/11, in the "age of terrorism." While we cannot completely remove these threats to external validity, we have tried to anticipate concerns related to these threats. Our student and nonstudent studies, in the United States and in Mexico, have provided us with data on a broad range of subjects in two different countries, one of which has experienced a major terrorist attack and one that has not. In addition, the use of students in our cases often represents a least-likely case, given their particular characteristics. We also made use of survey data drawn from more general samples, where possible, and these corroborate our experimental findings. With respect to the second limitation, if we find effects by just reminding people of past attacks and warning them of future attacks, we feel relatively confident that the effects during an actual crisis will likely be much more pronounced. Finally, while our experiments took place after 9/11, this is also the case for existing survey data relevant to our purposes. We attempt to overcome the problem associated with the overall elevated concerns about terrorism by comparing the terror threat condition to a "good-times" condition, in which we explicitly attempted to lower concerns about terrorism so that they might better approximate those that would have been found in a pre-9/11 world.

Experimental Design

In all of our studies, participants were randomly assigned to experimental conditions, which vary by study. All of the studies had a Terror Threat condition, which was designed to increase concerns of a terror attack, and a Good Times condition, which was designed to diminish concerns of such an attack. Some studies had a pure control group, which was not exposed to any treatment. Others contained groups exposed to different types of threat, such as an economic crisis. The medium through which the treatment was delivered was either an audiovisual media presentation or a newspaper article.

The basic procedure in all of the studies was to recruit subjects to a lab (or classroom), have them fill out a survey with basic demographic and attitudinal information, expose treated groups to some type of media message, and then measure our key variables of interest in a post test. We then assess our arguments by comparing responses to particular questions across subjects in the different experimental conditions.[3]

Since we only had the opportunity to expose people to a relatively short treatment, we knew the treatments had to be somewhat strong, especially if we wanted to get a sense of political behavior in extreme circumstances, such as an actual crisis. We also wanted to present subjects with information that they would likely encounter in a crisis context. Thus, we began by creating audiovisual treatments that were about a minute and a half in length. We modeled the presentations after media clips commonly seen on news Web sites, which combine a slideshow of images with a voiceover. Thus, the narration provided the cognitive information we wanted to convey, while the pictures were intended to help influence emotions such as worry about a terrorist attack (e.g., Brader 2005, 2006; Huddy and Gunnthorsdottir 2000).

The texts for the narrations were drawn primarily from news and political reports and edited together by the authors. We obtained most of the images from online news archives. In some cases, we used text boxes with quotes (which were read within the narration). The voiceovers were done by a male professional voice actor, and the images and narration were edited together by a professional editor. Since our U.S.-based studies were conducted in a computer-based experimental lab, it was easy to put up dividers between terminals and use headphones to ensure that subjects were only able to watch their assigned treatment on the computer screen. Lacking a computer lab for our study in Mexico, we could not use this form of treatment, and instead used mock newspaper articles that consisted only of text and which were about one page in length (500 words). We then used this form of treatment in two of the U.S.-based studies, in order to compare the effects of the audiovisual versus the newspaper treatment. We suspected that the effects would be stronger with the audiovisual treatments, since they contained images, and we test this expectation later in the chapter.

With respect to the content within the treatments, any information we presented needed to be credible in order for subjects to take it seriously. Thus, in creating our treatments, we collected and compiled most information from various newspaper articles and political reports; we did, however, take a generous editor's prerogative and assembled this information to create the starkest case possible and, further, we at times took a nonjournalist's prerogative and created select "facts."[4] We compiled this resulting text together either into a narrator's script or a mock newspaper article. We generally included information on past events, such as the terrorist attacks of 9/11 and in Britain, and future threats issued by Al Qaeda, as well as indicators of a lack of preparedness for a future terrorist attack. As we mentioned previously, almost all of the pictures (with the exception of a few graphs) for the audiovisual treatments were copied from real Web sites and were thus authentic.

An important benefit of this type of treatment is that it is packaged in a way similar to what individuals would see as they are exposed to information about terrorist attacks in their everyday lives. Thus, the treatments are high in external validity. One downside to presenting treatments in this way is that we cannot isolate exactly what it is about the treatments that might be driving any differences we find between conditions. This is in contrast to studies like those conducted by scholars of Terror Management Theory (TMT) who ask treated groups to write down thoughts about their own death (Landau et al. 2004; Pyszczynski, Solomon, and Greenberg 2002). They can then attribute any differences between treated and control groups to reminders of mortality. In our study, we cannot for example say if it is reminders about past attacks, the threat of future threats, or information about a lack of preparedness that is causing the shifts in attitudes, evaluations, and behavior. However, individuals in the real world are unlikely to be exposed to terror-threat news that does not include a combination of all of this information. It is also worth noting that the content across the treatments varies so that, for example, our Good Times condition does not reflect the terror-threat treatment by talking about how terrorism is *not* a concern. Methodologically our research approach shares a kinship with issue framing studies, in which the treatments received by participants vary in content in nonequivalent ways.[5] Given the nature of the research questions we are attempting to answer, we believe it is worth the sacrifice of some precision in exchange for greater external validity.

Terror Threat Treatment

The Terror Threat treatment sought to make the possibility of another terrorist attack salient in the subject's mind. The audiovisual presentation contained frightening politically relevant images and information regarding terrorism. Below is the text of the narration used in the 2004 election study (US04s):

(1) As we enter the fall of 2004, the worries of U.S. security officials are increasing. (2) Intelligence analysts say recent and credible information strongly suggests Al Qaeda is committed to carrying out a full-on attack in the United States. (3) On September 11, 2001, Al Qaeda's attacks killed nearly 3,000 (4) men, women, and children, and injured over 6,000 more. U.S. security officials are bracing for a series of attacks at least (5) twice this magnitude, and likely greater. (6) Secretary of Homeland Security Tom Ridge delivered this news in a recent press conference, calling it "sobering information." (7) Over the last year, terrorist activities and communications have increased. (8) Al Qaeda is reported to have been very pleased with the results of a series of train bombings in Madrid, among other recent attacks around the world. (9) Intelligence

officials indicate significant lapses in security at airports, nuclear plants, ports, bridges, dams, and water treatment facilities. In light of all this, (10) the CIA is warning Americans that "al Qaeda has people in the United States on the verge of mounting a large-scale terrorist attack." (11) With anti-Americanism around the world on the rise, and (12) increased chatter on terrorist networks, U.S. citizens are bracing for an imminent attack at home (13) and feeling less secure.

As this narration was read, various images (numbered when they emerge) appeared on the computer screen (which can be found in Web Supplement C). The background for all of the pictures was black. Image 1 appeared when the first sentence was read and consisted of a black screen with the following statement in white font "U.S. Officials Warn Attacks Are Likely." Image 2 was another black screen with a Homeland Security logo and had text that stated, "Al Qaeda is committed to carrying out a full-on attack in the United States." Several tragic pictures from 9/11 (images 3, 4, and 5) accompanied the narration about this event. As subjects heard about Ridge's press conference, a picture of him appeared along with the terror-threat level color-coded system (image 6). A picture of terrorist strikes around the globe (see image 7) appeared with the following sentence, while a picture of the train bombing in Madrid (image 8) appeared when that event was mentioned. As lapses in security were being discussed, image 9 tried to convey how underprepared the United States was for an attack by overwhelming the field of vision with different photos of ports, dams, water treatment facilities, and so on. Image 10 was another black screen, this time with a CIA logo warning Americans that "al Qaeda has people in the United States on the verge of mounting a large-scale terrorist attack." As the narrator read "with anti-Americanism around the world on the rise," a picture of an Arab-looking individual burning the U.S. flag appeared on the screen (image 11), followed by a picture of suspected terrorists (image 12). The narration ended with a collage of pictures from 9/11 and anti-American protestors (image 13).[6]

The audiovisual presentations conducted in the summer and fall of 2005 (US05ns and US05s, respectively) were almost identical, except we revised the narration to take into account the different time period. At that point, Tom Ridge had stepped down, so we replaced his image and department with a picture of Alberto Gonzalez, the U.S. attorney general. Moreover, Al Qaeda had claimed responsibility for more targets around the world, so we revised the discussion of Madrid to encompass these other attacks as follows: "Al Qaeda is reported to have been very pleased with the results of bombings that have been carried out against civilians in Iraq, Madrid, Egypt, and London."

We used a newspaper version of the Terror Threat treatment in the Mexico study, as well as in the fall 2006 and spring 2007 U.S. studies (US06s and US07s). The mock newspaper articles for each study can be found in Web Supplement C.[7] The main difference between the audiovisuals and the news articles is the absence of images and the presence of more detailed information in the latter. In the Mexico article, for example, subjects were told that "A raid on a London terrorist hideout on May 9, 2006, resulted in the capture of computer files that identified Mexican hotels, financial interests, and the subway system on a list of future Al Qaeda targets." In the 2006 U.S. student study, subjects read, "In a March briefing this year, investigators indicated 'real concern' about the theft of 7,000 pounds of fertilizer in Contra Costa County. In August, the U.S. Coast Guard reported bomb threats to Bay Area bridges."

Overall, then, both the audiovisual and article versions of the Terror Threat treatment sought to make salient potential terrorist attacks in the minds of our subjects. They were intended to approximate a real crisis condition, in which an individual would be exposed to information from the media concerning the danger posed by an imminent terrorist threat.

Good Times Treatment

The Good Times treatment sought to reduce concerns about potential threats or crises. The audiovisual treatment exposed subjects to happy images and positive information about the state of the United States and its citizens. We specifically did not mention anything about terrorism, so as not to prime subjects to think about the threat. Even if we reported on progress in this domain, bringing up the issue might cause subjects to recall their worry of future attacks. The benefit then of the type of Good Times treatment we use is that it is devoid of any references to terrorism and should better reflect times of general prosperity and well being. The drawback is that we can only say that against a backdrop of positive information about general indicators, a terror threat leads to changes in attitudes, evaluations, and behavior. We cannot isolate specifically what it is between the differences in the stimuli that is leading to the shifts. However, we will demonstrate later that we do find that our treatments act as intended: they increased concerns of a terror attack in one group and diminished them in the Good Times group.

As may be apparent to some readers, we modeled this treatment after the "Morning Again in America" ads by Ronald Reagan in 1984. Below is the text for the narration used in the study preceding the 2004 U.S. election (US04s):

(1) Our country is experiencing a time of prosperity and well-being. Americans are (2) enjoying increased disposable income as the country enters these good times. (3) Federal Reserve Chairman Alan Greenspan recently declared a "positive upswing" in the economy. (4) And, with low interest rates, home ownership is on the rise. (5) State officials across the U.S. have reported increases in standardized test scores for those in kindergarten through 12th grade. (6) In addition, a recent government report noted that more young people are going to college than ever before. (7) With opportunities for these young graduates increasing, the youth of today is finding the workplace more rewarding and diverse. (8) Advances in medicine and technology are enhancing the length and quality of life in the United States. (9) Experts report that, by most measures, our environment is cleaner than it was two decades ago. (10) Officials note that these changes, plus more active lifestyles, are decreasing health problems for many people. (11) Overall, more Americans report in surveys that they are healthier and happier than ever before. (12) Americans are justifiably proud of the advances made by their country and confident in what lies ahead for their children.

As this narration was being read, various images (numbered when they emerge) appeared on the computer screen (which can be found in Web Supplement C). The background for all of the pictures was now yellow. Image 1 was the first screen that appeared when the first sentence was read (labeled "1" in narration) and contained the title "Good Times in America" and pictured young boys playing the all-American sport of baseball. In the second image, subjects saw a picture of people shopping (image 2). As they were learning about the positive upswing in the economy, image 3 showed Alan Greenspan and a graph with arrows pointing up. A picture of a house under construction and a happy couple then greeted them in image 4 as the narrator read that more people are buying homes. As subjects heard about test scores increasing, image 5 showed two pictures of teachers with students in a classroom, which was followed by a photo, image 6, of a college campus. Image 7 then presented a collage of photos of college graduations, with hats flying in the air, as new students enter the more exciting and diverse workforce. A woman at a microscope appeared in image 8 as the narrator mentioned advances in science and technology, while a pristine lake appeared in image 9 as subjects were told about improvements in the environment. A collage of Americans exercising greeted the viewer in image 10 to reflect that the country is healthier than ever before, followed by a chart indicating increases in happiness in the United States (image 11). The final set of images contained another picture of children, as well as a picture of fireworks erupting at a professional baseball game.

As should be clear from the description, the Good Times treatment was designed to make people feel good about the country and the future. The audiovisual presentations conducted in the summer and fall of 2005 (US05ns and US05s) were again almost identical, with minor changes for the time-period differences (e.g., taking out a reference to Greenspan).

We again used a newspaper version of the Good Times treatment in the Mexico study (MEX06s), as well as the fall 2006 and spring 2007 U.S. studies (US06s and US07s). All three can be found in Web Supplement C. In the newspaper article in Mexico, subjects read that "with respect to the world economy, Mexico has become more competitive and has been able to attract more foreign direct investment, according to a recent report by the OECD." Subjects learned about the improved situation in California in the fall 2006 article: "With declines in unemployment and increased job opportunities for the public, especially among new college graduates, California's macroeconomic picture is 'looking rosy,' says Dermott Watson of the California Institute for Economic Research (CIER)."

Again, the overall intent of these treatments was to diminish concerns about threats among subjects exposed to this condition. We sought to approximate a real condition of relative well-being, calm, and prosperity in which the news stories to which individuals would be exposed would contain upbeat information and images.

Other Threat Treatments

In a few of our experimental studies (in both the United States and in Mexico), we introduced an economic threat treatment as a point of comparison.[8] Similar to the Terror Threat treatment, the alternative threat treatment was designed to elevate concern and worry, this time with respect to an economic threat. Some of the studies had an audiovisual treatment for the economic threat, while others had a newspaper article. To give a sense of the economic treatment, we present the narration from the economic threat audiovisual treatment (and the corresponding images can be found in Web Supplement C) used in the summer of 2005 study.

As the Fall of 2005 approaches, U.S. officials are warning that the nation's economy is in trouble. According to the non-partisan Economic Policy Institute, the United States has "just experienced the sharpest loss of jobs in a cycle since the Great Depression." Nearly half of all Americans know someone who has lost their job. Even among those who are employed, the rising costs of health care and education are making it difficult for American families to get ahead. Housing prices are a significant concern; according to Federal Reserve Chairman Alan Greenspan, they have reached "dangerous levels." And, safety nets that might cushion against economic problems are dangerously thin. In addition to declines in personal savings, all sides foresee that the nation's social security program will stop paying out within our lifetimes. Adding to this bleak portrait are soaring oil prices, a natural gas shortage, and unprecedented demands for electricity that have Americans bracing for record levels of inflation and a severe energy crunch. A recent bi-partisan congressional task force reports that—quote—"there are few options available to us in the short term to forestall inevitable pain for millions of Americans." With the domestic infrastructure in trouble and the dollar continuing its slide amidst threatening shifts in the global economy, Americans are facing a prolonged economic recession and feeling less secure.

Participants

Our experiments were conducted over a three-year period beginning in 2004, using student and nonstudent subjects in both the United States and Mexico. If our results are consistent across student and nonstudent subjects, then that enables us to make broader generalizations to the population as a whole. Since our arguments are meant to be general for citizens in democratic systems facing the threat of future terrorist attacks, we ran studies in the United States and Mexico, which differ on a few important dimensions. First, one country has been hit by a lethal international terrorist attack, while the other has not. Second, the United States is more developed politically and economically than its neighbor to the south. If we find a similar pattern of results in the two countries, that would indicate that it is the threat of future attacks, not necessarily a country's resources or past experience with an attack, which causes shifts in citizen attitudes, evaluations, and behavior. Furthermore, a similar pattern across the countries would suggest that this process is likely to occur among democracies that vary with respect to their political and economic situation.

Table 2.1 provides details on each of these studies, including the time period in which the study was conducted, the subject population, whether it was during an election, the form of compensation, and whether the study was computer-based or paper and pencil. Our shorthand notation to indicate each study is to first list the country (US or MEX), then year (04, 05, 06, or 07), then whether it had student (s) or nonstudent (ns) subjects.

As is clear from the table, the studies were in the field at various points in time from the fall of 2004 to the spring of 2007. The vast majority of the studies were conducted with students in the United States, though one of the studies contained a sample of U.S. nonstudents (occasionally referred to as "adults" simply to distinguish them from students), and another had a sample of students in Mexico. Two of the studies took place during an election context: the 2004 U.S. presidential election and the 2006 California gubernatorial election. The Mexico study took place two and a half months following the July 2006 election. For the student-based studies in the United States, participants were recruited from undergraduate social science classes at a large public university in northern California in exchange for class credit. For the adult study, research subjects were recruited from three populations: residents of two northern California towns and employees of a large university in northern California.[9] The adult participants were compensated thirty dollars for their time. In Mexico, students at a private university in Mexico City were recruited using flyers and were compensated eighty pesos for participating in the study.[10] All of the U.S. studies were conducted on a computer and the Mexico study was paper and pencil.

Table 2.2 presents the distribution of subjects in each study across the different experimental conditions. It also indicates the form of the treatment: audiovisual or newspaper article. All of the studies contained the Terror Threat and Good Times treatments, and all except the first contained another type of threat condition. All of these were an economic threat condition, with the exception of US06s. After the third study, we stopped using a pure control group. Our decision to eliminate this group came from the fact that our principal interest lies in comparing nonthreat conditions to threat conditions. As we had expected, those in our control groups reported average levels of concern about terrorism which fall in between the Terror Threat and Good Times conditions. These latter two groups, then, provide us with the most leverage with respect to assessing our project's arguments.[11] Given random assignment, the distribution of subjects across each experimental condition is similar, with the exception of US05ns, which has a higher number of subjects in the Good Times condition.[12]

Table 2.1. Details on the experimental studies

Study	N	Month/Year	Population	Election Context	Compensation	Form of Study
US04s	311	10/2004	Student	Y	Extra credit	Computer
US05ns	418	08/2005	Nonstudent	N	Monetary	Computer
US05s	201	10/2005–11/2005	Student	N	Extra credit	Computer
MEX06s	299	09/2006	Student	N[a]	Monetary	Paper
US06s	253	10/2006	Student	Y	Extra credit	Computer
US07s	237	05/2007	Student	N	Extra credit	Computer

[a] The Mexico study took place two and one-half months following the election.

Table 2.2. Distribution of subjects across conditions and form of treatment

Study	Good Times	Terror Threat	Other	Control	Form of Treatment
US04s	104	99		108	Audiovisual
US05ns	145	98	82	93	Audiovisual
US05s	51	49	53	48	Audiovisual
MEX06s	99	101	99		Newspaper
US06s	85	75	93		Newspaper
US07s	88	85	64		Newspaper

In table 2.3 we present some basic demographic information on the sample in each experimental study, as well as descriptive statistics for some political behavior and predispositions measures. To get a sense of how our samples differ with respect to the more general population, we compare the values in our U.S. experimental studies to those in the 2000/2002/2004 ANES panel study and the 2004 time-series study. Since panel studies are sometimes not perfectly representative, we chose to look at both. Finally, we compare the Mexico experimental sample characteristics with those of a national sample in the CIDE-CSES public-opinion survey in Mexico.

Turning first to the U.S. studies, the main demographic variable that is different in most of our experimental studies compared to the general population is age, since we use mostly student samples. The average age of most of our subjects ranges from twenty to twenty-one in the student samples, and is forty-six in the adult U.S. sample. The latter is very similar to the average age in the 2004 ANES survey, forty-seven. The percent female in the U.S. studies is similar to the value in the 2004 ANES study, though we do have slightly more females (63%) in the adult U.S. study (US05ns). With respect to race and ethnicity, the percentage of whites in our adult sample (76%) is very close to the percentage in the 2004 ANES study (73%). However, our U.S. student samples contain a higher proportion of Latinos and Asians, and fewer whites. Across all our study samples we have fewer African Americans represented compared to the national survey data. If we turn to political indicators, the percentage of Democrats in our U.S. studies ranges from a low of 47 percent in US05ns to a high of 61 percent in US07s, compared to about 32 percent in the 2004 ANES. We are closer to the 2004 ANES in most of our studies with respect to the percentage of Republicans. If we turn to political interest, the values are very similar across our studies, ranging from 2.3 to 2.6 (on a three-point scale), and are comparable to the values in the 2004 ANES (2.3). Finally, with respect to political sophistication indicators, our samples are slightly higher in political sophistication compared to the more general population in the 2004 ANES. We will later recall some of these key differences, especially with respect to partisanship, when we consider generalizing from the experimental results presented in later empirical chapters. For now, we should note that since many of our dependent variables measure factors such as authoritarian attitudes, militant foreign policy preferences, and evaluations of Republican leaders, it may be that our more Democratic and younger samples provide a relatively more difficult test case for our arguments.

If we compare the 2004 ANES to the 2000/2002/2004 ANES panel

Table 2.3. Mean values on demographic and dispositional variables, by sample and conditions

Variable	US04s	US05ns	US05s	US06s	US07s	ANES Panel	ANES 2004	MEX06s	Mexico CIDE-CSES
Age	20	46	n/a	21	21	55	47	20	40
Female	52%	63%	54%	47%	45%	57%	53%	36%	51%
White[a]	42%	76%	58%[b]	51%	43%	85%	73%	N/A	N/A
Asian	35%	8%	29%	23%	24%	1%	2%	N/A	N/A
Latino	11%	6%	14%	14%	19%	2%	7%	N/A	N/A
African American	0%	1%	4%	2%	3%	7%	15%	N/A	N/A
Democrat–U.S. PRD–Mexico	57%	47%	54%	53%	61%	36%	32%	10%	18%
Republican–U.S. PAN–Mexico	20%	24%	22%	19%	14%	35%	29%	40%	22%
PRI–Mexico	N/A	N/A	N/A	N/A	N/A	N/A	N/A	15%	15%
Interest[c]	2.6	N/A	N/A	2.3	2.4	2.3	2.3	2.3	2.0
Political Knowledge[d]	0.7	0.7	0.8	n/a	0.4[e]	0.3	0.5	0.6	0.6

[a] We leave other race out of the table.

[b] The race categories from this study were not mutually exclusive. Subjects could indicate more than one racial or ethnic group.

[c] The interest scale ranges from 1 to 3, with higher values indicating more interest in the campaign, though the exact wording varied by year.

[d] We constructed this measure from three political information questions that were closely matched on our survey and the 2004 NES: whether the respondent knew which party had the most members in the U.S. House, what job two people hold (Tony Blair, William Rehnquist/John Roberts, Rumsfeld/Gates). The two people varied across studies depending on office vacancies. Correct responses were coded as 1, while incorrect responses were coded as 0. We then created an additive scale that ranges from 0 to 1. We used comparable questions in the Mexico study. One of the questions from the CIDE-CSES study was similar, though the other two ask about terms for members of Congress and who is in the chambers of Congress.

[e] This is likely lower because we asked about Robert Gates, who had recently been appointed secretary of defense.

study, we find some minor differences. Subjects in the panel study are slightly older, more partisan, and less politically knowledgeable than those in the 2004 ANES study. There is also a higher presence of women and whites in the panel study. Both samples have about the same levels of political interest. Finally, if we compare our Mexico student sample to the sample in the CIDE-CSES study, we find that the CIDE-CSES sample is older, identifies more with the left-leaning Partido de la Revolucíon y Democratica (PRD) and less with the right-leaning Partido Acción Nacional (PAN), and has more females than the student sample. We will also bear these differences in mind when we discuss our findings for each study.

Procedures

Student subjects in the United States were recruited via announcements in political science classrooms, nonstudent subjects were recruited via mailings, and students in Mexico were recruited via flyers. All three recruitment methods indicated that we were conducting a study about public opinions on current events. While the method of recruitment varied, the procedures were similar in all of the experimental studies. Subjects reported to the experimental lab (or reserved classroom for the Mexico study) in order to participate. For the computer-based studies, once students were individually seated in front of a computer terminal, a research assistant initiated the computer program. The program first randomly assigned participants to either the control (status quo) group (if applicable), or one of the treatment groups.[13] The first thing to appear was a screen with study information and the study followed. In the paper-and-pencil study in Mexico, research assistants first had subjects read the information sheet and then randomly handed out surveys to the students.[14]

In the first part of the survey, subjects were asked some basic sociodemographic questions and political background variables. If the subjects were assigned to one of the treatment conditions, these questions were followed by instructions to put on headphones and watch a short presentation for the audiovisual form of the treatment or instructions to read the newspaper article. Participants were instructed to listen to or read the article carefully since they might be asked questions about the presentation/article later in the study. After exposure to the treatments (or not for those in the Status Quo condition, which proceeded immediately to the next set of questions), subjects completed a short survey, which included questions related to our key arguments, which will be discussed more in depth in the chapters that follow. Upon finishing, subjects read an additional study information page in which we gave more details about the study and were then compensated with money (U.S. adult study and Mexico student study) or class credit (U.S. student studies).

Did the Treatments Work?

Before we go any further, it is important to assess whether our treatments had the intended effects, increasing worry about terrorist attacks among those exposed to the Terror Threat treatment and decreasing worry among those in the Good Times condition. After exposure to the treatment, we asked respondents to indicate how worried they felt that there would be terrorist attacks in that country in the near future on a scale that we have coded to run from 0 to 1, with higher values indicating more worry.[15] In addition to exploring whether average levels of worry were higher among those in the Terror Threat treatment relative to Good Times across all of the studies, we also explored differences across the version of the treatment. That is, did the audiovisual treatments lead to higher levels of worry? One might suspect that the combination of information and images is more powerful than text alone. Furthermore, we explored differences across country context. Here our preliminary expectations included the notion that overall worry would be higher in the United States compared to Mexico, since Mexico has not experienced international terrorist attacks on its soil.

If we turn to figure 2.1, we find that for the whole sample (all studies pooled together), average worry about terrorist attacks is significantly higher among those in the Terror Threat condition, .445, compared to those in the Good Times condition, .390 ($p \leq .01$ according to a t-test). We also find that this relationship holds for both versions of the treatment and across countries.[16]

Does it matter if the treatment is audiovisual- or newspaper-based? In the figure, it appears that worry about terrorist attacks is higher among those in the United States exposed to the audiovisual treatment, .520, compared to those exposed to the newspaper version of the treatment, .491. Worry is also higher among those in the Good Times audiovisual treatment, compared to the newspaper version.[17] If we look at the difference in worry between Terror Threat and Good Times, it is actually the same for the audiovisual and newspaper versions of the treatment. The Terror Threat treatment is shifting subjects by about the same amount, relative to Good Times, even if the mean levels of worry are higher in the audiovisual version.[18] Thus, it appears that both versions were equally

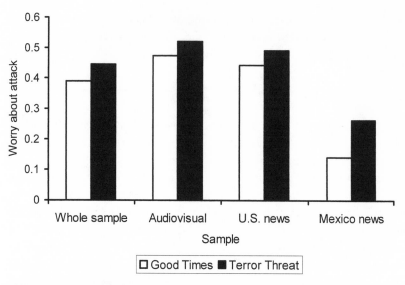

Figure 2.1. Mean worry about terrorist attacks by condition, version, and country

successful in increasing worry about terrorist attacks, relative to the Good Times condition.

Finally, we compared the differences in worry about terrorism among those in the United States and Mexico. Here we compared Mexico to the U.S. study that also used newspaper articles as the form of the treatment. As we expected, worry about terrorist attacks is significantly lower in both the Good Times and Terror Threat conditions for Mexico compared to the United States (according to t-tests). However, it appears that the Terror Threat condition is more effective in increasing worry, relative to Good Times, in the case of Mexico.

In sum, these results show that the treatments did have the intended effects on respondents, increasing concerns of a terrorist attack among those who viewed the Terror Threat treatment relative to those exposed to the Good Times treatment. Furthermore, these effects obtain regardless of the form of the treatment. Finally, worry about terrorist attacks was lower in Mexico compared to the United States.

In addition to exploring the effect of the Terror Threat condition on worry about future attacks, we wanted to confirm, as we outlined in chapter 1, that the Terror Threat condition influenced a range of different emotions. To measure emotions, we relied on the PANAS mood battery developed by Watson et al. (1988), which, when included, was positioned toward the end of our studies. The twenty-item battery consists

Table 2.4. Factors from emotion battery by condition

| Factor | Emotions Loading Highly | Mean Factor Value | | P-value on difference of means tests (GT vs. TT) |
		Good Times (GT)	*Terror Threat* (TT)	
Anxiety	Afraid, Scared, Nervous, Guilty, Ashamed, Distressed	−0.078	0.117	0.03
Positive Affect	Determined, Enthusiastic, Inspired, Proud, Strong	−0.063	0.102	0.06
Anger	Irritable, Hostile	−0.020	0.007	0.75
Interest	Alert, Attentive	−0.001	−0.013	0.88

of showing the subject an emotional term, such as "enthusiastic," and asking the respondent to indicate the degree to which he or she is feeling that emotion at the present time (see the appendix for wording). Using principal-components factor analysis, we find evidence of four distinct, underlying emotional dimensions (though two are just at the 1.0 Eigenvalue standard cutoff). For those interested in technical details, please see Web Supplement A, Table 2.b, for rotated factor loadings. In table 2.4, we show the average factor value for each underlying emotion for those in the Good Times and Terror Threat conditions, as well as whether the average value is significantly different between these two groups. Several emotions load highly onto the first underlying dimension,[19] which we label Anxiety, including afraid, scared, nervous, guilty, ashamed, and distressed. These were many of the emotions we discussed in the last chapter that should emerge during contexts of terror threat. As expected, individuals in the Terror Threat condition (.117) are significantly more anxious compared to those in the Good Times condition (−.078).

We label the second factor Positive Affect and several emotions load highly onto this factor, including active, determined, enthusiastic, excited, inspired, interested, proud, and strong. The average value on this factor is higher in the Terror Threat condition (.102) compared to the Good Times condition (−.063), and these differences are meaningful. This suggests to us that, given that the battery was placed at the end of the survey, individuals already had time to develop and make use of coping strategies that buoyed this set of positive emotions. This interpretation is bolstered by the host of evidence we will present in future chapters regarding the employment of these coping mechanisms. In short, we find that individuals exposed to the Terror Threat condition report feeling relatively more proud, strong, and inspired. The emotions hostile, irritable, and upset load highly on the third underlying dimension, which we label Anger, and the emotions alert, attentive, and interested load highly on a fourth factor, labeled Interested. While the values on Anger are higher among those in the Terror Threat condition compared to the Good Times group, and the reverse pattern holds for Interested, these differences are not very meaningful.[20] In sum, exposure to the Terror Threat condition, compared to the Good Times condition, affected a host of emotions and left individuals feeling more anxious and strong and, to a lesser extent, angry and less interested. The range of emotional responses is consistent with the uncertainty introduced by the threat condition as well as our expected tendency for individuals to adopt bolstering stances. One may argue that the evidence may just point to people being more aroused in general when given the threat context; however, this argument lacks strong support in the fact that we only find significant differences between the Terror Threat condition and Good Times for the dimensions related to anxiety and positive affect and not for those related to anger and interest.

Since we introduced an economic threat in some of our studies, we were also interested in determining if worry about the economy increased among those in the Economic Threat treatment group. We replicated the previous analysis for the Good Times and Economic Threat treatment groups for a question about worry about the economy, which runs from 0 to 1, with higher values indicating more worry. These results are presented in figure 2.2. Turning first to the whole sample, those exposed to the Economic Threat treatment are significantly more worried about the economy, .617, compared to those in the Good Times treatment, .544 ($p \le .01$ in a t-test). This relationship again holds across the different versions of the treatment and for both countries.[21] Again, we find that the form of treatment is not consequential. Finally, worry about the economy is higher in Mexico for both the Good Times and Economic Threat conditions, compared to the U.S. news version. This is as we would expect in that problems with the economy were salient in the Mexico election that occurred a few months prior to the study and, furthermore, Mexico had experienced severe economic crises in the recent past (e.g., the 1995 peso crisis). In sum, our Eco-

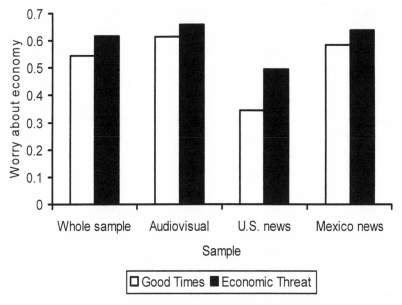

Figure 2.2. Mean worry about the economy by condition, version, and country

nomic Threat treatment also worked as intended, increasing worry among those exposed to the treatment, relative to the Good Times group.

Survey Data

In addition to the experiments, we make select use of survey data. Essentially, we draw on surveys that have reasonable indicators of worry about terror threats as well as questions pertaining to the three coping mechanisms. We will discuss each dataset in turn.

A survey that we are able to employ in our study of all three coping strategies is the ANES 2000/2002/2004 panel study, which consisted of five waves: a 2000 pre-election survey, a 2000 post-election survey, a 2002 pre-election survey, a 2002 post-election survey, and a 2004 post-election survey. The dataset included 1807 completed cases, though the number of observations is lower for some waves compared to others. The main reason we use the panel study is that the 2002 and 2004 waves of the study included a question that captures one's subjective determination of the likelihood of future terrorist attacks and a host of dependent variables relevant to each proposed coping strategy. A nice feature of the panel is that we can compare changes in evaluations and behavior over time in response to assessments of future terror threats. However, the panel also has some downsides. For one, the questions asked are not as extensive as those asked in the regular ANES time-series studies. Second, panel studies are generally less representative than cross-sectional studies because of panel attrition (losing subjects along the way). As we indicated earlier, those in the panel are slightly older, less politically knowledgeable, more partisan, and there is a higher presence of women and whites compared to the 2004 time-series study. Finally, panels can suffer from panel conditioning, meaning the process of being interviewed at one point in time may influence responses in the next interview, leading to potentially biased inferences. While we recognize these potential problems, we still use this study because it is the best available for our purposes.[22] Most importantly, the ANES time-series studies do not contain adequate questions on terror threat, while the panel does ask about individual perceptions of the likelihood of future terrorist attacks.[23]

In addition to this survey, we were able to place relevant questions on a national survey conducted in 2006 in Mexico, the CIDE-CSES survey project, led and implemented by Ulises Beltrán of CIDE and of BGC, Ulises Beltrán y Asociados. The national, face-to-face study was in the field from July 23 to August 2, 2006, a few weeks following the presidential election. We were able to put both charisma and leadership evaluation questions onto this survey.

With respect to the final strategy for dealing with crisis, relations with other nations, we employ survey data collected at the national level within both the United States and Mexico through the CCFR, the one with Mexico cosponsored with CIDE and COMEXI. The studies for both countries in 2004 and 2006 contain almost identical questions (though they are context sensitive) to allow for comparison. The 2004 U.S. survey was implemented by Knowledge Networks, Inc., over the Internet from July 6 to 12, 2004, and included a national sample of 1,195 U.S. citizens. The 2006 study, implemented by the same organization, was in the field from June 23 to July 9, 2006, and included a national sample of 1,227 U.S. citizens. The surveys for Mexico that we use were conducted as part of the *México y el Mundo 2004* and *2006* studies, conducted by the Centro de Investigación y Docencia Económicas (CIDE), the Consejo Mexicano de Asuntos Internacionales (COMEXI), and the CCFR. Both were implemented by BGC, Ulises Beltrán y Asociados. The face-to-face 2004 survey was conducted July 9–19, 2004, with a representative sample of 1,500 individuals, while the 2006 survey was conducted from July 22 to July 27, 2006, with a representative national sample of 1,499 individuals. Both surveys contained questions measuring worry about a terror attack as well as questions concerning foreign policy opinions. We also use some questions from the ANES panel study when looking at this strategy of coping.

Conclusion

In this chapter, we have discussed the methods and data we employ to test our arguments. The use of experimental data allows us to have a high degree of internal validity in looking at the relationship between terror threat and the three coping strategies. The use of survey data provides a means of increasing the external validity of our experimental results. Overall, this "triangulation" of research methods allow us to demonstrate the strength of our findings with respect to different types of data.

Having concluded this methodological tour whereby we describe the method, the means, and the immediate results of our crisis creation enterprise, we now turn to discussions of the insights we glean from the data described here. We begin in the next chapter with the first strategy of coping, modifying one's views of and relations to others. More specifically, in chapter 3, we demonstrate a link between terror threat and authoritarian and related attitudes.

3

Love Thy Neighbor?
Terror Threat and the Social Fabric

> If you want to be part of our nation's stand against those who
> murder innocent people for the sake of murder . . . love a neigh-
> bor like you'd like to be loved yourself.
>
> President George W. Bush, February 16, 2002

The days and months following 9/11 saw countless displays of love
for one's country. Individuals sported the American flag on t-shirts,
pins, and bumper stickers. The media followed suit with displays
ranging from journalists' statements and accessories to television
spots such as the Ad Council's public service advertisement showing citizens of different colors, with different accents, and of different ages stating "I am an American."[1] Such "rally 'round the flag"
reactions were further expressed in soaring approval ratings for
President Bush and Mayor Giuliani, as well as increased approval
ratings for leaders such as Britain's prime minister, Tony Blair. Individuals in the post-9/11 time period appeared to hold greater
levels of identification with the country (Moskalenko, McCauley,
and Rozin 2006), as well as greater trust in government, political
leaders, and law enforcement (Skocpol 2002). More evidence suggests that Americans, post-9/11, felt more cooperative and more
interested in public affairs (Putnam 2002). Moreover, Americans
tended to evaluate traditional American racial and ethnic groups
(African American, Hispanic, Asian, and white Americans) somewhat more favorably following 9/11 than they did in years prior

(Traugott et al. 2002). Taken alone, these bits of evidence might lead one to conclude that terrorist threats strengthen a country's social fabric.

Yet, two facts caution us against concluding that terrorist threats lead to the flourishing of social trust and engagement. In the first place, scholars have noted that tendencies to express attitudes that might foster social harmony have not necessarily translated into similar behaviors. Thus, while stories of volunteerism following 9/11 were made salient in the news, a survey fielded in 2002 found no evidence of a "surge" in the number of people involved in volunteer work (Traugott et al. 2002). Instead, television viewing increased significantly following 9/11. Despite reports that appear to indicate greater social cohesion, many Americans turned inward, toward their television sets, following the terrorist attacks (Putnam 2002; see also Schuster et al. 2001). These tendencies were and have been accompanied by even more ominous developments. Some Americans displayed less tolerance toward perceived outsiders following 9/11. For example, anti-Islamic hate crime incidents in the United States, recorded by the FBI, catapulted from 28 in 2000 to 481 in 2001.[2] The threat of terrorist attacks also led to greater levels of ethnocentrism and less support for the rights of Arabs and Muslims in the U.S. (e.g., Davis 2007; Huddy et al. 2005).

How exactly might assessments and relationships among individuals shift in times of terrorist threat? In this chapter, we turn to the first coping strategy outlined in chapter 1. More specifically, we consider the relationship between the threat of a terrorist attack and the expression of attitudes and policy preferences that reflect decreased social trust, decreased sympathy for out-groups, increased intolerance, and increased punitiveness. We provide evidence that terrorist threats contain the potential to rupture, not mend, a country's social fabric. As we will show in particular in the second part of the chapter, this tendency may be more prevalent among one set of individuals than another: those with high authoritarian predispositions.

The question at the core of this chapter is the following: to what extent do individuals facing crisis conditions—in particular, the threat of terrorist attacks—cope by becoming relatively more uncooperative, unsympathetic, and even hostile in their relations with others and with respect to their preferences over policies that govern other individuals? In an analysis of survey data collected in the year prior to and years after 9/11 we will show evidence that terrorist threat decreases social trust and, to some extent, lowers sympathy for societal out-groups (gays and illegal immigrants). While these results are revealing, they have some shortcomings; in particular, it is difficult to confirm a precise cause-and-effect relationship and, moreover, we are unable with these data to test whether one subgroup of individuals (those predisposed toward authoritarianism) is more likely to use this particular coping strategy. We therefore describe, in the second part of the chapter, a series of findings based on three experimental studies—two of which were conducted in the United States and one of which was conducted in Mexico. With these results we demonstrate a causal effect for terrorist threat on expressed authoritarian attitudes; at the same time, we show that this relationship exists primarily for those who are predisposed toward authoritarianism.

Threat and Social Harmony

Like other collective crises, in the face of a terrorist threat there is little an individual can do to resolve, or "control," the situation. Thus, individuals may pursue any of a number of coping strategies. In chapter 1 we argued that one potential coping mechanism involves increased levels of distrust, intolerance, and punitiveness. Another way to state this is to say that individuals become less trusting and more *authoritarian* in times of threat. By expressing such attitudes (and, potentially acting on them as well), individuals have a mechanism by which they can restore feelings of calm and control.

But not necessarily all individuals will express more authoritarian attitudes to the same degree. One possibility is that this coping strategy will be mostly reserved for those who are predisposed toward authoritarianism. Recall that authoritarian predispositions are stable predispositions that capture the degree to which one values group unity and obedience, as opposed to individual autonomy and diversity. Authoritarian attitudes, in contrast, are expressed opinions that relate to moral, political, and racial intolerance, as well as punitiveness toward out-groups. In times of relative well-being and calm, authoritarian predispositions may lie dormant; there is relatively less need to insist upon order and sameness under such conditions. If true, then we would expect that it is primarily among those who value group unity and obedience at the expense of autonomy and diversity that we see the highest expression of intolerant and less sympathetic attitudes in times of threat.

We thus begin with two general expectations. The first is simply that perceptions of threat—in particular, terrorist threat—are associated with greater levels of distrust, intolerance, and punitiveness. The second is that the relationship is driven primarily by one particular subgroup of individuals: those high in authoritarian predispositions. As noted above, we begin the empirical portion of this chapter with a discussion of a set of analyses of survey data. Panel survey data from the ANES (2000/2002/2004) allow us to examine the extent to which, among the general public, individuals worried about terrorism became more or less friendly and trusting toward their fellow man. Survey data from the CCFR complements these analyses, revealing the extreme extent to which the terrorist threat induces preferences over punitive policies, in this case the use of torture. We then turn to a discussion of analyses of data from three similar experimental studies, one that used a nonstudent U.S. adult sample, one that used a U.S. student sample, and one that used a Mexico student sample. With these data we are able to show that terror threats tend to increase authoritarian attitudes, but principally for those with authoritarian predispositions.

In addition to documenting the above consequences of the terrorist threat, we are able to compare the effects of terror threat to those of another type of threat, economic crisis. While some have considered the effect of economic threat on authoritarian attitudes (e.g., Doty, Peterson, and Winter 1991; Feldman and Stenner 1997; Rickert 1998; Sales 1973), few have closely examined terrorist threats. This is understandable given that, as of 9/11, we live in a changed world. Further, most experimental research has either combined different types of crisis into the same treatment or only examined one type of threat (as exceptions, see Feldman and Stenner 1997, and Stenner 2005). While the literature leads us to expect that a terrorist threat would induce similar effects, we began this undertaking without strong expectations as to whether effects would be more pronounced for a terror threat. We are able to gain leverage on this issue by comparing the effects of two different crises, terrorism and economic downturn, both of which are highly relevant to today's political world.

Survey Data Evidence

Does the specter of a terrorist threat place significant stress on a society's social fabric through the expression of increased authoritarian attitudes and behaviors? If so, we would expect that perceptions of threat would be closely related to a variety of indicators. First among these is social trust and related measures of one's confidence (or lack of confidence) in the good intentions of other people. While trust in others is not typically considered a defining characteristic of authoritarian attitudes, it arguably undergirds core components of authoritarianism: intolerance of difference, and punitiveness. A second relevant group of indicators pertains to societal out-groups. If threat causes individuals to circle the wagons, we might expect to see more hostility — or at least colder feelings — expressed toward certain out-groups. Finally, if individuals react to threat by seeking order and discipline, we should find that those who feel threatened are more apt to prefer a stronger stance against delinquency and, moreover, to permit harsher interrogation tactics in the treatment of suspected wrongdoers. We examine these expectations in a series of analyses using data mostly from the ANES 2000/2002/2004 panel study.

Trust

The ANES panel study contains two sets of questions asking respondents the extent to which they trust other individuals, including their neighbors. The first battery of questions gives us insight into general social trust while the second offers us a lens through which to view an individual's attitudes toward his or her more exclusive social community. Given the outpouring of patriotism following 9/11, one might expect that terrorist threat increases levels of trust in general or, at the very least, among neighbors. We find exactly the opposite.

In both 2000 and 2002 researchers asked the same individuals whether they agree or disagree with these statements: "you can't be too careful in dealing with people," "most people would try to take advantage of you if they got the chance," and "most of the time people are just looking out for themselves."[3] In general, individuals are more likely to agree with the first statement and less likely to agree with the latter two statements (see the values in note 4). If we consider simply average levels of distrust across the two years, there is very little change to report. In 2002 individuals show a slightly greater tendency to report that "you can't be too careful in dealing with people"; on the other hand, they are somewhat less likely to agree with the other two negative statements about individuals. None of these differences, though, are all that statistically reliable, which suggests that 9/11 and the looming threat of another terrorist attack had no effect on overall levels of social trust among the American public.[4]

Things change, however, once we move beyond the aggregate-level statistics and instead analyze general feelings of distrust from two other perspectives. First, in 2002, what effect did fear of another terrorist attack have on individuals' reported levels of social trust? Second, did fear of another terrorist attack in 2002 decrease the level of social trust an individual initially reported in 2000? We model trust and change in trust as a function of Terror Attack, measured by a question to which respondents indicate how likely they believe it is that the United States will suffer another attack as serious as those on 9/11. Higher values, on a four-point scale, mean the individual believes a future terrorist attack is more likely. In each analysis we also take into account other factors that might influence trust, in order to attempt to isolate the effect of concern about terrorism. More specifically, we include measures of political predispositions (party identification and ideology) and basic sociodemographic indicators (age, education, income, gender, and race).

If fears of a terrorist attack increase social distrust, we expect to find that Terror Attack has a positive and statistically reliable effect in both sets of social trust analyses (levels and change). The full results of our analyses are contained in Web Supplement A, tables 3.a and 3.b. Here we summarize those results. In the analyses predicting levels of distrust in 2002, terror threat has a statistically meaningful and positive effect for the question asking about whether you can't be too careful in dealing with people (Social Distrust 1) and for the question asking whether people are mostly just looking out for themselves (Social Distrust 3). For Social Distrust 1, moving an individual from thinking future terrorist attacks are not at all likely to thinking attacks are very likely results in a 23.4 percentage point increase in the probability of indicating that you can't be too careful in dealing with other people.[5] For Social Distrust 3, the change in predicted probability is smaller, but still substantively meaningful: 11.4 percentage points. Turning to an analysis of whether individuals are less trusting in 2002 relative to 2000, we find that Terror Threat has a positive and statistically reliable effect on individuals' beliefs that you can't be too careful in dealing with people. In other words, believing (in 2002) that a terrorist attack is more likely changes one's evaluation of other people *toward greater levels of social distrust.*

Perhaps individuals become more distrusting of others, in general, in response to terrorist threat but they increase their confidence in the benevolence of those who are socially proximate to them, their neighbors. Again our evidence suggests the opposite. In both 2000 and 2004 individuals were asked to what extent (1) people they generally see in their neighborhood are just looking out for themselves, (2) those people try to take advantage of others, (3) they treat each other with respect, and (4) they are honest. It is worth noting that trust in neighbors, on average, is expressed at fairly high levels. Across the two years, and considering all survey participants who answered the question, the average response ranges between roughly 3 and 4 on a five-point (1 to 5) scale for the first three questions and a four-point scale for the fourth question, where higher values indicate higher levels of trust. Looking at these average values across time, three years out from 9/11, individuals on average are apt to be relatively more suspicious of their neighbors than they were in the year prior to the terrorist attacks. On two out of the four variables, average levels of trust drop in small but significant ways.[6] Specifically, on the third neighbor trust variable (Neighbor Trust 3) the average response falls from 4.09 in 2000 to 3.98 in 2004; on the fourth variable (Neighbor Trust 4) the average response falls from 3.24 to 3.18. In short, after 9/11 the social fabric of the most geographically proximate social circles had decayed, not become stronger.

As we saw with the general social trust measure, conclusions based on aggregate-level analyses might not tell us the entire story. We therefore examine the determinants of individual-level opinions about neighbors in the same way we did with respect to the general social trust measures.[7] Once again the full tables of results are contained in Web Supplement A, tables 3.c and 3.d. Considering, first, whether in 2004 concerns about another terrorist attack on U.S. soil positively or negatively affect individuals' evaluations of their neighbors, we find a negative and statistically reliable relationship for three of the four measures (the exception is Neighbor Trust 4). Specifically, the more an individual thinks a future attack will occur, the more likely she is to report that her neighbors are mostly just looking out for themselves, trying to take advantage of others, and failing to respect others. Figure 3.1 shows how trust is predicted to shift when one moves from the lowest level of perceived threat to the highest. Considering those three analyses for which the Terror Attack variable is statistically significant, this effect ranges in size from −.18 (Neighbor Trust 3) to −.32 (Neighbor Trust 1) units. Do these results coincide with actual individual-level opinion shifts in the years following 9/11? To better assess this we again analyzed the difference in individual-reported opinions across 2000 and, in this case, 2004. For each of the same three measures of confidence in neighbors significant in the first set of analyses, we find that concerns of a terrorist attack in 2004 predict a decline in trust across the two time periods.[8] Figure 3.1 shows the predicted effects of moving from the lowest to highest value on the Terror Attack indicator for these variables: Neighbor Trust 1, Neighbor Trust 2, and Neighbor Trust 3. Especially in this case where the theoretical range of the dependent variable is much greater (from −4 to 4), the substantive effects are small yet, reliable. In short, the evidence substantially supports the conclusion that the threat of a terrorist attack *negatively affects neighborhood trust.*

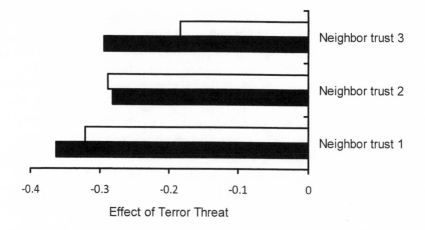

Figure 3.1. Maximum predicted effect of terror threat on neighbor trust
Note: The figure is based on analyses of ANES 2000/2002/2004 panel data; full results available in the Web Supplement A, tables 3.c and 3.d. Bars show the effect on the dependent variable when Terror Threat is moved from its minimum to maximum value across the four-point scale.

Feelings toward Groups

If people become less trusting of others when they are threatened by a terrorist attack, do they also feel colder toward specific groups of individuals? We have noted already that some scholars have found evidence that feelings toward standard "American" groups increased following 9/11. Thus, on average individuals if anything expressed warmer feelings toward African, Asian, Hispanic, and white Americans following 9/11 (Traugott et al. 2002).[9] This general shift might have occurred as a result of two processes—a surge in patriotism (at least in expressed patriotism) and a concentration in the media on bringing Americans together. Recall, for example, the post-9/11 "I am an American" television spot. The objective clearly was to foster social solidarity. The spot featured the elderly, the young, families, single persons, individuals with accents, and individuals of different racial and ethnic backgrounds. It ended with a visual depiction of the Latin phrase *E pluribus unum* and its translation, "out of many, one."

What about groups that some might not consider to be standard "American" groups? In particular, what about homosexuals and immigrants? One expression of authoritarianism is increased intolerance toward societal out-groups. Homosexuals and immigrants can be categorized as out-groups, groups that are perceived by some as belonging outside the specter of mainstream America. Immigrants are an interesting group to examine for additional reasons. The 9/11 hijackers were foreign-born. Immigrants, as well, may fall outside the positive cascade of patriotic feelings. Despite the United States' origins as a country of immigrants, those coming from other countries in the post-9/11 era might be more likely to be perceived as threats to the country's resources, if not the country's security as well.

The conclusion we draw is that feelings toward these groups decrease in the face of terrorist threat. In all three waves of the survey (2000/2002/2004), participants in the ANES panel study were asked to report their feelings toward gays using the classic feeling thermometer measure. The feeling thermometer taps affective ratings of individuals or groups, by having respondents rate the degree to which they feel cold or warm toward that object on a scale from 0 to 100 (degrees). We examine feelings toward gays in two sets of analyses. First, we consider whether concern about another terrorist attack in 2002 (2004) predicts feelings toward gays in that same year. Second, we consider whether concern about a terrorist attack predicts individual shifts in feelings toward gays across 2000 and 2002 (2004). We again include the same battery of controls in all analyses as we did in those analyses reported already in this chapter. The full results of these analyses are available in Web Supplement A, Table 3.e.

Summarizing the findings from these analyses, we find strong evidence that concern about terrorism affected feelings toward gays in the immediate aftermath of 9/11, but that this link decayed several years out from the terrorist attacks. In our analyses of the 2002 data, we find that concern about a terrorist attack significantly predicts feelings toward gays such that the more concerned one is, the colder one reports feeling toward gays. For each increase in concern about a terrorist attack (on the four-point Terror Attack variable), feelings toward gays decrease by 1.8 units on the feeling thermometer. This finding is mirrored in analyses that examine changes in feelings between 2000 and 2002. Individuals who in 2002 feared a terrorist attack were significantly more likely to have shifted their evaluations of gays toward colder feelings compared to those who did not fear another terrorist attack. In a similar set of analyses conducted using the 2004 data, we find that this effect appears to have mostly deteriorated. The Terror Attack variable no longer predicts feelings toward gays in 2004 and, while negative and not entirely unsubstantial in strength, the coefficient on the variable falls outside of traditional significance cutoffs in the analysis of changes in individual opinions from 2000 to 2004. Thus, while we find evidence that fear of another terrorist attack drives hostility—or at least lack of warmth—toward this particular societal out-group in the immediate aftermath of a large terrorist attack (9/11), this relationship decreases over time.

Turning to immigrants, we also find evidence of a link between concern about another terrorist attack and lack of support for this group. In this case, we do not have classic feeling thermometer measures. Rather, in all three waves of the survey, individuals were asked whether they thought federal spending on tightening border security in order to prevent illegal immigration should be increased, kept the same, or decreased. If terror threat causes individuals to become less friendly toward immigrants, than we would expect to find that the threat measure is associated with preferences for increasing border security in the post-9/11 era. And, indeed, this is what we find. Thus, in analyses of individuals' opinions in both 2002 and 2004, we find that the Terror Attack variable significantly and positively affects preferences over federal spending in this issue area (see Web Supplement A, Table 3.f). Figure 3.2 illustrates these effects, focusing on the predicted change in falling into the highest value on this dependent variable: preferring a spending increase. In the case of the 2002 data, a change in concern about a terrorist attack from the lowest to the highest value on the four-point scale results in an estimated 6 percentage point increase in the probability of expressing an opinion in favor of increased border policing in order to halt the inflow of unauthorized immigrants. In 2004 this effect is a whopping 18 percentage points.

Two words of caution seem appropriate in interpreting these results. First, we do not find similar evidence that terror threat is related to individual shifts in opinion across the two time periods, 2000 to 2002 and 2000 to 2004. Moreover, it could be that individuals' preferences over the border, and the connection between these preferences and concern about terrorism, are driven by fears of allowing terrorists in and not hostility toward immigrants in general. We cannot conclusively determine this one way or another. However, a question asked in 2000 and 2004 gives us at least some additional insight into this question. Individuals were asked whether they believe the number of immigrants legally permitted to enter the country should be increased, kept the same, or decreased. In analyses of opinions over this question in 2004, we find that concerns about terrorism are significantly related to preferences over admitting fewer immigrants (see Web Supplement A, Table 3.g). Thus, it appears there is some evidence that fears of terrorism are associated with reduced support for immigrant populations. We again, though, do not find support for an effect of concern

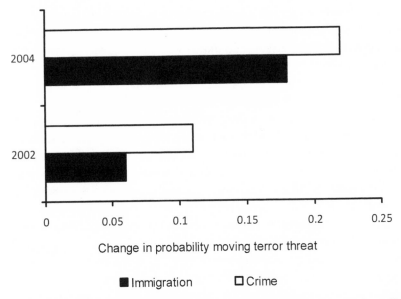

Figure 3.2. Maximum predicted change in probability of preferring increased spending
Note: The figure is based on analyses of ANES 2000/2002/2004 panel data; full results available in the Web Supplement A, tables 3.f and 3.h. Bars show the effect on the dependent variable when Terror Threat is moved from its minimum to maximum value across the four-point scale.

about terrorism (from 2000 to 2004) on individual shifts in preferences over immigration policy. Therefore, we cautiously assert that there is a link between terrorist threats and anti-immigrant preferences, but one that falls short of a strong and indisputable causal connection. We return to the issue of immigration again in chapter 6, in the context of border security.

Punitiveness

Another expression of authoritarianism in times of terror threat concerns punitive attitudes. Advocating harsh treatment of general delinquents and, as well, suspected terrorists is one way that individuals can assert—by proxy—some degree of control over the uncertain and relatively insecure situation that surrounds them in times of perceived terrorist threat. In addition to the above-discussed question about increasing federal spending for border security, participants in the 2000/2002/2004 ANES panel study were asked whether they believed that federal spending on dealing with crime should be increased, kept the same, or decreased. While this is not exactly an ideal measure for punitiveness since it concerns spending and not policies, it was the best available proxy. Our complete results are again available in the Web Supplement A (Table 3.h), and they mirror those for immigration. In analyses of opinions in 2002 and 2004, we find strong evidence that concern about terrorism is associated with preferences for greater spending on dealing with crime in those time periods. These effects are illustrated in figure 3.2, which shows effects for this dependent variable that are even stronger in each year than those found for immigration. However, we do not find a statistically reliable relationship between Terror Attack and changes in opinions on crime over time. Thus, the causal story lacks strong support, but we nonetheless can conclude that those who feared another terrorist attack on U.S. soil in the years after 9/11 were also likely to support increased spending on crime.

We have one additional, and improved, lens through which we can examine punitiveness. In a 2006 national survey of the United States conducted by the Chicago Council on Foreign Relations, respondents were asked whether they approved of using torture to get information from suspected terrorists. Individuals who believe that international terrorism is a "critical threat" are significantly more likely to approve of the use of torture, even after controlling for other likely predictors: ideology, education, income, and gender (see Web Supplement A, table 3.i for full results). Lacking a panel study setup, we cannot test whether such concern about terrorism leads to shifts in opinion over time. Nonetheless, once again, we have some evidence that concern about terrorism is associated with a more hard-handed approach to crime in general and terrorism more specifically.

In all, we find evidence in these survey data analyses that connects concerns about terrorism in the post-9/11 era to decreased social trust and to various indicators of authoritarianism, including lack of support for certain societal out-groups (gays and immigrants), and increased punitiveness. This evidence is compelling, but not quite as conclusive, nuanced, or robust as we would prefer. First, while it is a good measure, the ANES survey measure asking about terrorist attacks does not directly capture *worry* about pending threats. An individual might conceivably believe a terrorist attack is likely (and report that on the ANES survey) but not be worried about the attack. Perhaps the individual believes that he is sufficiently insulated along geographic, economic, and other relevant lines from such an attack. The central argument we made in chapter 1 is that it is a combined cognitive and affective (anxiety-provoking) reaction to threat that leads individuals to adopt certain coping strategies. Second, even controlling for factors such as party identification, ideology, and other relevant factors, we might still be uncertain over the extent to which we can make causal claims on the basis of the survey data analyses. To some extent, the panel study allows us greater confidence than we might otherwise be able to assert (by examining differences across time), but even here we do not always have the confidence to declare a clear, causal connection. Third, an important body of literature relevant to the discussion in this chapter has suggested the possibility that reactions to threat are not necessarily uniform when it comes to these attitudes; rather, those predisposed toward authoritarianism may be more likely to express such attitudes in times of threat. Fourth, the survey data do not allow us to examine whether other types of threats behave similarly or differently compared to terrorist threats.

Experimental Evidence

We respond to some of the limitations we have identified in the survey data analyses with a series of three experimental studies.[10] First, we examine the effect of terrorist threat on general authoritarian attitudes. Second, using one of the three experiments, we examine the effect of terrorist threat on additional indicators of authoritarianism, more specifically, intolerance and punitiveness. In each case we compare our findings for terrorist threat to another threat type, economic. We further demonstrate that authoritarian predispositions moderate the effect of threat. Our assertion here is that the threat of terrorism activates the effect of authoritarian predispositions on authoritarian attitudes, relative to times of well-being. Put differently, our argument is that the effect of threat is not constant across individuals. One particular group of people is more likely to employ the first coping strategy than others: those predisposed toward authoritarianism.

Authoritarian Predispositions

Authoritarian predispositions are considered stable aspects of one's personality attributable to one's genetic profile, upbringing, or both. To measure these traits, a set of scholars has proposed using questions related to one's beliefs regarding the treatment and raising of children. The assumption is that the degree to which one advocates a hard-handed approach or not is suggestive of one's very basic core values and beliefs. We follow this work and measure Authoritarian Predispositions using three questions on child-rearing values (Feldman and Stenner 1997; Stenner 2005). As noted, such values are believed to reflect an individual's core values, with respect to "authority and uniformity versus autonomy and difference," regardless of political or social context (Stenner 2005, 23). A prompt preceding the set of questions asks subjects to select which one of a pair of qualities it is more important to encourage in children. The first pair of qualities is "a child obeys his or her parents" versus "a child is responsible for his or her own actions." The second pair is "a child has respect for his or her elders" versus "a child thinks for him- or herself." The third pair is "a child has good manners" or "a child has good sense and sound judgment." Not surprisingly, responses to these questions tend to "hang" together, and we are able to create a single measure, which is scored such that lower values indicate more individualistic child-rearing beliefs and higher values indicate more authoritarian child-rearing beliefs.[11]

In the Mexico study we included the three childrearing questions alongside three additional questions. In recognition of the criticism that childrearing questions may not be particularly relevant to college students, Stenner (2005) proposes that researchers analyzing student subjects use a battery of word-choice questions to tap authoritarian predispositions. Borrowing from this research, we asked our subjects in the Mexico study to answer not only the childrearing questions but also a battery of questions in which they were to choose the word within a pair that they find relatively more appealing: obey or question; rules or progress; obedience or curiosity.[12] We then created a single additive predisposition index from all six items (three childrearing and three word-choice questions), coded such that higher values indicate higher levels of authoritarian predispositions, and which showed good reliability.[13]

Authoritarian Attitudes

As a first test of whether those predisposed toward authoritarianism are more likely to express intolerant, punitive, and related attitudes in times of threat, we investigate the effects of threat and authoritarian predispositions on a general measure of authoritarian attitudes. To measure Authoritarian Attitudes, we again follow Stenner (2005) and use a reduced twelve-item form of Altemeyer's (1988) Right Wing Authoritarianism (RWA) scale and a seven-point Likert response set. Stenner (2005) argues that these items from the RWA scale measure particular expressions of social and political intolerance, rather than underlying predispositions. The seven-point Likert response set allows individuals to indicate, for each statement, the extent to which they agree or disagree. The specific items range from relatively moderate attitudes such as "life imprisonment is justified for certain crimes" to more extreme antideviant expressions such as "Once our government leaders give us the 'go ahead,' it will be the duty of every patriotic citizen to help stomp out the rot that is poisoning our country from within." They also contain positive statements about, for example, the protection of "the rights of radicals and deviants" (see the appendix for full question wordings). This reduced form of the RWA scale, thus, attempts to capture attitudes related to moral and political tolerance.[14] We created an additive index of the measures that is coded such that higher values indicate more authoritarian attitudes.[15] The variable is nearly continuous and bounded at 1 and 7.

To test the argument that conditions of crisis activate the effect of authoritarian predispositions on authoritarian attitudes, we use multiple variable regression analysis. We model authoritarian attitudes as a function of exposure to the experimental conditions (the Good Times condition serves as the baseline), the authoritarian predisposition measure, and the interaction of the authoritarian predisposition measure and each experimental condition. The interaction terms are included in order to discern whether predispositions are indeed activated in times of threat.[16]

The complete set of results from these regression analyses is shown in table 3.1. To assist in the interpretation of these results, we discuss them in combination with graphs showing predicted authoritarian attitudes, by level of authoritarian predisposition and each of the three treatment conditions.[17] We expect to find that the slope, or effect, of authoritarian predispositions is significantly greater among those in the two threat contexts compared to the nonthreat content. This would lend support to the theory that authoritarian predispositions are activated in times of crisis.

The analyses provide clear support for our argument in all cases. For US05ns (U.S. nonstudent sample, summer 2005), while authoritarian predispositions are activated in the Good Times and Economic Threat conditions, we find that the effect of authoritarian predispositions is much higher during times of terror threat. At the same time, the effect of authoritarian predispositions on authoritarian attitudes is similar for those in the Economic Threat condition compared to those in Good Times. These results are reported in table 3.1 but can also be seen in figure 3.3. The lines for Economic Threat and Good Times show that there is some, but minimal, difference in authoritarian attitudes (y-axis) among those at low and high values on the authoritarian predispositions variable (x-axis). In contrast, when exposed to the terror threat, those high in authoritarian

Table 3.1. Threat, authoritarian predispositions, and authoritarian attitudes

	US05ns Coefficient (Std. Err.)	US05s Coefficient (Std. Err.)	MEX06s Coefficient (Std. Err.)
Constant	3.205**	2.340**	3.182**
	(0.201)	(0.126)	(0.164)
Status Quo	−0.049	−0.215	
	(0.094)	(0.144)	
Terror Threat	0.052	0.093	−0.102
	(0.083)	(0.148)	(0.158)
Economic Threat	−0.122	0.003	−0.150
	(0.102)	(0.138)	(0.144)
Authoritarian Predispositions	0.113++	0.089	0.303
	(0.053)	(0.114)	(0.294)
Authoritarian Predispositions · Status Quo	0.092	0.165*	
	(0.073)	(0.091)	
Authoritarian Predispositions · Terror Threat	0.327++	0.334++	1.040++
	(0.061)	(0.081)	(0.330)
Authoritarian Predispositions · Economic Threat	0.101+	0.206++	0.966++
	(0.073)	(0.090)	(0.329)
Ideology	0.331**	0.281**	0.145**
	(0.026)	(0.028)	(0.030)

Education	−0.045		
	(0.029)		
Political Sophistication	−1.086**		
	(0.136)		
Political Interest			−0.245**
			(0.056)
PAN PID			0.513**
			(0.090)
PRI PID			0.406**
			(0.125)
PRD PID			−0.134
			(0.131)
N	384	201	291
R-squared	0.59	0.48	0.38

Note: Values in cells are the results of OLS analysis with robust standard errors. One-tailed hypothesis tests used for *Terror Threat* and *Economic Threat*, *Authoritarian Predispositions*, and interactions among these variables; one-tailed statistical significance thresholds indicated as follows: ++$p \leq 0.05$ and +$p \leq 0.10$. Two-tailed hypothesis tests used for all other variables; two-tailed statistical significance thresholds indicated as follows: **$p \leq .05$ and *$p \leq 0.10$. Coefficients presented for the interaction terms are the slope of the effect of authoritarian predispositions within that condition (status quo, terror threat, economic threat).

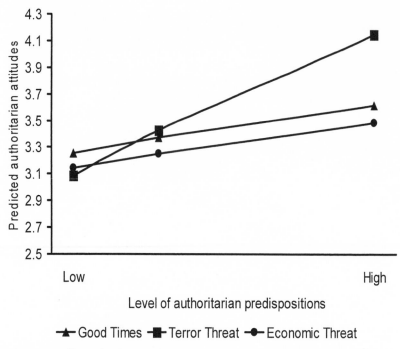

Figure 3.3. Effects of authoritarian predispositions on authoritarian attitudes, conditioned by experimental conditions, US05ns
Note: The figure is based on output from analysis reported in Table 3.1. Lines show the predicted level of authoritarian attitudes at different levels of authoritarian predispositions for each experimental condition.

predispositions show a much greater level of authoritarian attitudes; those low in authoritarian predispositions show just a slight tendency to adopt even more liberal stances. In short, the terror threat condition brings about an activation of authoritarian predispositions that is consistent with our expectations.

The results of US05s (U.S. student sample, fall 2005) are similar with respect to the Terror Threat condition. In fact, the effect of Terror Threat is nearly identical to that shown in figure 3.3 and so we do not graph it here. Thus, not only is the effect of authoritarian predispositions relatively higher among those exposed to the Terror Threat treatment but the magnitude of this effect is consistent across both studies. In this case, though, we also find evidence that authoritarian attitudes are also somewhat activated by the Economic Threat (compared to Good Times). At the same time, this effect is substantially smaller than that found for the Terror Threat condition. Finally, the authoritarian predisposition measure is not

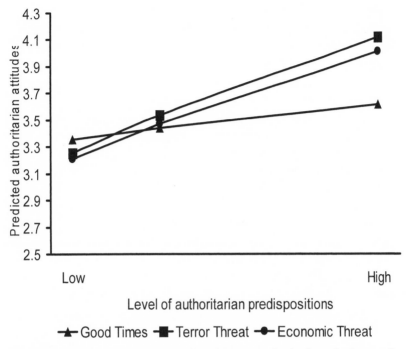

Figure 3.4. Effects of authoritarian predispositions on authoritarian attitudes, conditioned by experimental conditions, MEX06s
Note: The figure is based on output from analysis reported in table 3.1. Lines show the predicted level of authoritarian attitudes at different levels of authoritarian predispositions for each experimental condition.

meaningfully related to authoritarian attitudes when times are going well (Good Times). Thus, in this case, authoritarian predispositions are only activated in times of threat.

We recreate this graph a second time, to show results for MEX06s (Mexico student sample, fall 2006) in figure 3.4. Once again, we find that the effect of authoritarian predispositions is activated in the Terror Threat condition, while it is not for those in the Good Times condition. However, in this case, the effect of authoritarian predispositions in the two threat conditions is fairly similar. Thus, unlike the first two studies, when comparing across threat types, we do not find a relatively stronger effect for the threat of terrorist attacks in the Mexico study.

In summary, all three studies provide strong and consistent support for our expectations. Under conditions of terrorist threat, individuals predisposed toward authoritarianism express greater levels of social and political intolerance. We further see, across all three cases, that there is only minimal movement by those with more liberal predispositions in the opposite direction. Thus, our results differ somewhat from work by Stenner (2005) and others, which suggests that in times of threat each "side" (authoritarian and liberal) will move, attitudinally, toward its respective pole.[18] Rather, the action in our studies is among those who are already predisposed toward authoritarianism.

In terms of comparing across types of treats, in our two U.S. studies we find that conditions of security threat activate authoritarian predispositions to a greater degree than conditions of economic threat. This is consistent with scholarship in the field of Terror Management Theory (TMT), which suggests that threats to one's mortality should have a more significant effect on individuals' attitudes. In contrast to these results, in the case of Mexico, both crises appear to activate equally authoritarian predispositions. We offer the conjecture that this may be because the memory of recent economic crises in Mexico made the possibility of another recession appear a relatively more tangible threat to one's well-being, whereas Mexico has not been a victim of international terrorist attacks. But we offer this only as speculation. In any case, the results clearly suggest that—in terms of anticipating the relative effects of different crisis conditions—it is at least possible that it is not only the type of threat that matters (one primarily physical and the other primarily financial), but also the country context in which this threat is issued.

Additional Analyses: Intolerance and Punitiveness in the Mexico Case

The experiment in Mexico provides us with a way to extend our analyses in more ways than one. First, as we have just demonstrated, the basic effects of terrorist threat in terms of our first coping strategy are not geographically bound to the United States. Second, the treatments in the Mexico experiment were mock news articles while those in the 2004 and 2005 U.S. studies were audiovisual news segments. This allows us to show that, not only do our results hold across countries, but they hold across different representations of similar treatments. Finally, and most relevant to this subsection, we were able to insert on the Mexico experiment two additional questions tapping intolerance and punitiveness. In the first place, we included a set of questions that taps Tolerance of Disliked Groups. In so doing, we followed a research technique advanced by Sullivan, Piereson, and Marcus (1978, 1982) and begin by asking subjects to indicate a group of individuals that they "like the least." We provided subjects with a list of what might be thought of as likely suspects but also allowed subjects to indicate a group not on the list.[19] We then asked respondents the degree to which they supported allowing the identified group to do the following: make a speech in my city; protest against the government; hold a rally; run for office; and teach in public schools. We created an additive scale, ranging from 1 to 7, in which higher values indicate higher tolerance.[20] Given this coding, we expect a negative effect for authoritarian predispositions.

With respect to the punitiveness measure, we should first note that crime is a highly salient issue in modern-day Mexico. Public opinion data from the CSES-CIDE Mexico 2006 national survey show that 17 percent of respondents identified some aspect of public insecurity (e.g., kidnapping, drug-trafficking, violence) as one of the two most important problems facing the country. The question we included in our study asked participants to indicate which of two options for dealing with street crime comes closest to their views. The "hard on crime" option read (here in English): "it is important for police to do whatever it takes to stop these crimes, even if this violates the rights of those accused of committing a crime." The "soft on crime" option read "it is important for police to protect the rights of those accused of committing a crime, even if it gets in the way of stopping these crimes." The dummy variable, Soft on Crime, is coded such that we again expect a negative effect of authoritarian predispositions on opinions on this issue.

We evaluate the relationships among threat, authoritarian predispositions, and these measures tapping intolerance and punitiveness, as we did in the previous set of analyses. The full results of the statistical models are available in our Web Supplement A (see Table 3.j). In order to assess our argument, we again graph the effect of authoritarian predispositions on each policy preference, by experimental condition, in figures 3.5 and 3.6. The effects in the figures show us how an individual's value on the given policy shifts when we move an individual across the range of low to high authoritarian predispositions. The results across both figures provide strong support for the contention that threat moderates the effect of authoritarian predispositions on these attitudes. We find that the Terror Threat condition activates the effect of authoritarian predispositions on tolerance and stances on crime, while the Good Times condition does not. Those exposed to the terrorist threat become increasingly less tolerant *and* take a harder stance on crime (noted by the downward sloping lines) as individuals score higher on the authoritarian predispositions measure.

Turning to the Economic Threat condition, we find that the effect of authoritarian predispositions among those exposed to the Economic Threat

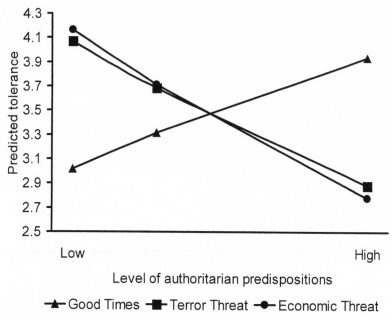

Figure 3.5. Effects of authoritarian predispositions on tolerance, conditioned by experimental conditions, MEX06s
Note: The figure is based on output from analysis reported in Web Supplement A, table 3.j. Lines show the predicted level of tolerance at different levels of authoritarian predispositions for each experimental condition.

is substantively meaningful for the Tolerance dependent variable. In fact, it parallels what we find in the Terror Threat condition. Thus, these results—combined with those for expressed authoritarian attitudes—suggest that authoritarian predispositions are activated in expected ways in times of economic crisis in Mexico, with respect to at least some relevant preferences. To summarize these findings we could say that terrorist threat has a consistent influence but the influence of economic threat is not inconsequential.

Conclusion

In this chapter we have presented an ample amount of evidence that threats, in particular those pertaining to terrorism, significantly stress a country's social fabric. The argument and results presented in this chapter add new perspectives and evidence to the general literature on conditions of threat and authoritarianism. Stepping outside of the narrow domain of our analyses and graphs, and their relevance to a mostly academic audi-

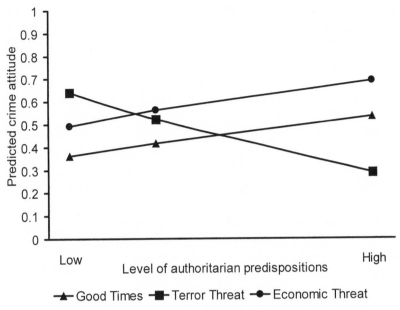

Figure 3.6. Effects of authoritarian predispositions on crime attitudes, conditioned by experimental conditions, MEX06s
Note: The figure is based on output from analysis reported in Web Supplement A, table 3.j. Dependent variable is coded so that higher values indicate a softer stance on crime. Lines show the predicted level of crime stance at different levels of authoritarian predispositions for each experimental condition.

ence, our results have potential implications for the quality of democracy. Briefly put, the results suggest that the social fabric on which a democracy rests may be put at risk in times of crisis. Under such circumstances, we find that individuals, or at least selected individuals, become less trusting, less sympathetic toward out-groups, and more intolerant and punitive than they would be under better environmental conditions. One could argue that these attitudinal shifts are harmless in that they may be only fleeting. Yet, our analyses suggest that the relationship between terror threat and some of these tendencies persists several years after 9/11; we return to this question of the duration of effects in the conclusion. One could also argue that these attitudinal shifts help safeguard the country. For example, given the difficulty of identifying terrorists, it might be self- and even nation-preserving to become more suspicious of others in times of terrorist threat.

And yet, even if we accept such arguments, we would still conclude that these attitudinal shifts represent a risk to democracy due to their significant potential to result in the infringement of certain rights for the supposed sake of the collective. For example, we find that terrorist threat is linked to less sympathy toward an out-group that is arguably irrelevant to the issue of terrorism: gays. We further find causal (experimental) evidence that terrorist threat (and, in Mexico, economic threat as well) leads certain individuals to express greater levels of authoritarian attitudes. To the extent that such individuals act on these attitudes in ways that are at counterpurposes to the resolution of the terrorist threat and/or in ways that degrade social cohesion, the democratic nation is arguably weakened both with respect to its quality and, potentially, security.

In the next chapter, we begin to explore the second strategy of coping, which relates to looking for and delegating leadership to those who appear capable of resolving the crisis situation. While the first strategy of coping has been shown to be most relevant for those high in authoritarian predispositions, the second strategy may be more broadly adopted by members of the mass public.

4

Holding Out for a Hero:
Looking for Leadership in Times of Terror Threat

In choosing a president, we really don't choose just a Republican
or Democrat, a conservative or a liberal. We choose a leader. And
in times of war and danger, as we're now in, Americans should put
leadership at the core of their decision.

Rudy Giuliani, August 30, 2004

The above quote by Rudy Giuliani at the 2004 Republican National
Convention addresses the meat of this chapter. The former mayor
of New York argues that evaluations of leadership abilities should
be *the* key determinant of individual voting decisions during threatening times. There are a number of reasons why people might rationally want to focus on strong leadership in times of threat. Strong
leaders may be better able to provide protection, restore a sense of
efficacy, and bring about a resolution to the given threat context.
But do people *actually* weight strong leadership more heavily in
their voting decisions during times of security crisis compared to
noncrisis settings? Giuliani asserts that they should. We examine
whether they do.[1]

First, though, we take a step back to the determinants of perceptions of strong leadership. In contrast to an arguably rational
response in the voting booth, we suggest that something more
purely psychological occurs with respect to leadership evaluations.
Giuliani's statement implies that people arrive at the voting booth
with fixed perceptions of the leadership capabilities of political

figures. We argue in contrast that people actually come to perceive the leadership qualities of select political figures differently during times of terror threat. As we indicated in the introduction, newsprint mentions of Giuliani, as well as Bush, as a "strong leader" tripled following the September 2001 terrorist attacks. At the same time, approval ratings soared for both figures. This preliminary evidence is consistent with our argument that people *project* additional leadership qualities onto certain political leaders in times of terror threat. Admittedly, though, with these somewhat anecdotal data we cannot rule out two alternative hypotheses: these increases were entirely due to people reacting to the actions of these leaders within the threat context and/or to political elites emphasizing their leadership skills.[2]

So, do individuals rate political figures more highly on strong leadership in times of terror threat because of their actions and/or rhetoric, or do individuals come to perceive stronger leaders just given the presence of a threat? The former is consistent with an instrumental response, while the latter suggests a more psychological desire to find a savior in times of threat. In the first part of this chapter we will hold the actions and rhetoric of political figures constant and examine whether individuals assess leadership qualities differently depending only on the presence or absence of a condition of crisis. More specifically, we ask, do individuals cope with terrorist threat by projecting *additional* leadership capabilities onto likely leaders? The answer, in short, is that they do, and this holds across different levels of office. We will further show that, in addition to projecting greater leadership onto certain individuals, the crisis condition causes people to downgrade their evaluations of rival leaders. In the second part of the chapter, we then turn to a second component of this coping strategy: weighting leadership more heavily in voting decisions in times of terror threat. As we have suggested, political actors and advisors in the 2004 U.S. presidential election designated leadership in times of terror as an important theme; their campaigns primed this issue and attempted to persuade citizens of the relatively greater strength of their own candidates in this regard. Was their intuition correct that voters would value leadership relatively more when confronting a terrorist threat? We find that individuals indeed weight leadership more heavily in times of terror threat compared to times of relative well-being and prosperity.

In this chapter we will demonstrate the extent to which individuals project leadership onto selected candidates during times of terror threat compared to "good times" using both experimental and survey data from the United States. More specifically, we look at the 2004 U.S. presidential election as well as the 2006 California gubernatorial election. Next we turn to the question of whether individuals weight leadership qualities more heavily in the voting booth, using the same data.

Terror Threat, Leadership Evaluations, and the Vote

The presence of a terrorist threat causes individuals to focus increasingly on questions of leadership. Under such conditions, individuals look for strong leaders who appear able to resolve the given crisis situation. By believing there exists a leader of heroic capacity, individuals are able to allay a range of negative emotions, such as feelings of inefficacy and insecurity, brought on by the crisis.

Yet, people are not only likely to look for a candidate with such traits, they are likely to project *additional* leadership capabilities onto selected figures. The desire to find a leader who will restore feelings of hope and provide protection compels individuals to see a stronger leader than they would otherwise perceive. In this effort to single out a heroic figure, people also *downgrade* the leadership capabilities of the selected leader's opponent.[3]

An important question, clearly, is who is this selected leader likely to be? In chapter 1, we argued that who would benefit (and who would lose) depends on a combination of three factors: personal background, party reputation, and whether the crisis is internal or external. Thus, under the threat of a terrorist attack, individuals might look to leaders with a military background. They may also consider the reputation of the leader's party on issues of national security. Finally, since most terrorist attacks are externally provoked, individuals will likely be motivated to blame external actors and rally around an incumbent.

If we apply these factors to the two cases we examine, the 2004 U.S. presidential election and the 2006 California gubernatorial election, we should find that George W. Bush and Arnold Schwarzenegger benefit from projections of leadership. First, both were incumbent candidates at the time of our studies. Second, both candidates are Republican, the party with a stronger reputation on the issue of terrorism (at least when our studies were conducted). With respect to personal factors, it is not obvious that Bush had an advantage over John Kerry, since Kerry had more *actual* military experience. However, his involvement in antiwar protests after returning from Vietnam opened the door for Swift Boat Veterans for Truth, a 527 group, to critique his military record during the election. With respect to the California election, Schwarzenegger's history as a bodybuilder and his action-hero movie roles could have given people the initial perception that he was a stronger leader than rival candidate Phil Angelides. If we take into account the balance of all three factors, we come to the expectation that under conditions of terrorist threat, individuals in these cases will cope by elevating their perceptions of Bush's and Schwarzenegger's leadership qualities and, in turn, deflating perceptions of Kerry's and Angelides' leadership qualities.

We assert that conditions of terrorist threat also cause people, on average, to weight these inflated leadership qualities more heavily in their voting decisions. A long line of scholarship on voting behavior shows that individuals typically select candidates on the basis of three factors: their party identification, their opinions on issues, and/or their assessments of the candidates' traits. The degree to which voters weight each of these three factors varies across individuals and across contexts. Voters will weight strong leadership more heavily in their voting decisions in times of terror threat compared to better times for two principal reasons (see chapter 1 for the full discussion). First, times of anxiety lead individuals to rely less on standing dispositions such as partisanship and more on factors relevant to the election, such as candidate traits and issues (Brader 2005, 2006; Marcus, Neuman, and MacKuen 2000). Second, a characteristic of the context we examine, terror threat, is that both candidates will have incentives to stake out a similar issue position: make the country safer. Therefore, following a Downsian logic (1957), citizens should look to other factors such as the leadership traits of the candidates. In times of terror threat, candidates' rhetoric and campaign strategies will often make traits more salient than issues and this may further lead to voters placing a heavy weight on candidate traits. The 2004 U.S. election was exactly such a situation: Bush, in particular, tried to make terror threat salient, and both candidates emphasized their leadership capabilities on the campaign trail. Nonetheless, we also consider that citizens, independent of elite priming, may select to place greater weight on leadership traits in times of terror threat.

Though our principal concern is the weight placed on leadership traits, some of our data also allow us to examine how the effects of issues and partisan identification vary across settings. With respect to the former, some works suggest that the effect of issues should increase (Marcus, Neuman, and MacKuen 2000) when individuals are anxious. However, our discussion above indicated that this may not be the case if candidates have incentives to take the same position on the issue of terrorism. Thus, we remain agnostic about the extent to which the importance placed on issues may increase, decrease, or remain the same in times of terror threat. With respect to partisanship, the literature suggests that partisanship should be weighted less under conditions of terror threat (e.g., Brader 2005; Marcus, Neuman, and MacKuen 2000).

Our study contributes to and extends existing research in a number of ways. First, few scholars have looked systematically at the relationship between contexts of terror threat and perceptions of leadership. Furthermore, of those who have, the literature is silent on who will benefit from projections. We explicitly take up the task of identifying the beneficiary of leadership projections under times of terror threat. Second, our study is the first that we know of to explore how the weights voters place on different criteria, such as candidate traits, shift in times of terror threat (relative to good times). Up to this point, scholars have mostly considered how individual level factors and campaigns condition the effect of traits on voting decisions.

Setting the Scene: The 2004 Presidential and 2006 California Gubernatorial Races

Before we turn to a discussion of our empirical results, we have a little more to say about the two election contexts that we explore in this chapter. We begin with the context of the 2004 U.S. presidential election and then turn to the 2006 California gubernatorial race.

The 2004 presidential election took place under conditions in which perceptions of crisis were both plausible and real. The fact that the United States was operating under the threat of terrorism was identified often by the media and by politicians. Readers may well remember that news reports suggested Al Qaeda was planning an attack against the United States in the period before or near election time. Vice President Dick Cheney was one particularly prominent voice issuing frequent warnings about terrorist activities:

> [T]hey're doing everything they can to find ways to strike us. . . . And you can imagine what would happen if we had an al Qaeda cell loose in the middle of one of our own cities with a nuclear weapon. The devastation that that would bring down on hundreds of thousands, maybe millions of Americans, obviously is something that you don't want to think about.[4]

As we discussed in the introduction to the chapter, many of President Bush's speeches and ads reminded citizens of 9/11 and his leadership in the war on terror. At the same time, Senator Kerry tried to convince the public that he had the requisite skills to lead the country through dangerous times.

Still, homeland security was not the only issue on citizens' minds. Individuals were also concerned about the economy and the situation in Iraq (Morin and Balz 2004). At the same time, circulating in the media were numerous positive indicators about the economy, health, and the environment. Thus, the electoral context was ripe for manipulation in a lab. The many different issues on the table, some threatening and some not, made it possible for a researcher (or, say, a pair of researchers) to selectively present information that would increase concerns of a terrorist threat for some individuals, while at the same time presenting other information that would diminish concerns of a terrorist threat among another set of individuals. It also made it possible, within this latter group, to credibly make salient conditions of prosperity and well-being. We followed exactly such a plan with our audiovisual treatments in the 2004 experimental study.

The 2004 election seemed like a natural test case in that the issue of terrorism was one of several salient issues in the campaign and it is something handled most clearly at the national level, by the executive. However, our arguments are general and may even hold in nonpresidential contests in which the terrorism issue is less salient. In order to examine how far our claims travel, we conducted a similar experiment in a different electoral context, namely, the 2006 California gubernatorial election (US06s: U.S. student sample, fall 2006).

The offices of president and governor are similar in that they are both executive offices. Thus, citizens may value leadership qualities in both contexts. The offices are different in that citizens are generally less interested in gubernatorial races compared to presidential races and so familiarity with candidate traits may be weaker. Furthermore, the issues that are relevant vary, with foreign policy and security issues being more relevant at the national than the state level. For these reasons, if our arguments are supported in this less likely case, then we are confident that the results are robust and generalizable to other executive offices.

The candidates in the 2006 California gubernatorial race included incumbent Republican Arnold Schwarzenegger and his Democratic challenger, Phil Angelides. Throughout the course of the campaign, Schwarzenegger led by a wide margin in the polls. Thus the race was nowhere near as close as the 2004 presidential election. Further, national security concerns were not a prominent issue in the election. This latter factor in particular should present us a more difficult test case, given that it may be more difficult to raise the salience of terrorist attacks in this context. At the same time, this factor provides us with an opportunity to see whether or not linkages among terrorism, leadership, and vote choice exist within a context in which the candidates, other political actors, and the media are not constantly priming terrorism and leadership.

Given our interest in comparing across two distinct contexts—times of threat and times of well-being—and given that we had established that a status quo group was likely to fall between these categories (see chapter 2), we selected to include only the Good Times and Terror Threat conditions for our 2006 study. In this case, the treatment was delivered in the form of a mock newspaper article.

Leadership Affected

In order to investigate the relationship between terror threat and leadership, we first had to identify some measure of people's perceptions of the leadership qualities of candidates. This task was made relatively easy in that for almost three decades the ANES has asked the following question: "In your opinion, does the phrase 'he provides strong leadership' describe Candidate X extremely well, quite well, not too well, or not at all?" Because it is a standard and well-accepted measure, we employ this question for each candidate in our experimental studies. The question was embedded in a battery of trait evaluations, in which subjects also evaluated the following phrases with respect to each candidate: "he is intelligent"; "he is moral"; "he cares about people like me"; and, "he is honest." We focus here on *relative* perceptions of leadership, and so we subtracted the challenger's leadership evaluation from the incumbent's. The Leadership Gap measure runs from −3 to +3, with higher values indicating better evaluations of the incumbent (Bush or Schwarzenegger) relative to the challenger (Kerry or Angelides). We also examine data from the ANES panel study, though we are only able to look at leadership evaluations of Bush, in which case the variable runs from 1 to 4.[5]

In our experiments, the key comparison group consists of individuals furthest removed from the context of a terrorist threat, those exposed to conditions of relative prosperity and well-being. We therefore compare how exposure to the Terror Threat condition relative to exposure to the Good Times condition (which serves as the baseline, or reference, condition) influences values on Leadership Gap. In our analysis of the ANES survey data, our indicator of terror threat is the same one that we used in chapter 3, which asks respondents to indicate on a four-point scale how likely it is there will be another terrorist attack (like 9/11) on U.S. soil, with higher values indicating more likely.

In addition, we also take into account an individual's party identification. Scholars have argued that partisan identification serves as a "perceptual screen" for incoming information (e.g., Bartels 2002; Campbell et al. 1960; Zaller 1992), making individuals more likely to accept information that is consistent with their identification and reject information that is inconsistent. The implication of this argument is that partisans may respond differently to the threat conditions when evaluating political leaders.[6] We therefore created measures for those who self-identified as Democrats, Republicans, and Independents. In each of our analyses we explore whether the effects of the threat treatment on perceptions of leadership qualities are the same for each partisan group.[7] In each of our analyses, we further include relevant control variables so that we can better isolate the effect of threat.

We first present analyses from the two experimental studies conducted during the 2004 presidential and 2006 gubernatorial elections, respectively. Turning first to the 2004 election, table 4.1 shows that exposure to Terror Threat increases values on the Leadership Gap measure relative to Good Times. Exposure to the terrorist threat audiovisual treatment increases evaluations of Bush relative to Kerry by about one-third of a unit. While the size of this effect does not appear extremely large, it is substantively quite meaningful when considering that the audiovisual treatment is only about one and a half minutes in length. Furthermore, we do not find evidence that the effect of the terrorist threat is different among our three partisan groups. That is, the effects we find on leadership perceptions are not unique to Republicans but, instead and perhaps surprisingly, are also found among Independents and Democrats.

The results for the 2006 California gubernatorial race are presented in the second data column of table 4.1. Once again the Terror Threat condition boosts leadership evaluations of the incumbent candidate. In this case the beneficiary is Arnold Schwarzenegger, and the loser is his principal challenger, Phil Angelides. Specifically, those in the Terror Threat condition end up .241 units higher on the Leadership Gap measure relative to those in the Good Times condition. We again do not find that partisans react differently to the threat context.

To summarize, in both of our experimental cases we find strong evidence that conditions of terrorist threat boost leadership evaluations of the incumbent Republican candidates relative to their Democratic challengers. Our evidence covers two levels of office and contexts across which

Table 4.1. Evaluations of Leadership Gap, US04s and US06s

Variable	Bush-Kerry US04s Coefficient (Std. Err.)	Schwarzenegger-Angelides US06s Coefficient (Std. Err.)
Constant	−0.279	2.057**
	(0.185)	(0.484)
Terror Threat	0.303++	0.241+
	(0.160)	(0.172)
Control	0.248	
	(0.168)	
Democrat	−0.510**	−0.456**
	(0.177)	(0.202)
Republican	1.746**	0.618*
	(0.214)	(0.327)
Female	−0.054	
	(0.135)	
Ideology		−0.310**
		(0.085)
Interest		−0.154
		(0.149)
N	299	159
R-squared	0.374	0.382

Note: Values in the cells are the results of OLS analysis with robust standard errors. One-tailed hypothesis tests are used for *Terror Threat* with statistical significance thresholds as follows: $++p \leq .05$ and $+p \leq .10$. Two-tailed hypothesis tests are used for all other variables; two-tailed statistical thresholds are indicated as follows: $**p \leq .05$ (two-tailed) and $*p \leq .10$ (two-tailed).

the salience of the terrorism issue varied. These results conclusively demonstrate a projection effect, since the experimental study holds constant any actions and/or rhetoric by Bush and Schwarzenegger across experimental conditions. Neither actions nor the leaders' rhetoric is discussed in either experimental treatment. That said, we recognize that one could question whether raising the issue of terrorism reminded people of Bush's actions on the terror front more than it did for those in the Good Times condition, and this therefore caused the shift in leadership perceptions. However, our second study leads us to reject this alternative interpretation. In this case we find an effect for Schwarzenegger, who did not play a key role in the immediate aftermath of 9/11.

Another question one might is ask whether citizens come to project more favorable traits in general, as perhaps they simply come to like certain leaders more. Or, as we are suggesting, are citizens looking to and projecting *particular* traits onto leaders in times of terror threat? We included other standard trait questions in our experimental studies and are therefore able to respond to this question. To do so, we constructed trait gap measures for intelligence, honesty, empathy, and morality. For each measure, we run the same analyses as we did for Leadership Gap (see Web Supplement A, tables 4.a and 4.b). In our 2004 study (US04s), we find that individuals in the Terror Threat condition perceive Bush as relatively more intelligent ($p = .047$, one-tailed) and more caring ($p = .076$, one-tailed) than Kerry compared to those in the Good Times group. However, the effects of the Terror Threat condition are greater for the Leadership Gap measure than they are for these other two traits. In the 2006 California gubernatorial election, we find that individuals in the Terror Threat condition perceive Schwarzenegger as relatively more moral ($p = .005$, one-tailed) and more honest ($p = .010$, one-tailed) than Angelides compared to those in the Good Times condition. In this case, the effects of the Terror Threat condition are not greater for Leadership Gap compared to these other two traits. It does appear then that projection of favorable evaluations occurs for *some* other traits, though not all. Furthermore, across both studies, the only trait that is consistently affected by terror threat is the leadership measure. In short, individuals focus significantly, but not exclusively, on strong leadership in times of terrorist threat.

Data from the ANES panel study from 2000/2002/2004 allow us to examine whether we can detect patterns, similar to those in our experiments, among a sample of people who better represent the mass public. The leadership evaluation question for Bush was asked in each wave of the study, so we can observe how individuals' evaluations of Bush's leadership qualities shifted over time (the study did not include a question about Kerry). In 2000 evaluations of Bush as a strong leader are around 2.71 (on the four-point scale) in 2000. These mean evaluations receive a boost, to 2.91, in the year 2002, and this difference is significant according to a t test ($p \leq .00$, two-tailed). In 2004, evaluations of Bush as a strong leader decline a bit to 2.81, but are still significantly higher than they were in 2000 ($p \leq .05$, two-tailed). Thus, at first glance, it appears that evaluations of Bush as a strong leader increased post-9/11 and stayed higher than pre-9/11 levels into 2004.

While these patterns in the data are suggestive, we cannot rule out the possibility that factors other than worry about terrorism are driving these increases in leadership evaluations after 2000. Recall that the 2002 and

2004 studies include a Terror Attack question. We can therefore use this indicator and take advantage of the panel nature of the data to examine how perceptions of Bush as a strong leader changed for the same individuals over time, given their perception of the likelihood of another terrorist attack. We look at the difference in perceptions of Bush's leadership between 2000 and 2002 and then between 2002 and 2004. Higher values mean that the individual came to see Bush as a stronger leader over time. Support for our argument would come in finding that differences in leadership perceptions increase among those who think that another terrorist attack is likely. Since we are analyzing survey (and not experimental) data, we attempt to isolate the effect of terror perception by controlling for potential confounding factors including partisanship, gender, age, race, education, ideology, and income.[8] We also assess whether the effect of the terror indicator on leadership evaluations varies for different groups of partisans. The results are presented in table 4.2.

We turn first to the difference in leadership perceptions between 2000 and 2002. As expected, the terror threat indicator is connected to changes in evaluations of Bush's leadership abilities. Thinking that attacks are more likely leads individuals to have a more positive evaluation of Bush as a strong leader in 2002 relative to their evaluation in 2000. Admittedly, the substantive effect is modest: the change in evaluations of Bush's leadership, moving from someone who thinks attacks are not at all likely to someone who thinks attacks are very likely, is only .18 units (the full scale ranges from −3 to 3). Contrary to what some might expect, we do not find any evidence that the effect of terror threat on leadership perceptions is different for different partisan groups.

Moving to the results for the difference in leadership evaluations between 2002 and 2004, we find that the terror threat indicator again is significant, though this time its effect is moderated by partisanship. More specifically, Independents who think attacks are more likely have higher evaluations of Bush's leadership in 2004 relative to their evaluation in 2002. However, Democrats with similar assessments of the likelihood of future attacks have slightly more negative evaluations of Bush's leadership capabilities (though these effects appear smaller than the boost that Independents give to Bush). Meanwhile, we do not find any effects for the terror indicator among Republicans. Thus, the decline in the leadership boost we observed in the mean leadership evaluations from 2002 to 2004 could be related to the more negative assessment among Democrats. This shift coincides with Democratic elites criticizing the administration's handling of the war on terror and the problems in Iraq. The results support our core

Table 4.2. Evaluations of difference in Bush Leadership, ANES panel data

	2002–2000 Coefficient (Std. Err.)	2004–2002 Coefficient (Std. Err.)
Terror Attack	0.060+	0.155++
	(0.046)	(0.091)
Democrat	−0.128	0.953**
	(0.096)	(0.346)
Republican	0.076	0.397
	(0.093)	(0.346)
Terror Attack · Democrat		−0.168++
		(0.096)
Terror Attack · Republican		−0.099
		(0.086)
Female	−0.241**	−0.127
	(0.079)	(0.091)
Age	0.004	0.000
	(0.003)	(0.003)
Asian	0.500	0.476
	(0.325)	(0.422)
Latino	−0.088	0.143
	(0.199)	(0.254)

African American	−0.328**	−0.030
	(0.140)	(0.072)
Mixed Race	−0.247	0.218
	(0.163)	(0.206)
Income	−0.048**	−0.020
	(0.021)	(0.024)
Education	−0.006	0.010
	(0.027)	(0.032)
Ideology	0.000	0.005**
	(0.001)	(0.002)
Constant	0.230	−0.440
	(0.257)	(0.357)
N	497	348
R-squared	0.061	0.090

Note: Values in the cells are the results of OLS analysis with robust standard errors. One-tailed hypothesis tests are used for Terror Attack and the interactions between Terror Attack and partisanship; one-tailed statistical significance thresholds indicated as follows: ++$p ≤ .05$ and +$p ≤ .10$. Two-tailed hypothesis tests are used for all other variables; two-tailed statistical thresholds indicated as follows: **$p ≤ .05$ (two-tailed) and *$p ≤ .10$ (two-tailed). Coefficients presented for the interaction terms are the slope of the effect of terrorism for that partisan group.

argument (connecting terrorist threat to shifts in evaluations), yet they differ from the results of our analyses of the experimental data and the 2000 and 2002 ANES panel data. In none of these cases did we find different effects across partisans. One reason for the difference may be that there is dual causality in the 2004 survey data in which Democrats who became more negative with respect to Bush's leadership came to think that he made the United States more vulnerable to future attacks. Given the possibility of endogeneity with the survey data in 2004, we have more confidence in the experimental results.

To conclude, we have seemingly conclusive evidence of the first step in the second strategy of coping: seeking and projecting leadership qualities onto certain political leaders. In considering whether this is an instrumental reaction or something more, we again note this method of coping would seem to be motivated by psychological needs. It is unlikely that people could articulate a rational reason for increasing their perceptions of someone's leadership evaluations just because there is a threat; nor, indeed, is it obvious that they are aware of these shifting leadership perceptions. Once these evaluations have been so shifted, do they also become more consequential in the voting booth? We evaluate this next.

Weighting Leadership in the Voting Booth

In analyzing vote choice we follow a similar strategy as we did above. We first turn to our experiments and, in this case, look at whether individuals in these studies weight the difference in leadership capabilities more heavily in their voting decisions. We then turn to an analysis of the ANES panel survey data in order to assess the generalizability of our findings.

In each of the two experimental studies, subjects were asked whether they intended to cast their vote for George W. Bush/Arnold Schwarzenegger (1) or John Kerry/Phil Angelides (0). To create a standard model of vote choice, we include measures of party identification (Party Identification), Leadership Gap, and a measure of issue stances. The Issues measure for 2004 is created from responses to four questions: defense policy, economic policy, perceptions of the nation's security, and perceptions of the nation's economy. For 2006, the questions were asked with respect to the state of California; we substituted spending on homeland security for defense spending, and we find two relevant clusters of issues, one of which accounts for policy positions, Issues 1, and another which takes into account perceptions of California's economy and security, Issues 2.[9] Higher values on party identification and the issues measure(s) should make a subject more likely to vote for Bush and Schwarzenegger. To evaluate our argument that the weight of leadership becomes more consequential in times of terror threat, our analyses include a measure that looks at the combination of the Terror Threat condition and Leadership Gap (interaction term), called Leadership Gap·Terror Threat. For 2004, we also include an interaction between Leadership Gap and the control group (Status Quo). To allow for the possibility that the weight assigned to issues shifts in times of terror threat versus good times, we also include interactions between each issue measure and the experimental conditions. Finally, in 2006, we are able to explore whether the weight of partisanship shifts in times of terror threat.[10]

The full results of our vote choice analyses are presented in table 4.3. If we look at the measures for partisanship, leadership, and issues on their own, we can see the effects among those in the Good Times condition. As one would expect, Republicans and those who evaluate the Republican's leadership capabilities more positively than those of the Democratic challenger are more inclined to vote for the Republican. This holds for both elections. In 2004 those who are more conservative in their issue opinions are more likely to vote for Bush.

The key question, however, is whether individuals weight *leadership* more given exposure to the Terror Threat condition. The answer is yes. Across both elections, we find clear evidence that subjects in the Terror Threat condition weight leadership more heavily into their voting decisions compared to subjects in the Good Times condition (see the significant and positive effect for Leadership Gap·Terror Threat). In 2004, we do not find this pattern among those in the Status Quo condition. Interestingly, for the 2004 election, issue opinions are weighted differently across the conditions, but the effects are such that those in the Terror Threat condition with more conservative-issue positions and more favorable retrospective evaluations are less likely to vote for Bush relative to their counterparts in the Good Times condition. Meanwhile, issues do not influence the voting decisions of those in the Terror Threat condition for the 2006 election. There may be several reasons for this result. First, as we argued earlier, candidates may be perceived to take similar stances on security, which causes individuals to look to other criteria, such as leadership. Second, even if subjects were motivated to seek out more information about candidate stances on terrorism, our study did not enable them to do so. Finally, for 2006, we find that subjects in the Terror Threat condition do not weight partisanship in their voting decisions, while those in the

Table 4.3. Analysis of Vote Bush (US04s) and Vote Schwarzenegger (US06s)

Variable	Coefficient (Standard Error)	Coefficient (Standard Error)
Leadership Gap	0.654++	0.836++
	(0.285)	(0.276)
Leadership Gap · Terror Threat	2.320++	1.420++
	(0.558)	(0.355)
Leadership Gap · Status Quo	0.401+	
	(0.256)	
Terror Threat	−2.696**	0.544
	(1.120)	(0.630)
Status Quo	−0.560	
	(0.603)	
Party Identification	0.602**	0.347**
	(0.144)	(0.100)
Issues 1	1.239**	0.214
	(0.575)	(0.248)
Issues 2		0.028
		(0.176)
Party Identification · Terror Threat		0.100
		(0.124)
Issues 1 · Terror Threat	−2.015**	−0.144
	(0.637)	(0.251)

Issues 1 · Status Quo	-1.352**	
	(0.416)	
Issues 2 · Terror Threat		0.026
		(0.220)
Constant	-3.103**	-1.939**
	(0.727)	(0.442)
N	251	143
Wald chi-squared	75.84	51.24
Prob>chi-squared	0.000	0.000
Pseudo R-squared	0.882	0.565
Percentage correctly predicted	98.0%	89.51%
Proportional reduction in error	0.919	0.659

Note: Values in the cells are the results of probit analysis with robust standard errors. One-tailed hypothesis tests are used for Terror Threat, Leadership Gap, and the interactions between Terror Threat and Leadership Gap; one-tailed statistical significance thresholds indicated as follows: $+p \leq .05$ and $+p \leq .10$. Two-tailed hypothesis tests are used for all other variables; two-tailed statistical thresholds indicated as follows: $**p \leq .05$ (two-tailed) and $*p \leq .10$ (two-tailed). Coefficients presented for the interaction terms are the slope of the effect of Leadership Gap within that experimental condition.

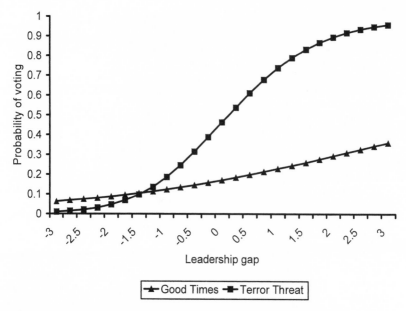

Figure 4.1. Predicted probability of voting for Bush at different values of Leadership Gap by condition, US04s
Note: The figure is based on output from analysis reported in table 4.3. Lines show the predicted probability of voting for Bush at different values on the Leadership Gap measure by experimental condition.

Good Times condition do. This finding is in line with other studies which show that individuals high in anxiety weight partisanship less in the voting booth (Brader 2005, 2006; Marcus, Neuman and MacKuen 2000).[11]

In order to better illustrate these results, we offer visual demonstrations of the predicted probability of voting for the Republican candidate across the different values of the Leadership Gap measure for those in the Good Times and Terror Threat conditions. The illustration for Bush is in figure 4.1, while the figure for Schwarzenegger is in figure 4.2.[12] In general, we expect to see that both lines increase across the values of Leadership Gap (since higher values mean more positive evaluations of the Republican relative to the Democrat); however, the line should be higher and steeper for those in the Terror Threat condition. Turning first to figure 4.1, this is exactly what we find. The predicted probability of voting for Bush increases dramatically at higher levels of the Leadership Gap measure among those in the Terror Threat condition. Leadership still matters under times of well-being, but less so. The increase among those in the Good Times condition is much less substantial.[13] If we turn to figure 4.2, we find the exact same

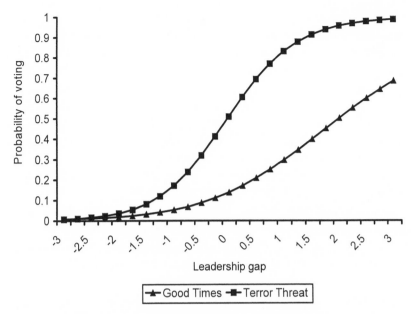

Figure 4.2. Predicted probability of voting for Schwarzenegger at different values of Leadership Gap by condition, US06s

Note: The figure is based on output from analysis reported in table 4.3. Lines show the predicted probability of voting for Schwarzenegger at different values on the Leadership Gap measure by experimental condition.

pattern for Arnold Schwarzenegger.[14] In short, the figures demonstrate strong support for our argument: in the face of a terrorist threat, voters accord greater weight to leadership traits compared to times of relative prosperity and well-being. While Giuliani said they should, we say they do.

One may wonder whether other trait evaluations become more consequential in times of terror threat relative to good times. To explore this possibility, we run the same sets of analyses as above, but instead of including Leadership Gap, one by one, we include each of the other trait gap measures: moral, intelligent, honest, and cares about people.[15] For 2004, the only trait for which we find an increased weight among those in the Terror Threat condition relative to those in Good Times is for morality perceptions. However, if we incorporate both leadership and morality perceptions in the same model, we find that the effect for morality among those in the Terror Threat condition washes out. For 2006, we do not find any cases in which individuals weight another trait more heavily in the Terror Threat condition relative to Good Times, though intelligence is close to significant.

The above set of results demonstrates exactly the mechanism that we expected to find linking terror threat conditions, leadership evaluations, and vote choice, but for a set of somewhat restricted samples. We have the means to probe the generalizability of these results again with the ANES 2000/2002/2004 panel study. This study asked for whom the respondent voted Bush (1) or Kerry (0). Our indicator of threat is, again, the question about how likely the respondent thinks it is that the United States will suffer a terrorist attack in the next twelve months. In this case, though, we create separate measures for each response (somewhat likely, likely, very likely), with someone thinking attacks are not at all likely being the baseline category.[16]

Our approach in the following analysis is to approximate a basic vote choice model similar to the one we estimated for the experiments (though here we have four levels of terror threat/nonthreat rather than just two). Our key measure is leadership evaluations of George W. Bush interacted with each threat dummy variable (Somewhat Likely, Likely, Very Likely). Because the survey did not include a question about Kerry as a strong leader, we are restricted to looking at how perceptions of Bush as a strong leader influence voting decisions at different levels of threat perceptions. To finish building this model, we include two other factors relevant to the vote: partisanship and ideology.[17] Since we are dealing with survey data, we also take into account gender, age, race, education, and income. The full results of our vote choice analyses are presented in Web Supplement A, table 4.g.

In terms of general results, we find that Republicans and conservatives are more likely to vote for Bush, as one would expect, as are females and those higher in income. Those with higher education, as well as Asians and African Americans, are less likely to vote for Bush. If we turn to our key measures of interest, we find that leadership evaluations exert a stronger effect on voting decisions among those who think attacks are somewhat likely, likely, and very likely relative to those who think future attacks are not at all likely. The difference in the effect of leadership on the vote across those who perceive no threat or some threat is also quite substantial. figure 4.3 shows that, among those who think attacks are not at all likely, moving from the lowest to highest leadership evaluation of Bush increases the probability of voting for him by about 69 percentage points. While high, the shift is even more substantial among those who think attacks are somewhat likely, likely, and very likely, resulting in increases of 91, 85, and 87 percentage points respectively. Thus we do not just observe those who think attacks are very likely weighting leadership more heavily in their

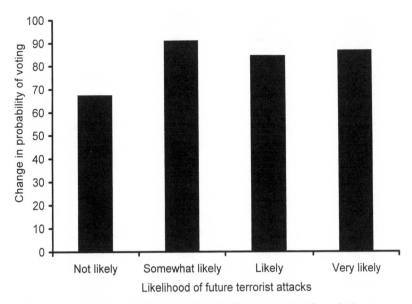

Figure 4.3. Change in the probability of voting for Bush moving from the lowest to highest leadership evaluation, by likelihood of future terrorist attacks
Note: The figure is based on output from analysis reported in Web Supplement A, table 4.g. Bars show the change in the probability of voting for Bush moving from the lowest to highest leadership evaluation across different values of the Terror Threat indicator.

voting decisions, but also those who think future attacks are somewhat likely.

These results are clearly consistent with our experimental results and our argument that individuals weight leadership more heavily in the voting booth during times of terror threat compared to other times. The fact that we obtain these results with a study that does not perfectly capture core elements of our hypothesis and experimental design leaves us soundly assured that the relationships we have identified among terror threat, leadership, and voting are robust, in particular that they hold among the more general U.S. population with respect to vote choice in the 2004 election.[18] In short, leadership matters in times of crisis—in more ways than one.

Discussion and Conclusions

What does it mean for the quality of democracy, if anything, that individuals project additional leadership qualities onto selected leaders in times of terror threat and then weight such qualities more heavily in the voting booth? With respect to the first, projecting leadership qualities onto a select figure while downgrading evaluations of another might simply be a relatively benign coping mechanism. Individuals' feelings of hope and strength are presumably at least partially restored by their belief in a distinctly capable leader. Taken alone, it might appear that this type of coping strategy is not especially problematic for the quality of democracy. The same might be said of the result, taken independently, of placing emphasis on leadership qualities in the voting booth. Some might instead argue that the quality of democracy is degraded if individuals focus on personality traits in times of crisis at the expense of other important considerations, such as issue positions or performance evaluations. This concern would comport with a more progressive conception of the ideal political role played by citizens, which includes learning about the issues of the day and voting based on assessments of such issues.

That said, others, such as Giuliani, might claim that the standards citizens use to elect leaders *should* vary during times of threat versus nonthreat. As we discussed in the introduction, during the colonial and founding eras, notions of good citizenship meant electing a person who is deemed a good leader (Schudson 1998). In short, we assert that in general this form of coping on its own does not pose a large threat to the quality (nor to the durability) of democracy, even if it means that citizens fail to live up to progressive ideals of policy-based voting.

What if we couple the projection of strong leadership qualities in times of threat with then weighting such qualities more heavily in the voting booth? In such a case, voters are placing greater emphasis on perceptions of traits that may not be accurate or, at the least, do not reflect perceptions under times of relative well-being. Such behavior arguably is more worrisome with respect to the quality of democracy than either of these two effects in isolation. We may be even more concerned about the quality of democracy if the newly elected, presumably strong leader begins to take actions that do in fact pose a threat to democratic institutions or processes and citizens not only turn a blind eye but actually proffer their support and acquiescence. We turn exactly to these issues in the next chapter.

5

Enabling Charismatic Leadership in Times of Terror Threat

> While other Presidents have profited from a large number of so-called rallies, few Presidents have presided over as many crises as Ronald Reagan. . . . Some of these involved direct actions taken by Reagan, such as the invasion of Grenada and the bombing of Libya, while some were initiated by others, such as the Achille Lauro and TWA hijackings. The Challenger space shuttle explosion and the bombing of the Marine Corps barracks in Lebanon were particularly tragic rally events. In addition, the President's own courage in the face of life-threatening personal peril (the assassination attempt and Reagan's 1985 cancer surgery) further solidified his support among the American people.
>
> David J. Lanoue, "The 'Teflon Factor'"

The above quote documents some of the unusually large number of crises that triggered "rallies" (boosts in support) on behalf of the charismatic U.S. president Ronald Reagan.[1] Reagan was dubbed the "Teflon president" owing to his ability to deflect criticism, negative evaluations, and even scandals. As the case of Reagan suggests, there appears to exist a strong compulsion to shield and champion charismatic leaders who hold office in times of threat. In sharp contrast to the proverbial glass ceiling that frustrates some individuals, Reagan appeared to float effortlessly above a "glass floor."[2] We believe two of the factors behind this remarkable ability are crisis and charisma. And, in some ways, Reagan was not all that unique.

Historically, deep national crises often coincide with the rise of strong and charismatic political leaders. Among those who governed in times of crisis are individuals widely hailed as great leaders, who exercised power with restraint and respect for democratic processes. A fine example is found in George Washington, who held office in a time of significant political and economic uncertainty. The hopes of a country were bound up in his administration. Yet, despite significant pressure to stay in office, Washington bowed to democratic principle and allowed for an alternation of power. Also among those who have emerged in times of crisis are individuals who ruled as malevolent dictators. Chief among these lies Adolf Hitler, whose rise to and expansion of power was buoyed by political, economic, and social unrest.

This is the second of two chapters focused on a second strategy of coping with threat, which entails looking for and delegating leadership to those who appear capable of resolving the crisis. We argue and provide evidence in this chapter for a specific set of relationships among threat, charisma, and evaluative and behavioral responses. Our argument is as follows. First, in order to restore feelings of hope, efficacy, control, and security, citizens both look for and *project* additional charismatic qualities onto particular leaders. This argument parallels that which we tested in the first half of the previous chapter, where we examined perceptions of strong leadership. Second, conditions of threat and perceptions of charisma motivate citizens to protect a selected leader's image even in the face of negative performance, to assist the leader by way of self-sacrificial behavior, and, in some cases, to prefer a greater centralization of power in the executive office.

We begin the chapter with a review of our expectations. We then walk through multiple pieces of evidence in support of our arguments. We look not only at different types of data but at data from two different countries, the United States and Mexico. More specifically, we included questions related to charisma on two experimental studies in the United States (US04s: U.S. student sample, fall 2004; US05ns: U.S. nonstudent sample, summer 2005) and one experimental study in Mexico (MEX06s: Mexico student sample, fall 2006). We also look at two studies in the United States without charisma measures (US05s: U.S. student sample, fall 2005, and US07s: U.S. student sample, spring 2007). In addition to the experimental results, we examine survey data in Mexico (2006 CIDE-CSES survey project). Whereas our experiments focus on terrorist and economic threats, in the latter analyses we look at a broader array of crises (threats to physical security, the economy, and political stability) and their relationship to perceptions of charisma.

Crises, Charisma, and the Consequences for Leadership

In chapter 1 we detailed a two-part argument concerning the relationships among crisis, charisma, and certain outcome variables. First, conditions of crisis motivate individuals to seek out, and find, leaders who appear stronger, more charismatic, and more unrivaled than they might otherwise be perceived. Such a projection of leadership qualities allows individuals to feel more hopeful and secure in the face of a threat. Madsen and Snow (1991) make this argument specific to charisma. In their seminal work on the charismatic bond, they theorize and then demonstrate using the case of Argentina's Juan Perón that crises in that country left individuals with a deep psychological need to place their faith in a presumed savior. Our work in this chapter follows in their footsteps, though we add the expectation that evaluations of the charisma of *rival* candidates will also shift in times of crisis as individuals attempt to single out one presumably heroic leader.

The second part of our argument is that crisis and charisma in turn elicit evaluative, attitudinal, and behavioral shifts in citizens. Such reactions may stem from psychological needs to maintain a feeling of security (e.g., by protecting the presumed savior's image). It is also possible that such reactions are the result of a goal-oriented, instrumental perspective whereby individuals seek to provide the leader the space and capacity with which to resolve the crisis condition. In chapter 1 we identified several possible outcomes arising from these tendencies. Specifically, both threat and charisma should motivate individuals to avoid blaming the leader for policy mistakes, to sacrifice their own resources on behalf of the leader and his or her cause, and—at least in some cases—to cede greater institutional authority to the leader.

The argument we are putting forward is one in which conditions of threat have both direct and indirect (via perceptions of charisma) effects on individuals' attitudes, evaluations, and behaviors with respect to selected leaders. In what follows we evaluate the various components of this argument using data from several experiments. Specifically, by drawing on data from both the United States and Mexico we gain insight into the generalizability of our claims (see chapter 2 for additional information on how the mode of treatment varied across these studies). With respect to the U.S. studies, by using data from four distinct studies, we are able to test whether our arguments hold across different subject types, across different measures of blame and self-sacrifice, and across time. The Mexico study allows us to examine some of these relationships in the context of a system with a relatively short history of competitive party politics. Differences in context across the two countries may play a role when we look at the effect of threat and charisma on preferences over the institutional balance of power and, specifically, executive strength.

Our work contributes to and extends existing research in a number of ways. First, this project represents one of the few systematic tests of the relationship between contexts of terror threat and perceptions of charisma and leadership. We also explore other types of crisis, such as economic decline, crime-induced public insecurity, and political uncertainty/conflict. In addition to terrorism being understudied, few have systematically looked at the relationship between these latter two threat types and perceptions of charisma. Furthermore, while the literature is silent on who will benefit from projections, we explicitly take up the task of identifying the beneficiary of charisma projections across different types of threat contexts. In addition, while previous work has suggested that charisma brings with it certain privileges (e.g., blame reduction, self-sacrifice, and power deference), we explicitly apply these ideas to the political context and, as well, examine multiple indicators of what these privileges might be. Finally, most of the more systematic quantitative work that does exist on the subject of threat and charisma has been carried out within the U.S. context alone. We add additional insight and support for our core arguments by examining data from Mexico alongside data from the United States.

Conditions of Threat Induce Shifting Perceptions of Charisma

Our first task is to demonstrate a robust link between conditions of threat and charisma. Since the study of charisma is rare in political science, we first clarify what we mean by the concept. Frequent references to the term *charisma* in the popular press suggest that the public possesses some general sense of what it is and that it is important. In classroom exercises, we asked students to create a list of charismatic leaders. Names such as Fidel Castro, Martin Luther King Jr., Adolf Hitler, Juan Perón, and Franklin Delano Roosevelt frequently make the list. If we restricted the exercise to contemporary politicians, we would expect the list to include persons such as Bill Clinton, Barack Obama, Rudy Giuliani, and Tony Blair.

But what is charisma exactly? Beginning with Weber's (1922/1947) classic work, scholars have theorized about charismatic leadership across a variety of disciplines. Two basic understandings of charisma stand out in current academic and popular texts. The first stems from Weber's definition of charisma as "a certain quality of an individual personality by virtue of which he is set apart from ordinary men and treated as endowed with supernatural, superhuman, or at least specifically exceptional qualities" (quoted in Eisenstadt 1968, xviii). In this conception, leaders are, or are not, inherently charismatic. If we look at charisma in this way, it is an elusive or at least ambiguous concept. How exactly does a researcher determine whether a leader is "superhuman"?

We adhere to a second, more concrete definition of charisma characterized by three principal features. First, charisma is an underlying construct derived from a bundle of specific traits and, as such, something that an individual can possess to a greater or lesser degree. This treatment of charisma is nearly ubiquitous in the study of organizational leadership and is increasingly used in political science (e.g., Bligh, Kohles, and Pillai 2005; Emrich et al. 2001; Pillai and Williams 1998; Pillai et al. 2003; Shamir 1994). Among scholars working in this tradition, a great deal of agreement exists with respect to the bundle of traits that make a leader more charismatic. Specifically, those who are more confident, caring, enthusiastic, goal-oriented, optimistic, and inspiring are considered to be more charismatic (e.g., Behling and McFillen 1996; Bryman 1992; Conger and Kanungo 1988; House and Howell 1992; Madsen and Snow 1991).

Second, the degree to which someone is perceived as charismatic is linked to evaluations made by *other* people (Conger, Kanungo, and Menon 2000). Thus, individuals might have different evaluations of the degree to which a particular leader is charismatic. For example, some people think Bill Clinton lights up a room, usually Democrats and some Independents, while Republicans perceive him through a less attractive lens. This notion that charisma is linked to the perceptions of others brings us to the third and related principal feature, which is that charisma is not simply an inherent personality trait, but is something that is malleable. While individuals may innately possess (or fail to possess) certain traits associated with charisma, the degree to which that individual is ultimately perceived as charismatic can be influenced by select factors. For one, perceptions of charisma can be influenced by personal efforts to adopt more charismatic characteristics (e.g., Cohen 1992). Leaders who articulate a compelling vision of the future or who project an outsider image might come to be seen as more charismatic (see Conger and Kanungo 1988).[3] Not only can people "learn" to be more charismatic, events going on in the world can also influence perceptions of charisma. This then brings us to our principal argument: in times of crisis individuals are more likely to perceive a selected leader as more charismatic.

Measuring Charisma

To measure charisma, we need to determine the extent to which individuals believe a selected leader possesses the various traits associated with that quality. Social scientists primarily in the field of leadership have generated and validated a battery of questions that ask individuals to evaluate leaders on the traits associated with charisma (Multifactor Leadership Questionnaire-5X Long Form; Bass and Avolio 1995). This battery of questions is widely used in studies of leadership (Awamleh and Gardner 1999; Tejeda, Scandura, and Pillai 2001), and is increasingly being used in studies of political leadership.[4] In all experiments in which we studied charisma, we included twelve statements related to perceptions of charisma.[5] In the case of the 2006 Mexico survey data, we used a subset containing five of these twelve questions given space constraints.[6]

For each question within the battery, subjects were asked to indicate the extent to which they agree with a given statement as it pertains to a given leader. For example, subjects in the United States were asked to indicate the degree to which they agree with the following statement: "George W. Bush articulates a compelling vision of the future." Another example is: "George W. Bush displays a sense of power and confidence." The trigger words used in the full battery are the following (and can be seen in the appendix): vision, pride, goes beyond self-interest, respect, power, values and beliefs, sense of purpose, moral and ethical, sense of mission, optimistic, enthusiastic, and confidence. As we have indicated, the battery of statements is intended to capture the degree to which individuals perceive the target (for example, George W. Bush) to possess the set of traits that is believed to underlie the latent concept of charisma.

To generate a single Perceptions of Charisma variable from responses to the individual statements, we added those responses together (and divided by twelve, for the experiment-based studies). This additive index runs from 1, indicating the lowest perception of charisma, to 6, indicating the highest perception of charisma. This variable has validity across all of our studies.[7]

Case-specific Expectations

In times of crisis, people seek a hero. But, in the specific cases for which we have data—the United States in 2004 and 2005 and Mexico in 2006—to whom will they turn? In chapter 1 we identified three factors that likely play a role in this process: perceived responsibility for the threat; the leader's partisanship; and, the leader's background. Where these dimensions appear to run in the same direction, we can easily establish an *a priori* expectation. Where some of the factors appear to favor one leader, while other factors favor another, our prognosticating abilities are more limited; when we find this to be the case, we candidly admit this and assert a softer (or no) set of initial expectations.

In our study of crisis and charisma in the United States, we examine two types of crises. First and foremost, we examine terrorist threat. In the US04s study, we are able to explore this with respect to both Bush and his electoral opponent, John Kerry, while in the US05ns study, we look at a Terror Threat condition and, as well, an Economic Threat condition. In this latter case, because it was a nonelection year, we only examine perceptions of Bush's charisma. As we already discussed in the previous chapter, we expect Bush to be the beneficiary (and Kerry the loser) of projections of leadership qualities in times of terror threat. Economic threats, on the other hand, should hurt perceptions of Bush's charisma. Classic works on retrospective voting tell us that people tend to blame the incumbent for poor economic performance (Fiorina 1981). Moreover, given their ownership of welfare and related issues (Petrocik 1996), Democrats may seem relatively more appealing in times of economic downturn. Thus, if economic threat indeed affects perceptions of charisma, then we expect this effect will be such that perceptions of Bush's charisma will be deflated relative to those in the Good Times condition.

We are also able to explore both terror and economic threats in the context of Mexico's 2006 presidential election. Until near the end of the twentieth century, Mexico was a one-party dominant state. In 2000 voters ousted the ruling party, the PRI, from the executive office and elected Vicente Fox of the PAN. The campaign for the next presidential election, in 2006, saw the PRI not only field their first presidential candidate as a party out of government, but that candidate (Roberto Madrazo) further played a relatively minor role in the election. Instead, the race came down to a neck-and-neck horserace between Felipe Calderón, candidate for the right-leaning and incumbent PAN, and Andrés Manuel López Obrador, of the left-leaning PRD. The exceptionally close contest resulted in both candidates declaring victory. At the time of our study, the Federal Electoral Institute (IFE) had certified the election results, confirming Calderón as the victor but protests claiming government-sponsored fraud were still being organized by López Obrador, who was also actively establishing a "parallel government." The postelection context, in short, contained some uncertainty over the future of Mexican politics.

Within this context, our study focused on the two frontrunners: Calderón and López Obrador. Our principal expectation is that the Terror Threat condition will increase perceptions of Calderón's charisma (relative to Good Times). Calderón is of the incumbent party, facing an external threat, and this should generate rally-like effects for his candidacy. Further, his party arguably has a stronger reputation on issues of public security, typically taking a harder stance on crime; this may transfer into expectations that his party can better handle issues of national security. In contrast, López Obrador is less likely to receive such a boost, given his challenger status, his party's less clear stance on issues of national security, and no personal factors in his own background suggesting he would be strong in this issue area. Individuals should react by deflating perceptions of López Obrador's charisma, as they pin their hopes on Calderón.

The expectations for our Economic Threat condition in Mexico are a bit more complicated. Both candidates talked about the importance of the economy during the election but highlighted different aspects of it. López Obrador focused on poverty relief among the more disenfranchised while Calderón, especially in later stages of the campaign, focused on job creation. Calderón's association with the incumbent party would suggest that those employing a standard economic voting calculus would hold him at least partially responsible for negative economic news. Given both of these factors, we begin with the expectation that people holding negative economic evaluations will perceive the left-leaning challenger López Obrador as more charismatic and the right-leaning incumbent party's candidate, Calderón, as less charismatic. We apply this expectation principally to our analysis of the 2006 CIDE-CSES Mexico national survey, in which we examine measures of economic, political, and public security threats (there is no indicator of terrorist threat in the survey).[8] Turning to expectations for the experiments (MEX06s), two factors combined point us to a different set of initial expectations. First, in this experimental study we have a larger sample of PAN supporters and those from advantaged backgrounds. Second, Calderón's campaign team ran a highly visible set of ads attacking López Obrador, suggesting that he was an economic risk for Mexico.[9] To the extent that Calderón's campaign was successful in raising concerns about López Obrador's abilities to manage the economy, especially among those higher in socioeconomic status, it might have helped offset the limitations of being connected to a right-leaning, incumbent party. In evaluating our experimental evidence, we begin with the soft expectation that the threat of economic decline will lead those individuals to project higher levels of charisma onto Calderón, at the expense of López Obrador.

While the survey data did not have questions concerning international terrorism, there were questions that enable us to test another type of physical threat that has become increasingly important in Mexican politics: public safety. Based on open-ended responses to a question on the major political problems confronting the nation we created an indicator of Public Security Threat.[10] With respect to which leader might benefit among those affected by a public security threat, we believe it is difficult to establish clear expectations. On the one hand, the PAN as the incumbent administration could be perceived as responsible for failing to ensure public security. On the other hand, the PAN has traditionally taken a stronger stance on the issue. Further, López Obrador, as mayor of the Federal District, could conceivably be held accountable for failings in at least that major metropolitan area. Consequently, we do not have strong expectations for which of the two might receive a leadership boost from individuals concerned about public insecurity and, instead, in this issue area we let the data speak for themselves.

Finally, another issue arguably stole the spotlight in the aftermath of the Mexican presidential election: accusations that the close contest between the two frontrunners was ultimately rigged in favor of Calderón. We examine this issue within our survey data analyses by way of a question that asks respondents whether they thought the presidential election was clean or not, on a five-point scale, with higher values indicating more negative evaluations (Election). Given Calderón's affiliation with the incumbent PAN administration, which was not immune to accusations of collaboration in fraudulent electoral activities in the postelection period and given that it was López Obrador who spearheaded those accusations (and thus quite clearly "owned" this issue), we expect that those who perceived the election as fraudulent will be more (less) likely to perceive López Obrador (Calderón) as a stronger and more charismatic leader.

In addition to including measures for our various threat conditions in our statistical analyses predicting perceptions of charisma, we also include measures of respondents' party identification, as we did in the previous chapter. We created measures for those who self-identified as Democrats, Republicans, and Independents for the U.S.-based studies, and for Panistas, Perredistas, Priistas, and Other/None in Mexico.[11] We again explore whether partisans respond differently to the threat conditions, this time with respect to perceptions of charisma.[12] In keeping with our analyses from previous chapters, we also include factors that were unevenly distributed across our experimental conditions (see chapter 2 for details on the results of these tests). Finally, since respondents in the Mexico survey data are not randomly assigned to experimental conditions, we controlled for age, gender, union membership, education, church attendance, race, region, ideology, and political efficacy.[13]

Charisma Affected

Do crisis conditions affect perceptions of charisma? The answer quite clearly is yes. We find strong support for such a conclusion across all three experiments that we examine and in our analysis of the Mexican survey data. To provide some structure to the discussion of our results we will split them by country, beginning with the United States and the case of terrorist threat, charisma, and George W. Bush and John Kerry.

In the first two data columns of table 5.1 we present the results of analyses of our 2004 student study. Exposure to the Terror Threat condition leads individuals in that treatment group to perceive Bush as .184 units more charismatic and to perceive Kerry as about .161 units less charismatic, compared to their peers in the Good Times condition. Two points are worth making about these results. First, while these shifts are moderate to small on the six-point Charisma scale, we find them nonetheless significant when considering the short duration of our treatment in the lab setting (a minute-and-a-half audiovisual presentation). Second, we find differences in baseline perceptions of Bush's and Kerry's charisma by partisanship, with Republicans rating Bush as more charismatic and Democrats rating Bush as less charismatic, compared to the Independent baseline. The reverse pattern holds for Kerry. However, and quite interestingly, we do *not* find that the effect of terrorist threat on perceptions of Bush's charisma is different for different partisan groups. Partisans of all stripes react similarly to the threatening context. That said, some partisans groups react differently to the treatment with respect to evaluations of Kerry. Namely, only Republicans and Independents in the Terror Threat condition have lower evaluations of Kerry's charisma, while there is no effect among Democrats.

Our 2005 nonstudent U.S. study acts as a robustness test for the findings pertaining to the effect of terrorist threat on perceptions of Bush. The key factors that differentiate this study from the 2004 study are the use of a nonstudent sample, the change in time (one year later), and the inclusion of an Economic Threat treatment alongside the Terror Threat and Good Times conditions. In this dataset, we found differences in levels of political information across our experimental conditions, and thus include this in our analysis. Furthermore, since much experimental work shows that people with different levels of political information sometimes react differently to incoming information (e.g., Druckman and Nelson 2003; Kam 2005; Miller and Krosnick 2000; Sniderman, Brody, and Tetlock 1991), we tested whether the effect of the treatments vary by political information level.[14] The results are in the third data column of table 5.1. The presence of interaction terms makes direct interpretation of the effects of threat not possible, so we graph the shift in perceptions of Bush's charisma given exposure to the Terror and Economic Threat treatments (relative to those in the Good Times condition) among individuals at different values of political information in figure 5.1. As the figure shows, terror threat increases Bush's charisma among those at lower values on the political information scale. The Terror Threat condition yields a .57 jump on the charisma scale for those at the lowest level of political information. The comparable effects for those at .25 and .5 on the political information scale are increases of .38 and .19, respectively. These effects are statistically significant, while the effects of Terror Threat wash away for those above .5 on the political information scale. We do not find any statistically meaningful effects for an economic threat on perceptions of Bush's charisma at any level of political sophistication. We again observe similar differences in baseline partisanship, with Republicans perceiving Bush as more charismatic and Democrats perceiving him as less charismatic. Furthermore, we do not find that partisans react differently to the threat conditions. We should pause to underscore the importance of this particular finding: across two studies we find evidence that *regardless* of one's partisanship, individuals facing a context of terrorist threat in 2004 and 2005 came to perceive George W. Bush as more charismatic than they would have under conditions of well-being and prosperity.

It is possible that the critical reader is still not impressed and instead is thinking: Is it really surprising that citizens living in a country that suffered such a lethal terrorist attack project charisma onto the person in office at the time of the attacks? How might individuals living in a country that has not experienced a terrorist attack respond to a Terror Threat condition? Our analyses of data from our fall 2006 Mexico student study (MEX06s) provide us with the ability to say that the effect of terrorist threat on the projection of charisma is not unique to the U.S. case.

In the analysis of our Mexico experiment, the results of which are shown in the last data column of table 5.1, we find that the Terror Threat condition boosts perceptions of Calderón's charisma and decreases perceptions of López Obrador's charisma, relative to the Good Times condition. Not only do we find the same pattern of results in Mexico, we find that the size of the effects for the likely beneficiary is *similar* to the U.S. results. The Terror Threat condition increases Calderón's charisma by .178

Table 5.1. Perceptions of charisma, US04s, US05ns, and MEX06s

Variable	US04s		US05ns	MEX06s	
	Bush Coefficient (Std. Err.)	Kerry Coefficient (Std. Err.)	Bush Coefficient (Std. Err.)	Calderón Coefficient (Std. Err.)	AMLO Coefficient (Std. Err.)
Constant	3.385**	4.207**	2.869**	3.124**	3.149**
	(0.138)	(0.121)	(0.228)	(0.219)	(0.278)
Terror Threat	0.184+	−0.161+	0.569++	0.178+	−0.362++
	(0.117)	(0.100)	(0.325)	(0.117)	(0.140)
Status Quo	0.059	0.277**	0.253		
	(0.137)	(0.107)	(0.328)		
Economic Threat			0.052+	0.161+	−0.301++
			(0.408)	(0.109)	(0.140)
Democrat/PRD	−0.180	0.753**	−0.287**	−0.584**	1.366**
	(0.149)	(0.126)	(0.109)	(0.199)	(0.182)
Republican/PAN	1.485**	−0.772**	1.441**	0.646**	−0.508**
	(0.167)	(0.151)	(0.129)	(0.106)	(0.129)
PRI				−0.035	−0.278
				(0.164)	(0.192)
Female	−0.087	−0.138			
	(0.109)	(0.089)			

	(1)	(2)	(3)	(4)	(5)
Education			0.065*		
			(0.038)		
Political Information			−0.174		
			(0.254)		
Terror Threat · Political Information			−0.755++		
			(0.441)		
Economic Threat · Political Information			−0.291		
			(0.552)		
Status Quo · Political Information			−0.248		
			(0.415)		
Political Interest				0.124*	0.010
				(0.070)	(0.088)
Ideology Conservative				0.108*	−0.052
				(0.037)	(0.044)
N	299	299	407	291	285
R-squared	0.35	0.42	0.41	0.28	0.29

Note: Results are from OLS analysis, with robust standard errors. Significance thresholds are as follows: $**p \leq .05$ (two-tailed); $*p \leq .10$ (two-tailed); $++p \leq .05$ (one-tailed); and $+p \leq .10$ (one-tailed). We use one-tailed tests where we expect a directional effect for a hypothesis and two tailed tests where we do not have directional expectations. Robust standard errors in parentheses.

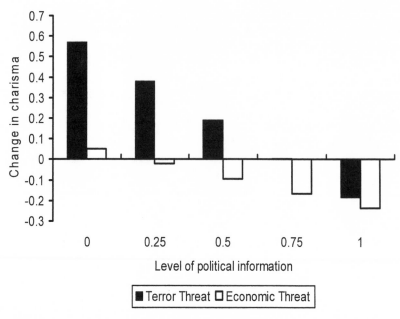

Figure 5.1. Effect of conditions at different values on the political information scale, US05ns
Note: The figure is based on OLS analysis reported in table 5.1. The bars show the predicted shift in perceptions of charisma for these two leaders, by level of political sophistication. Effects for Terror Threat are statistically significant at .5 and lower on the political information scale; effects for Economic Threat are not.

units, relative to the Good Times condition. Meanwhile, López Obrador receives a bigger drop in charisma from the Terror Threat condition, .362, than does Kerry (.161). Whereas in the U.S. case we did not see a statistically significant effect for the Economic Threat condition, we do find such an effect in Mexico. Recall that in this case we expected Calderón to receive a boost, and López Obrador to be harmed, by the Economic Threat condition. And this indeed is what we find. Finally, with respect to partisanship, we note that Panistas rate Calderón (López Obrador) higher (lower) on charisma, while the reverse holds for Perredistas. Just as in the U.S. case, while partisan groups have different baseline evaluations of the leaders, we fail to find evidence that the effects of the terror and economic threats are dependent on partisanship.

Data from the CIDE-CSES survey from Mexico allow us to expand our look at the effects of conditions of economic threat, as well as threats to political stability and public security, on perceptions of charisma among a nonstudent and more representative sample of that country. Given the

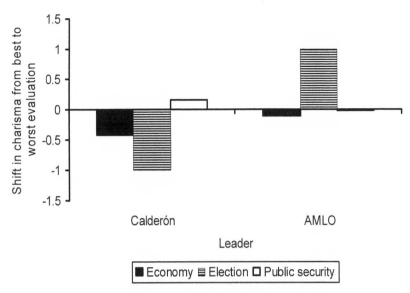

Figure 5.2. Effect of different types of threat on charisma, Mexico CIDE-CSES
Note: The figure shows the shift in charisma moving from the best to the worst evaluation of the economy, the election, and public security based on the OLS analysis reported in Web Supplement A, table 5.a.

more representative sample and given the wording on the economic threat question (retrospective evaluations), we expect a boost in López Obrador's charisma and a decrease in Calderón's charisma. We expect a similar effect for the political crisis measure and are agnostic as to the effect of our Public Security Threat indicator. Since we are working with survey data, we include a host of control variables, which we identified earlier. The results for the three threat indicators are illustrated in figure 5.2 (full results are available in Web Supplement A, table 5.a).

If we turn to our key variables and evaluations of Calderón, we find that the Economic Threat and Election Crisis measures have negative effects on perceptions of his charisma, while concern with physical security has a positive influence. Overall, these findings are consistent with our expectation that both economic and political crises should hurt Calderón in this sample. We were agnostic about the effects of concern with physical security, but the results suggest that those perceiving a crisis of security favor the incumbent party's candidate. Some of these effects are also quite substantial. For example, looking at figure 5.2, if we move from the best to the worst evaluation of the national economy, an individual's evaluation of Calderón's charisma declines by about half a unit (on the six-point scale).

The comparable effect for the political crisis issue (Election) is even greater, leading to almost a full-unit decline in perceptions of his charisma. The latter effect in particular is as strong as (and possibly just slightly greater than) the effects of one's partisanship. In contrast, the effects are more muted for the issue of Public Security in which there is only a modest increase in perceptions of Calderón's charisma (.15 units). With respect to López Obrador, the only threat measure that has a reliable effect is the political crisis measure. As expected, we find that this measure increases perceptions of his charisma.[15] This effect is also fairly substantial, nearly identical in size to that registered for evaluations of Calderón (but in the opposite direction).

It is a bit surprising that, in this first set of analyses, Economic Threat does not have the expected positive effect for evaluations of López Obrador's charisma. However, the economy measure only asks for very general evaluations and does not tap specific concern with more concrete economic issues. In a follow-up analysis with more specific economic indicators,[16] we find results more in line with our expectations: individuals who think that poverty has increased over the past year are less likely to perceive Calderón as charismatic and more likely to perceive López Obrador as charismatic (see Web Supplement A, table 5.a). We further find that those who think that unemployment has increased over the past year are also less likely to perceive Calderón as having high levels of charisma. For the purposes of our argument, the key point to take away is that only specific aspects of economic threat boosted López Obrador's charisma, even among the general population.

Stepping back to a more general evaluation of this first step in our overall argument about crisis and charisma, we conclude by noting that we detect ample support for a connection between these two factors across all three studies. The studies span country contexts, research methods, and sample types. Yet in each case we find evidence that, under conditions of threat (relative to better times), individuals cope by attempting to single out a heroic personality. They do so by projecting additional charismatic qualities onto a selected leader while deflating their perceptions of his opponent's charisma. We find evidence, in the U.S. case, of only a connection between terrorist threat and charisma, though we caution that our investigations here into other types of threat are limited. In the case of Mexico we find relationships between various indicators of threat and charisma and we find these linkages exist both within the narrow frame of our experiment and, as well, within survey data drawn from the general population of the country.

The Political Purchases of Crisis and Charisma

We now turn to the second empirical task of this chapter, which concerns demonstrating the effects of both crisis and charisma on a variety of evaluative, attitudinal, and behavioral indicators. Our argument is that conditions of terrorist threat have both direct and indirect (via charisma) effects on these outcome variables. Thus, in this section we first examine the extent to which conditions of threat directly affect blame attribution, willingness to sacrifice, and preferences over institutional design. We assess the first two sets of outcome variables using experimental data from the United States and we examine preferences over executive strength using data from both the United States and Mexico. Second, we test whether perceptions of charisma do indeed mediate the effect of threat. We know already, from the previous section, that terrorist threat significantly affects perceptions of charisma. To validate a mediating relationship we need two further pieces of evidence: a statistically significant relationship between Charisma and the outcome variable (when Terror Threat is also included in the model) and a smaller coefficient for Terror Threat in a model including Charisma compared to a model without Charisma.[17] We take care to note in the below discussions when we meet these criteria for a mediating relationship. Third, we are able in some cases to examine the effect of economic threat on the outcome variables of interest. Recall that in the U.S. case economic threat did not predict charisma; therefore, in this case we are only interested in whether there is a direct effect of economic threat, as an indirect effect has already been ruled out.

To what extent do terrorist threat and charisma lend a given leader, in this case President Bush, a Teflon-like shield against criticism for policy failures/weaknesses? In US04s (U.S. student sample, fall 2004), we asked respondents about Bush's responsibility for U.S. failures in Iraq. Just prior to receiving the question, subjects were first reminded that "recent reports from the Senate intelligence committee indicate that the CIA provided faulty information on the presence of weapons of mass destruction in Iraq, which was one of Bush's main justifications for the war." A follow-up question, Blame Attribution, then asked respondents to indicate, on a scale of one to five, to what extent they believe Bush is to blame for U.S. failures in Iraq, with higher values indicating more blame. We model Blame Attribution as a function of which experimental condition a subject was exposed to (the Good Times condition is the baseline), their partisan identification, gender, and perception of Bush's charisma.[18] Full results are presented in the first data column of table 5.2.

Table 5.2. Determinants of blame attribution, US04s (OLS) and US05ns (Probit)

	US04s	US05ns				
	Iraq Coefficient (Std. Err.)	Iraq Coefficient (Std. Err.)	CIA Coefficient (Std. Err.)	Homeland Security Coefficient (Std. Err.)	Environment Coefficient (Std. Err.)	Economy Coefficient (Std. Err.)
Constant	5.896** (0.193)	0.691* (0.411)	-0.922* (0.514)	0.180 (0.447)	0.004 (0.431)	0.845** (0.406)
Bush Charisma	-0.418++ (0.054)	-0.511++ (0.088)	-0.341++ (0.093)	-0.411++ (0.089)	-0.457++ (0.086)	-0.464++ (0.085)
Terror Threat	-0.278++ (0.114)	-0.160 (0.193)	-0.380++ (0.216)	-0.281 (0.629)	0.113 (0.195)	0.002 (0.190)
Status Quo	-0.235** (0.107)	-0.031 (0.195)	0.147 (0.210)	0.764 (0.513)	-0.036 (0.202)	-0.340 (0.212)
Economic Threat		-0.215 (0.203)	-0.172 (0.223)	-1.525+ (0.799)	-0.187 (0.218)	-0.232 (0.206)
Democrat	-0.001 (0.103)	0.459** (0.168)	0.475** (0.179)	0.341** (0.176)	0.170 (0.176)	0.232 (0.172)
Republican	-0.959** (0.183)	-0.261 (0.217)	-0.293 (0.355)	-0.286 (0.287)	0.035 (0.268)	-0.095 (0.262)
Female	-0.086 (0.096)					

	(1)	(2)	(3)	(4)	(5)
Education	0.192**	−0.024	0.066	0.107*	0.036
	(0.059)	(0.068)	(0.066)	(0.063)	(0.059)
Political Sophistication	0.233	1.615**	−0.062	−0.090	−0.487
	(0.291)	(0.392)	(0.450)	(0.319)	(0.310)
Security · Political Information			0.168		
			(0.829)		
Status Quo · Political Information			−1.253*		
			(0.684)		
Economic Threat · Political Information			1.720++		
			(1.047)		
N	299	407	407	407	407
R2/Pseudo R2	.49	0.23	0.16	0.12	0.13
Prob>F/Prob>chi2	0.000	0.000	0.0000	0.000	0.000

Note: Coefficients in cells are the results of probit analyses, except for US04, which is OLS, with robust standard errors. One-tailed hypothesis tests used for Bush Charisma, Terror Threat and Economic Threat; one-tailed statistical significance thresholds indicated as follows: $++p \leq .05$ and $+p \leq .10$. Two-tailed hypothesis tests used for all other variables and analyses; two-tailed statistical significance thresholds indicated as follows: $**p \leq .05$ and $*p \leq .10$.

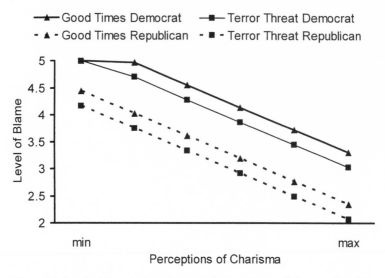

Figure 5.3. Level of blame assigned to Bush for Iraq, by condition, partisanship, and charisma, US04s
Note: The figure is based on output from analysis reported in table 5.2. Lines show the predicted level of blaming Bush for failures in Iraq at different values on perceptions of Bush's charisma by experimental condition.

The results support our claims about both a direct and an indirect effect of terrorist threat on blame reduction, in this case. Figure 5.3 displays the predicted level of blame assigned to Bush, given varying perceptions of charisma for those in the Good Times and those in the Terror Threat conditions, by partisanship (Democrats vs. Republicans).[19] Conditions of terror threat have clear, direct effects on blame assignment. As the figure shows, at each level of perception of charisma and for each partisan group, those in the Good Times condition assign greater blame to Bush compared to those in the Terror Threat condition.[20]

As figure 5.3 also shows, perceptions of Bush as a charismatic leader are related to a greater willingness to overlook weaknesses—the downward sloping lines in the figure indicate that perceptions of charisma decrease tendencies to blame Bush for failures in Iraq. For example, our analyses predict that in times of terror threat Republicans who perceive Bush to have no charisma assign a level of blame equal, on our scale, to about 4.2 units. In contrast, their peers who perceive Bush to have maximum levels of charisma assign a significantly lower level of blame, equal to about 2.1 units. Moreover, we find evidence of charisma mediating the relationship between terror threat and blame attribution. Exposure to the threat of a terrorist attack causes individuals to increase their perceptions of Bush's charisma (compared to good times); these higher perceptions of charisma, in turn, reduce the amount of blame that is assigned to Bush for policy mistakes in this issue area; and the effect of terror threat on blame attribution is reduced when charisma is included in the model (for the model without charisma see Web Supplement A, table A5.b).

Finally, as expected, the baseline levels vary by partisan group, with Republicans being generally less willing to assign blame compared to Democrats. However, we also see that in some cases Democrats assign *less* blame to Bush than Republicans.[21] While partisans have differing baseline tendencies to blame Bush for policy mistakes/weaknesses, both high perceptions of charisma and conditions of terrorist threat compel individuals of all types to become less willing to blame Bush for failures in Iraq.

Does a tendency to shield a given leader from responsibility for policy failures extend beyond domains that are closely connected to the executive and his policies? In both the US05s (U.S. student sample, fall 2005) and US05ns (U.S. nonstudent sample, summer 2005) studies we asked subjects to assign primary responsibility for a series of policy problems and failures to the U.S. Congress, President Bush, the media, the Democratic Party, the Republican Party, or some other actor. The particular policy problems we considered were Iraq, the leaking of an agent's name by the CIA (a reference to the 2005 Valerie Plame scandal), homeland security, the environment, and the economy (see the appendix for full question wording). In the US05s study they were also asked about responsibility for failures in the aftermath of Hurricane Katrina. We coded each of the questions so that a value of 1 is assigned to indicate that President Bush is selected as the most blameworthy, and a value of 0 was assigned to all other responses. In general, our respondents are more willing to blame Bush for problems in Iraq than the other four issue areas (58.5% compared to 21–23% for the other issues; see Web Supplement B for more details).

The US05 student study did not contain measures for charisma, but we can look at the direct effect of terror threat on propensities to blame Bush for policy failures. We find that those in the Terror Threat condition appear significantly less likely to blame Bush for policy failures on the CIA scandal, homeland security, and the environment (for full results see Web Supplement A, Table 5.c). In these three cases, the substantive effect of the Terror Threat variable is moderate but important in size: exposure to the Terror Threat condition causes individuals to become approximately 12 to 14 percentage points less likely to blame Bush for that respective policy failure than they would otherwise. Considering our Economic Threat condition, we find a significant, and negative, effect only with respect to the environment. The substantive effect is similar, though just slightly larger, than that of Terror Threat.

The US05 nonstudent study also included questions about charisma, so we can explore whether charisma and security crisis, individually or jointly, affect blame attribution over these issue areas. In our analyses for the six policy areas, we model blame as a function of perceptions of Bush's Charisma; the experimental conditions (the baseline is the Good Times condition); Republican or Democrat partisanship (the baseline is no or other partisanship); political sophistication; and, the respondent's self-reported level of education. As before, we test for whether individuals at different levels of political sophistication respond differently to our treatments. We find this to be the case only once, for "Bush Blame Homeland Security," so we only model this conditioning relationship for that measure. The results are presented in the remaining data columns of table 5.2.

Interestingly, we find a significant direct effect for terrorist threat on blame attribution in only one case, that of the CIA scandal.[22] Individuals exposed to the Terror Threat condition are just under 7 percentage points less likely to blame Bush for the leaking of a CIA agent's name relative to those in the Good Times condition (based on the results in table 5.2). Recall that this is one of the issue areas for which we also find an effect within our student study; it thus appears that those exposed to Terror Threat conditions feel particularly compelled to protect a given leader against accusations of wrongdoing. In this same case we find clear evidence of an indirect effect as well, via perceptions of charisma. Among those in the Terror Threat condition, moving from the minimum to the maximum value of perceptions of Bush's charisma leads to a 24 percentage point decline in the probability of blaming Bush for failures in this arena. As with the case of Iraq with the study in 2004, we find support for a mediating relationship with charisma.[23]

In contrast to the limited effectiveness of Terror Threat for the remaining measures, the Charisma variable has a negative and statistically significant relationship with blame across all of them. These effects are also quite substantial. For example, the effect of moving from the minimum value to the maximum value on charisma is to decrease the likelihood of an individual blaming Bush for Iraq by 78 percentage points![24] Even the smallest effect of a 24 percentage point decline (for the CIA leak) is still quite substantial, yielding a clear demonstration of the Teflon-like quality that protects those who are perceived as charismatic.[25] Moreover, the fact that the Charisma variable is significant in all of the analyses suggests that this protective effect is robust to multiple issue areas. While we cannot conclusively determine if this is indeed a causal connection (given that Charisma was not a treatment variable but, rather, measured in the same post-treatment survey as were the blame dependent variables), the results are consistent with theoretical perspectives that link perceptions of charisma to reduced willingness to blame particular leaders.[26]

The US05ns study also contained an economic threat treatment. Like the Terror Threat condition, the Economic Threat condition is also significant once, this time for the Homeland Security Blame variable and in conjunction with the Political Sophistication variable. The effect of the interaction is such that those who are exposed to the Economic Threat condition *and* are politically sophisticated are more likely to blame Bush for problems with homeland security than those who are exposed to that same crisis condition but are not politically sophisticated. Given that the Economic Threat condition did not have a direct effect on perceptions of Bush's charisma, there is no indirect effect of the economic crisis on any of the blame variables.

To conclude, the studies analyzed here provide substantial evidence that the threat of a terrorist attack causes individuals to reduce tendencies to blame a given leader for policy failures. In the case under analysis here, the recipient of this Teflon shield was President Bush in the fall of 2004 and the fall of 2005, among student and nonstudent subjects and across a variety of issue areas. We find expected effects for charisma on blame reduction across a wide range of issues. We find evidence of direct effects of terror threat on blame reduction for only some issues, and in these cases it appears that charisma plays a mediating role. Overall, these results leave us with strong support for our basic argument. In comparing terrorist threat to economic threat, we find a much weaker relationship for the latter; it does not have an indirect effect (given that it does not affect perceptions of charisma in the U.S. cases studied here) and its direct effects are limited to a few isolated cases.

Charisma, Crisis, and Willingness to Sacrifice for the Leader's Cause

We now turn to the question of whether, and to what extent, crisis and charisma affect willingness to self-sacrifice. To refresh, our argument is that heightened perceptions of charisma and the terrorist threat make individuals more likely to engage in self-sacrificial behavior. One of our goals in this section is to assess the extent to which that willingness to self-sacrifice extends, or does not extend, beyond the immediate needs of the leader. We first examine willingness to put forward one's own resources on behalf of the leader's campaign. We then analyze willingness to sacrifice one's own resources on behalf of policies that, to varying degrees, are related to the leader's agenda. Once again we examine these questions with respect to the leadership of President George W. Bush, and we evaluate the extent to which the effects of crisis are direct and/or indirect via perceptions of charisma.

To examine willingness to sacrifice one's own resources for Bush's campaign, we return to our first study, US04s. We needed a plausible measure of (self-reported) willingness to self-sacrifice and so we asked respondents to indicate how many of four campaign-related activities (make phone calls to get out the vote, attend a rally, drive this candidate's supporters to the polls, and contribute money to the campaign) they were willing to engage in on behalf of George W. Bush. We added individuals' responses together to create a Self-Sacrifice measure which ranges from zero to four acts. The mean value on the variable (and standard deviation) is .57 (1.06), and the distribution is skewed toward 0, the modal value.[27]

To test whether terrorist threat and charisma affect self-sacrifice, we regress Self-Sacrifice on Bush Charisma, dummy variables for the Terror Threat and Status Quo conditions (baseline category is Good Times), partisanship, and a dummy variable indicating gender.[28] In this case we did find that partisans react differently to the experimental conditions, and so we include measures to allow for this relationship (interactions between partisanship and the treatment conditions). The full results are presented in the first data column of table 5.3. Based on these results, in figure 5.4 we graph the predicted level of sacrifice (generated using CLARIFY), on the five-point scale (0 to 4), for Democrats and Republicans, in the Good Times and Terror Threat conditions, respectively. In the first case, we see that the direct effect of terror threat (compared to good times) varies across partisan groups. For Democrats, we observe no difference across times of terror threat and times of nonthreat. While we do not plot them here, the same is true for Independents. Republicans, on the other hand, show a relatively greater tendency toward self-sacrifice in the face of a terrorist threat, compared to their average predicted sacrifice levels in nonthreatening times. Thus a Republican who views Bush as highly charismatic *and* who has *not* been exposed to the terror threat condition reports a willingness to engage in just under two acts on behalf of Bush; his counterpart in the Terror Threat condition is predicted, on average, to be willing to participate in

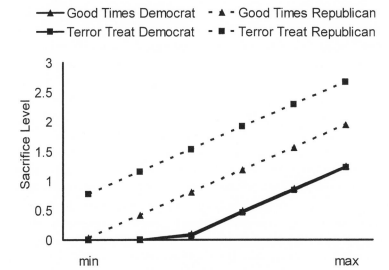

Figure 5.4. Level of sacrifice for Bush, by condition, partisanship, and charisma, US04s
Note: The figure is based on output from analysis reported in Web Supplement A, table 5.e. Lines show the predicted levels of sacrifice at different values on perceptions of Bush's charisma by experimental condition.

just over 2.5 acts. In short, we find the expected effect for terror threat, but only for Republicans.[29]

Turning to charisma, as the graph shows, perceptions of charisma are clearly and strongly related to levels of sacrifice. All four lines slope upward, such that the more Bush is perceived to be charismatic, the more willing individuals are to sacrifice their own resources on his behalf. Moving from minimum to maximum perceptions of charisma increases the self-sacrifice level by over one full act. This effect, then, is substantively quite meaningful and the evidence overall supports the assertion that charisma partially mediates the relationship between terrorist threat and self-sacrifice, in this case.[30]

With strong evidence that conditions of terror threat and charisma both contribute to individuals' willingness to sacrifice their own time and personal resources to help elect a selected leader (in this case, Bush), we now consider the question of whether these self-sacrificial tendencies carry beyond that specific domain, to the leader's policy agenda and/or on behalf of national issues more generally. In the US05ns study we asked respondents a total of six questions concerning to what extent they would support a personal income tax increase in order to pay for more spending on the following: the mission in Iraq, homeland security, the environment, education, social security, and welfare programs. Respondents indicated their support or lack of support on a seven-point scale where higher values indicate greater support. Of these issue areas, homeland security and Iraq were most closely linked to President Bush's agenda at the time. We therefore expect that perceptions of Bush's charisma and the Terror Threat variables will have positive effects on these measures.

We have less clear expectations for the effects of Bush's charisma and the threat variables on the remaining four policy areas. While Bush did prioritize education and Social Security at different points in his administration, he did not advocate a policy of greater spending. Furthermore, the Republicans and Bush are not known for supporting increases in social welfare spending nor for spending on the environment. Those who perceive Bush as more charismatic may then be less supportive of increasing spending in these domains via a personal income tax increase. Moreover, spending in these domains is unlikely to help resolve a security crisis and may be considered to be diverting money from more important sources. This speculation suggests that we might even expect negative effects of the charisma and Terror Threat variables in these domains. If instead individuals respond to security crises by rallying around the country in a general sense, and seeking to maintain and restore the greatness of the country, then we could see a positive relationship between, at the least, conditions of terror threat and preferences over taxation to support these four remaining policy areas.

What direct effects do the Terror and Economic Threat conditions have on levels of sacrifice across these variables? The answer in this case is "not very substantial or reliable" ones. The results of our analyses, predicting self-sacrifice, are presented in the remaining data columns of table 5.3.[31] Across all six issues, the Terror Threat variable is not a statistically significant predictor of these types of self-sacrifice, when Charisma is included in the model. Interestingly, the Economic Threat variable is significant in the case of the Environment. It has a direct, positive effect; for some reason that honestly eludes us, those exposed to the Economic Threat condition are more likely to favor a personal income tax increase on behalf of spending for the environment.

To the extent that there is any story to tell with respect to these measures of self-sacrifice, it is a story that must include charisma. The first thing to note in table 5.3 is that the Charisma variable is a statistically significant predictor in each of the six analyses. In order to easily assess the substantive meaningfulness of these results, we calculated the maximum effect of charisma (obtained by moving from minimum to maximum perceptions of Bush's charisma) on each of the six Self-Sacrifice measures. We begin with the results for the two policy areas most clearly related to Bush's own agenda: Iraq and Homeland Security. The Bush Charisma variable has a substantial, positive effect in both cases. Moving from the minimum value on Bush Charisma to the maximum value increases one's support for a personal income tax for the mission in Iraq by just over two units on the seven-point sacrifice scale. The comparable effect for Homeland Security is .85. Not only are these fairly substantial effects, but it is important to keep in mind that the analyses control for partisanship. Further, in these cases—Iraq and, to a lesser extent, Homeland Security—all of the conditions are met to substantiate charisma as a mediating variable connecting terrorist threat to self-sacrifice.[32] Turning to the remaining four dependent variables, we find that the Bush Charisma variable is negative and significant. Thus, those who perceive Bush as relatively more charismatic exhibit a relatively greater tendency to eschew policy proposals that seemingly conflict with his political objectives: personal income tax increases on behalf of welfare- and environment-oriented programs. Overall, we have evidence that charisma increases tendencies to sacrifice on behalf of policies closely connected to the leader. Our evidence also suggests that increased perceptions of charisma decrease support for policies not associated with the leader or, more specifically, policies that might be considered in an unfavorable light by that leader.[33]

Thus, combined with our first analysis concerning self-sacrifice (within the US04s study), we conclude that charismatic bonds induced by security crises leave individuals relatively more eager to sacrifice their own personal resources on behalf of the leader and his agenda. Individuals, in times of crisis, tend not to be content to wait passively for the "hero" to save the day; rather, they are willing to adopt a more proactive role, sacrificing their own resources to help elect and discriminately assist the leader they've deemed most capable of resolving the crisis. But how far are they willing to go in terms of assisting in the resolution of the crisis? In the next and final section of this chapter, we consider the relationship between threats and preferences over the executive-congressional balance of power.

Crises and Preferences over Democratic Design

Do conditions of threat and/or charisma cause individuals to adopt preferences for greater executive power? We tested for this possibility in two studies: first, the MEX06s (Mexico student sample, fall 2006) study that

Table 5.3. Determinants of self-sacrifice, US04s and US05ns

	US04s		US05ns					
	Campaign Activities Coefficient (Std. Err.)	Iraq Coefficient (Std. Err.)	Homeland Security Coefficient (Std. Err.)	Social Security Coefficient (Std. Err.)	Welfare Coefficient (Std. Err.)	Education Coefficient (Std. Err.)	Environment Coefficient (Std. Err.)
Constant	-1.164** (0.231)	1.024** (0.326)	2.734** (0.381)	4.892** (0.467)	3.107** (0.465)	4.366** (0.472)	3.933** (0.436)
Bush Charisma	0.383++ (0.062)	0.403++ (0.069)	0.165++ (0.086)	-0.231** (0.095)	-0.322** (0.095)	-0.302** (0.100)	-0.307** (0.091)
Terror Threat	0.113 (0.149)	0.193 (0.155)	0.224 (0.186)	-0.183 (0.198)	0.120 (0.184)	0.124 (0.206)	-0.027 (0.201)
Status Quo	0.497** (0.238)	0.057 (0.143)	-0.003 (0.194)	-0.371* (0.195)	-0.049 (0.194)	0.114 (0.210)	0.157 (0.207)
Economic Threat		0.161 (0.179)	0.046 (0.203)	-0.169 (0.223)	0.183 (0.221)	0.208 (0.202)	0.369* (0.202)
Democrat	0.039 (0.108)	-0.135 (0.127)	0.318* (0.162)	0.712** (0.187)	0.568** (0.186)	0.748** (0.186)	0.697** (0.185)
Republican	0.734** (0.233)	0.912** (0.217)	1.087** (0.228)	-0.190 (0.243)	-0.594** (0.242)	-0.090 (0.259)	-0.455* (0.257)
Status Quo · Democrat	0.07 (0.096)						

Status Quo · Republican	0.583						
	(0.378)						
Terror Threat · Democrat	−0.04						
	(0.0.103)						
Terror Threat · Republican	0.731++						
	(0.305)						
Female	0.080						
	(0.089)						
Political Sophistication		−0.307	−0.807**	0.110	1.025**	0.306	0.513*
		(0.248)	(0.310)	(0.311)	(0.293)	(0.322)	(0.303)
Education		−0.047	−0.044	−0.046	0.108*	0.131**	0.164**
		(0.048)	(0.058)	(0.061)	(0.061)	(0.060)	(0.059)
N	299	407	407	407	407	407	407
R-squared	0.54	0.35	0.17	0.14	0.29	0.19	0.26

Note: Coefficients in cells are the results of OLS analyses, with robust standard errors. One-tailed hypothesis tests used for Bush Charisma, Terror Threat and Economic Threat—for analyses of Campaign Activities, Iraq, and Homeland Security; one-tailed statistical significance thresholds indicated as follows: ++$p \le .05$ and +$p \le .10$. Two-tailed hypothesis tests used for all other variables and analyses; two-tailed statistical significance thresholds indicated as follows: **$p \le .05$ and *$p \le .10$.

we discussed previously in this chapter; second, a study conducted with student subjects in the United States in spring 2007 (US07s). The context of each of these studies is highly relevant to any interpretation of our results. Recall that by the time of our Mexico study, the right-leaning candidate of the incumbent PAN party, Felipe Calderón, had been officially certified as the winner, though uncertainty remained over whether or not his opponent, Andrés Manuel López Obrador, would accept this result and demobilize his supporters. In the case of the U.S. study, by the spring of 2007, President Bush's popularity had decreased significantly (see the approval ratings reported in the introduction, for example). His approval ratings at this time were significantly lower than in 2004 and 2005, when studies discussed earlier in this chapter took place. This context, therefore, allows us to probe into the duration of the public's willingness to defer to a selected leader in times of crisis.

How do we investigate preferences over executive strength? In each of these studies, we included two measures of preferences for a strong executive. The first, Strong Executive, asks respondents to indicate which of two options they most agree with: the president should be more powerful than Congress (which we code as 1) or Congress should be more powerful than the president (which we code as 0).[34] In Mexico the mean on this variable is .35, meaning that 35 percent of the sample on average preferred a relatively stronger executive than Congress. In the United States, the mean is .12; clearly, far fewer U.S. study participants, compared to participants in Mexico, believe the president should be stronger than the Congress. The second, Presidential Powers, is derived from a set of questions that asks respondents to consider whether the president should be allowed to act without the approval of Congress with respect to four activities: declaring war; negotiating treaties and international agreements; traveling abroad; and making important decisions in international organizations.[35] We create an additive measure scaled from 0 to 4, where 0 captures "no acts" and 4 captures "four acts" on which the president should be allowed to act without congressional approval. In Mexico the mean value is 1.24. It is again lower, though not remarkably so, in the U.S. study: 1.01.

For Mexico, to analyze the effects of terror threat and charisma, we regress the two executive strength variables on the two measures of charisma (for Calderón and for López Obrador), exposure to the experimental conditions (Good Times serves as the baseline), and partisanship. For the U.S. case the model is the same except for charisma measures, which were not asked in this study. The results are presented in table 5.4.[36]

In the case of Mexico, we find that terror threat is a positive and meaningful predictor of both executive strength measures. With respect to the Strong Executive variable, compared to those in the Good Times condition, those exposed to the terrorist threat are 11.5 percentage points more likely to express a preference for a president who is stronger than Congress. With respect to the Presidential Powers variable, an individual exposed to the Terror Threat condition reports, on average, a willingness to grant .25 additional acts to the president, without the need of congressional approval (compared to a similar individual in the Good Times condition). Thus, we find strong support for the notion that, when exposed to a terrorist threat, compared to times of relative well-being and prosperity, individuals become more willing to cede additional power to the executive. Quite interestingly, we do not find reliable or substantively important effects for the Economic Threat variable. Thus, it appears that the effect of threat in this study is limited to the security crisis.[37]

With respect to a relationship between charisma and preferences over executive power, we find some, but limited support. Specifically, the only instance in which charisma is a statistically reliable predictor of such preferences is in the case of perceptions of Calderón's charisma, for the Presidential Powers variable only. In this one case, charisma has a fairly substantial effect: moving from minimum to maximum evaluations of Calderón's charisma results in an approximately 1.5-unit move on the five-point dependent variable. In other words, individuals (experiencing this move across the charisma scale) become willing to grant Calderón roughly one and a half more acts without congressional approval. These results also provide us with evidence that charisma can play a mediating role in the relationship between terrorist threat and preferences over executive strength.[38]

We note a few reasons to remain skeptical of the absolute generalizability of these findings. First, while we have detected the anticipated link between conditions of security crisis and preferences over institutional design in the case of Mexico, we have found this with respect to a case where our subjects are right-leaning on average and where the president-elect is similarly right-leaning. It may be that this is a most likely case for finding a relationship between terrorist threat and preferences over executive strength. It may also be a least likely case for finding a link between economic crisis and those same preferences. If, for example, a left-leaning candidate, who by virtue of his or her ideology has more "ownership" over issues of social welfare, was in the executive office *and* we sampled a more left-leaning population, it is possible that we might find evidence of increased preferences for a strong executive under conditions of economic threat. Further, a similar qualifying note should be made about the results

Table 5.4. Preferences over executive strength, MEX06s and US07s

	Mexico (MEX06s)		United States (US07s)	
	Executive Strength Coefficient (Std. Err.)	Presidential Powers Coefficient (Std. Err.)	Executive Strength Coefficient (Std. Err.)	Presidential Powers Coefficient (Std. Err.)
Constant	-0.994*	-0.015	-1.101**	1.150**
	(0.587)	(0.344)	(0.246)	(0.139)
Calderón Charisma	0.029	0.294++		
	(0.104)	(0.062)		
López Obrador Charisma	0.076	0.014		
	(0.089)	(0.058)		
Terror Threat	0.334++	0.237++	-0.183	-0.249++
	(0.198)	(0.130)	(0.283)	(0.150)
Economic Threat	0.000	0.045	-0.160	-0.221+
	(0.202)	(0.130)	(0.283)	(0.146)
PAN/Republican	0.465**	0.096	0.788**	0.621**
	(0.205)	(0.137)	(0.310)	(0.249)
PRI/Democrat	0.251	-0.151	-0.270	-0.124
	(0.261)	(0.172)	(0.263)	(0.141)
PRD	-0.718*	-0.169		
	(0.381)	(0.216)		
Political Interest	-0.205*	-0.046		
	(0.121)	(0.082)		

Ideology	0.129**	0.003	
	(0.065)	(0.044)	
N	279	283	237	237
(Pseudo) R-squared	0.08	0.13	0.09	0.08

Note: Coefficients in cells are the results of probit analyses for Executive Strength and OLS analyses for Presidential Powers, with robust standard errors. One-tailed hypothesis tests used for both Charisma variables, Terror Threat and Economic Threat; one-tailed statistical significance thresholds indicated as follows: ++p ≤ .05 and +p ≤ .10. Two-tailed hypothesis tests used for all other variables and analyses; two-tailed statistical significance thresholds indicated as follows: **p ≤ .05 and *p ≤ .10.

for the charisma variables. In this case, the fact that it is perceptions of Calderón's charisma that are significant (in the one case) may have to do with the fact that he had been declared the victor and/or the fact that our sample is more right-leaning than the Mexican population in general.

We do not have limitless data with which to respond to the above discussion. However, we can examine one additional issue, which concerns the extent to which—across time—individuals are willing to defer power to a given executive in times of terrorist threat. We can do so with data from a study conducted in the United States in 2007. On the one hand, there is ample evidence that the U.S. public (and the U.S. Congress) has supported a strengthening of the executive office in the post-9/11 era. This lends some support to the notion that there is a connection between conditions of terrorist threat and preferences over executive power in the U.S. case. However, the public's and other governmental branches' tolerance for the consolidation of power in the executive office appeared to be wearing thin by 2007.

Table 5.4 also contains the results of analyses in which we predict the two measures of preferences over executive power for the U.S. case. In the analysis of whether the president should be more powerful than Congress, we do not find any effect for either exposure to the Terror Threat or Economic Threat condition. If we turn to the analysis of the powers a president should be authorized to exercise without congressional approval, we find that subjects in both the Terror Threat and Economic Threat conditions are *less* supportive of executive power relative to subjects in the Good Times condition. In each case, exposure to the threat causes individuals to decrease the extent to which the president can act without congressional authorization by just under one quarter of a unit.

Conclusion

Terrorist threat causes individuals to perceive leaders differently than they would under better times; in some contexts, other threats can similarly affect charisma perceptions. Furthermore, terrorist threats and charisma perceptions have important consequences with respect to blame attribution, self-sacrifice, and (in some cases) preferences over executive power. With respect to the last consequence, we found divergent results across the Mexican and U.S. cases and, while we cannot be certain of the reasons for this, we suspect that timing and context are both important factors causing individuals exposed to terrorist threat in the case of the United States in

2007 to desire *decreased* executive power (compared to those in the Good Times condition).

We conclude from our analyses that the combination of terrorist threat and charisma has significant implications for democratic processes. When confronted with a security crisis (in the form of a terrorist threat at least), individuals not only *will* themselves to find strong leaders, but they express a further willingness to protect and assist that leader. Aspects of these tendencies may place democracy at risk. Some might claim that for a democracy to work effectively citizens do not need to analyze every single policy issue and know where each party stands, they just need to be able to make evaluations of how the current administration is doing with respect to big issues (e.g., Fiorina 1981; Riker 1982). Our results suggest that under conditions of security crisis, such evaluations may very well be biased. In the first place, individuals tend to perceive the select leader as more charismatic and in turn are less likely to blame him or her for policy failures. In the second place, the crisis context will also directly make the individual less likely to blame that leader. At the extreme, these relationships may be especially troubling under conditions in which the particular flawed policies that a select leader is pursuing threaten to harm the quality of democracy. For example, some individuals question the human rights record of the Bush administration in the war on terror.

The particular indicators of self-sacrifice that we examine in this chapter do not seem to put much, if any, stress on democracy. In fact, it may be reasoned that such behavior shows that citizens respond admirably to crises, showing a willingness to act selflessly to promote a resolution to threats and related negative conditions. That said, an increased likelihood to engage in self-sacrificial behavior may pose a threat in the case of individuals mobilizing in support of a leader with an agenda that threatens democratic institutions. We need not shed any ink describing how a centralization of the executive at the expense of the legislature might place democracy at risk. One need only turn to the Federalist Papers for an eloquent argument to this effect (likely more eloquent than we would be able to make here).

This chapter concludes our journey through the various outcomes related to the second method of coping, which we began in chapter 4. With an array of experimental and survey data, we have demonstrated strong support for our arguments with respect to this coping mechanism. In short, in chapter 4 we demonstrated that conditions of terrorist threat (relative to times of well-being and prosperity) cause individuals to *project* additional leadership tendencies onto likely leaders and, as well, become more inclined to base their voting decisions on these heightened leadership qualities. In this chapter we have shown that, once he or she is elected, individuals seek to protect the selected leader, by forgiving his policy mistakes, and to assist the selected leader, by sacrificing their own resources on his behalf, and in some cases, by supporting increased institutional powers for the executive office. We turn now, in the next chapter, to our final method of coping, which relates to how individuals react and respond to other nation-states.

6

Engage Abroad, Protect at Home

Our first priority must always be the security of our nation. . . .
We will win this war; we'll protect our homeland. . . . America
is no longer protected by vast oceans. We are protected from attack only by vigorous action abroad, and increased vigilance at
home.

President George W. Bush, 2002

In the above quote from the 2002 State of the Union address, President Bush clearly outlined the need for dual objectives in the war
on terror. The president's statement captures the essence of our
third proposed coping strategy for dealing with conditions of terror threat. As Bush's speech identified, the first goal is to engage
abroad in order to ensure that nations are not allowed to harbor
and support terrorists, that terrorist training camps are shut down,
and that terrorists are brought to justice. The second goal is to protect at home, pursuing measures such as securing the border and
improving airport security.

To varying degrees, the pursuit of these objectives in a post-9/11
world has been advocated by the White House, supported by politicians, accepted abroad, and welcomed by the public. For example,
support for the campaign in Afghanistan has been broad among
the U.S. public, the U.S. Congress, and allies in other countries. The
U.S. public was initially supportive of the war against Iraq, as was
the vast majority of the U.S. Congress, although the president had

a smaller "coalition of the willing" from other nations. In general, the interventionist approach advanced by the Bush administration was lauded in its initial stages. Yet, by 2006, opinion had become increasingly skeptical of President Bush and his agenda, especially with respect to the war in Iraq (though this agenda remained unchanged).[1]

Immediately following 9/11 widespread support surfaced among the public and government officials for many policies related to protecting the homeland. A majority of Americans believed that it was necessary to sacrifice some personal freedoms for the sake of the war on terrorism. For example, in a September 2001 poll, 55 percent surveyed stated it was necessary to sacrifice civil liberties to fight terrorism; in contrast, only 35 percent reported it was not necessary.[2] Forty-five days after 9/11, Congress concurred by passing the USA PATRIOT Act, which received broad support in both chambers. The act included giving federal officials much greater authority to track and intercept communications at home and abroad, a policy affecting both citizens and noncitizens. The act also gave law enforcement officers greater power to detain and remove immigrants suspected of terrorist activities. A year later, the Homeland Security Act of 2002 was passed, which created the Department of Homeland Security and led to the restructuring of many agencies to coordinate information sharing with respect to terrorism. According to a 2006 Gallup Poll, a vast majority, 77 percent, of the U.S. public believed the changes to airport security made by the department have been effective.[3] While the reauthorization of the USA PATRIOT Act was more controversial, a CBS/*New York Times* poll found that about half of the public, five years out from 9/11, still found the act to be a necessary tool in the war on terror.[4] Since 9/11, the issue of immigration reform has also been front and center, with the resulting debate characterized by a focus on the need to improve border security. In 2005 the House of Representatives passed HR 4437, which sought to create a 700-mile fence along the U.S.-Mexico border and criminalize undocumented immigrants and persons assisting them. In contrast to some of the other homeland security measures, the bill sparked massive waves of protest among immigrants and immigrant rights advocates.

Anecdotal evidence clearly indicates that, following 9/11, members of the U.S. public for the most part acquiesced to a foreign policy marked by these dual objectives of engaging abroad and protecting at home. This chapter investigates the extent to which such foreign policy preferences are selected, advocated, or otherwise championed by individuals facing a terrorist threat. In what follows, we first review the argument we proposed in chapter 1. We then turn to analyzing preferences for engaging abroad, using survey and experimental data from both the United States and Mexico. Next, we examine preferences concerning protecting the homeland, again using survey and experimental data from both countries. We close the chapter with a discussion of the results and their implications for democracy.

Terrorism Leads to Dual Objectives in Foreign Policy

The rise of international terrorism represents a unique type of crisis from a foreign policy perspective. Unlike classic international threats, international terrorist groups are often dispersed organizationally and geographically, which makes tracking members, their resources, and their plans extremely difficult. In order to cope with anxiety and negative emotions stemming from a terrorist threat, we expect that individuals will adopt foreign policy preferences focused on two objectives: protect at home and engage abroad. By "protect at home," we mean policies aimed at enhancing security within the nation state, such as restricting immigration and ceding some domestic freedoms. By "engage abroad," we refer to preferences over taking a more active role in international affairs, both in general and with respect to security issues.

In developing this argument, we place our work within a long line of scholarship on foreign policy and foreign policy opinions. Such research documents that citizens are capable of having clear opinions on foreign policy, which take into account information on relative power and security threats. While these opinions can be influenced by elite rhetoric, they do not necessarily depend only on elite framing (see our discussion, with relevant citations, in chapter 1). This research further categorizes the types of foreign policy stances that individuals might adopt. In general, there are at least two distinct dimensions to foreign policy opinion: general internationalism and the nature of state involvement, be it cooperative or militant (Maggiotto and Wittkopf 1981; Wittkopf 1986; but see Chittick and Billingsley 1989; Chittick, Billingsley, and Travis, 1990, 1995).[5] Combining these two dimensions, we can imagine a tree in which the first branching represents whether someone is internationalist or isolationist. Internationalists want to take an active role in world affairs while isolationists oppose international involvement of any type. We can then subdivide the internationalist branch into those who are accommodationists or hardliners. Accommodationists are those who favor cooperative international involvement but oppose militant internationalism, while hardliners favor militant internationalist involvement but oppose cooperative internationalism. More recent refinements to the initial dimensions include clarifying the form of internationalism, as either unilateral or multilateral in nature (Chittick and Billingsley 1989; Chittick, Billingsley, and Travis 1995; Russett 1990).

Within this framework, we suggest that individuals faced with a terrorist threat will become more internationalist in their foreign policy preferences, advocating the pursuit of *both* militant and nonmilitant means to eliminate the threat. We also expect that given the nature of terror threats, these preferences will be relatively common across countries, such that many countries will be interested in cooperative endeavors to handle the threat. However, the form of the internationalism should vary across countries, depending on resources. For example, we do not explore unilateral foreign policy attitudes in Mexico since the country does not have the requisite resources to pursue this type of engagement. If members of the public take into account countries' strategic positions when forming preferences, then they would not consider unilateral actions by Mexico to be feasible.[6] In the case of the United States, on the other hand, we are able to explore whether the form of internationalism tends toward support for certain unilateral or multilateral policies. At the same time that individuals become more internationalist in times of terror threat, we expect them also to concentrate energies on defending the homeland through a variety of security measures. Simply put, individuals facing a terrorist threat are likely to feel more secure to the extent that their government is pursuing policies aimed at home and abroad.

A relevant question, especially given our earlier references to Bush's rhetoric concerning the dual objectives, is to what extent these attitudinal shifts are simply a response to elite framing. That is, *if* individuals facing a terrorist threat do indeed adopt policies consistent with those of the Bush administration, how can we discern whether this is not simply a framing effect whereby individuals mimic elites' policy stances? In order to gain leverage on this question, we examine responses to terrorist threat in Mexico alongside our analyses of the United States. The issues of foreign and domestic policy responses to international terrorism are not nearly as salient in Mexico. Thus, finding that Mexicans behave similarly to U.S. citizens in the face of terrorist threat provides greater justification for asserting that this is not simply a preference adopted as a result of elite framing but rather a more universal coping mechanism adopted in response to the threat of terrorist attacks.

Another relevant issue is whether alternative solutions are theoretically plausible. While protecting the homeland will always be an important goal in the face of terrorist threat, is it not possible that some people may become more isolationist rather than internationalist? In the case of Spain in 2004, citizens responded to terrorist bombings by demanding that the administration reduce its commitments to the global "war on terror" by withdrawing troops from Iraq. We believe that a flight response is more the exception than the norm, especially in the context of a pending threat. A pending terrorist threat is likely to lead not only to fear but to a host of negative emotions, including anger, which scholars have demonstrated is linked to more militant foreign policy stances (Huddy et al. 2005). It is possible, however, that a prolonged crisis may lead to significantly greater levels of anxiety, which may lead to a preference for flight (Huddy et al. 2005). In later analyses we will provide evidence suggesting that both timing and emotions condition responses to terrorist threat.

In investigating the general effect of terror threat on citizens' foreign policy preferences, our work adds to scholarship on foreign policy opinions. It is commonly accepted that citizens become more militant in the face of international threat (see, for example, Herrmann and Tetlock 1999; Jentleson 1992; Jentleson and Britton 1998; and Kushner Gadarian 2008). Few studies, however, have focused on the relationship between terrorist threat and support for cooperative international endeavors, which combined with preferences for military action would signal a true turn toward general internationalism. A select number of studies have shown that domestic populations, under a potential security threat, may mobilize to affect international cooperation (Evangelista 1995; Knopf 1998).[7] However, these works do not examine individual-level opinion formation and expression in the face of a terrorist threat.

With respect to protecting at home, some existing studies demonstrate a link between terrorist threat and increased support for policies that protect the homeland. Citizens who are more worried about terrorism are more willing to trade civil liberties for greater security (Davis 2007; Davis and Silver 2004a; Huddy et al 2005). Furthermore, those with high levels of worry are more willing to increase surveillance on Arabs and Arab Americans, increase security checks on Arab visitors, and decrease visas to Arab countries (Huddy et al. 2005). However, only a small number of studies have examined how terrorist threats affect preferences over border security and immigration policy. We examine a greater range of policy preferences in the U.S. context and extend our scope beyond U.S. borders.

We explore our expectations using both survey and experimental data for the United States and Mexico. We examine foreign policy preferences in the United States using two national surveys conducted by the CCFR as part of their Global Views research program. The first survey relied on a national sample of U.S. citizens in 2004 and the second survey used a national sample in 2006. Likewise, in the case of Mexico, we take advantage of two national surveys of Mexican public opinion, one conducted in 2004 and the other in 2006. Both surveys were conducted by CIDE, COMEXI, and the CCFR—the first as part of the Global Views research program and the second as part of the México y el Mundo 2006 study. Both surveys provide a number of questions that allow us to examine preferences toward engaging abroad and protecting within. We consider preferences toward general internationalism, security engagement, and specific policies to combat international terrorism. For protecting within, we look at questions concerning immigration and border control policies.

We also included a broad series of international engagement and homeland protection questions on experiments in the United States in the spring of 2007 (US07s) and in Mexico in the fall of 2006 (MEX06s). On these two studies, we replicated some of the same types of questions from the survey data. In three additional experiments (US05ns, US05s, and US06s), we included a few questions related to international engagement and homeland protection and we make use of these select data where appropriate. As we present our experiment-based results, the reader should assume we are referring to either US07s or MEX06s, unless stated otherwise.

Evidence of a Turn toward Internationalism

In this section we assess empirical evidence relevant to our first expectation: individuals become selectively supportive of international engagement under conditions of terror threat (compared to times of well-being and prosperity). We begin the section by taking a broad look at preferences over internationalism versus isolationism. We then turn to preferences over general militant engagement. Finally, we explore support for policies that are more specific to the issue of terrorism.

Isolationism versus Internationalism

In the face of terrorist threat, does the public become more inclined to engage with the rest of the world or prefer to retreat from it? All of the studies we examine here include a question tapping individuals' general disposition toward international involvement. The question, Active in World Affairs, asks respondents whether they believe it is best for their country to be "active in world affairs" (coded as "1") or "stay out of world affairs" (coded as "0"). This question thus separates internationalists from isolationists in general terms, consistent with classic works on these dimensions.[8]

Turning first to the survey data, we explore support for our argument by examining the relationship between the Active measure and a measure based on a question asking whether or not respondents consider "international terrorism as a grave threat." This dummy variable, Terror Threat, serves as our proxy for concern about international terrorism. The full results, including those for control variables, are shown in table 6.1.[9] In both countries and for both years of available data, we find that individuals who perceive international terrorism as a grave threat are more likely to prefer being active in world affairs. How meaningful is this link? In the case of the United States, those who perceive a terror threat (relative to those who do not) are approximately 15.8 percentage points more likely to support taking an active role in the world in the 2004 study and 10.3 percentage points more likely to support taking an active role in the 2006 study.[10] The comparable effects in Mexico are a 12 percentage point increase in 2004 and an 18 percentage point increase in 2006. Overall, these are pretty substantial effects.

Turning to the experiment-based data, we can assess whether a similar relationship holds by simply reporting and comparing the proportion of subjects who support being active in world affairs in the Terror Threat and Good Times conditions.[11] In Mexico we find that the proportion who support being active in world affairs is slightly higher among those in the Terror Threat condition (46%), relative to those in the Good Times condition (42%), but these differences are not statistically meaningful. In the U.S. case, we actually find that subjects in the Terror Threat condition were slightly less supportive of being active in world affairs (47%), compared to those in the Good Times condition (58%), but again, these differences are not statistically meaningful.

We thus find strong survey evidence that individuals across both countries (across two years of data) become more supportive of being active in world affairs given the presence of a terrorist threat. However, the results from the experimental studies are inconclusive. One potential reason for the weaker results for the experimental data in the United States is that by spring of 2007, overall levels of anxiety were higher, given engagement in Iraq. As we indicated earlier, it could be that emotions moderate the effect of the terror threat in the realm of foreign policy preferences. We return to consider this possibility later in this chapter. For now, we note that the overall evidence, while not entirely consistent, is more supportive than not

Table 6.1. Preferences over being active in world affairs in the United States and Mexico, 2004 and 2006

	Mexico		United States	
	2004 Coefficient (Std. Err.)	2006 Coefficient (Std. Err.)	2004 Coefficient (Std. Err.)	2006 Coefficient (Std. Err.)
Terror Threat	0.493++ (0.082)	0.307++ (0.093)	0.425++ (0.094)	0.286++ (0.088)
PAN	−0.037 (0.094)	0.275** (0.094)		
PRI	−0.109 (0.109)	0.122 (0.087)		
PRD	−0.301** (0.110)	0.222 (0.137)		
Ideology			0.017 (0.030)	−0.007 (0.032)
Education	0.056** (0.018)	0.118** (0.017)	0.136** (0.037)	0.083** (0.025)
Female	0.062** (0.021)	−0.305** (0.072)	−0.174** (0.080)	0.019* (0.010)
Income	−0.141* (0.075)	−0.011 (0.031)	0.014 (0.027)	−0.085 (0.078)
Constant	−0.235* (0.133)	−0.615** (0.132)	−0.176 (0.189)	−0.120 (0.188)
N	1281	1331	1130	1196
Chi² statistic	84.523	106.651	40.21	35.13
Chi² probability	0.000	0.000	0.000	0.000

Note: Coefficients in cells are the results of probit analyses, with robust standard errors. Significance thresholds are as follows: $**p < .05$ (two-tailed); $*p < .10$ (two-tailed); $++p \le .05$ (one-tailed); $+p \le .10$ (one-tailed). We use one-tailed tests on Terror Threat as the hypotheses are unidirectional and report robust standard errors.

of our argument that conditions of terrorist threat lead to an increased internationalist orientation among members of the general public.

Security Engagement

While individuals may have a more international outlook in the face of a terror threat, how do they think their country should involve itself in world affairs? Does the public become more supportive of cooperative militant actions in general? Furthermore, how does concern about terrorism affect preferences over the form of international involvement? That is, are citizens in a resource-rich country like the United States more inclined to support unilateral or multilateral efforts? These questions form the core of this section.

To tap into multilateral militant policy preferences, we look at questions concerning support for a cooperative United Nations peacekeeping force. The UN peacekeeping question in the United States and Mexico surveys is different enough to make direct comparisons inappropriate. In the Mexico surveys, the question relates to support for Mexican troops participating in a UN peacekeeping force, while in the U.S. surveys the question relates to support for a standing peacekeeping force. For each question, the possible response options are support (coded as "1") or oppose (coded as "0"). In the experiments, we use the same question in both countries, which asks subjects the extent to which they agree (on a seven-point scale) that their country should participate in a UN peacekeeping force if asked to do so by the UN.

Turning first to the survey data, we find that individuals who perceive international terrorism as a grave threat are more supportive of engaging militarily in UN peacekeeping operations. The results of our probit analyses are presented in table 6.2. Transforming these results into substantive effects, Mexicans who perceive international terrorism as a grave threat (relative to those who do not) are 12.1 percentage points more likely to support contributing to a UN peacekeeping force in the 2004 study and 12.5 percentage points more likely to do so in the 2006 study. Meanwhile, those in the United States who perceive a grave terror threat are 9.7 percentage points more supportive of having a standing UN peacekeeping force in the 2004 study and 8.1 percentage points more supportive in the 2006 study. In both countries, for both sets of survey data, we find strong evidence that conditions of terror threat lead to more support for multilateral militant endeavors.

To determine whether these findings hold for our experimental studies, in figure 6.1 we compare average support for participating in a UN peacekeeping force by experimental condition for each country. In Mexico we see that subjects in the Terror Threat condition are more supportive of participating (mean = 4.4) in a UN peacekeeping force, compared to those in the Good Times condition (mean = 3.6). These differences are statistically meaningful. Thus, exposure to the Terror Threat condition pushes the average participant from having lukewarm opposition to lukewarm support for participating in a UN peacekeeping force. In the U.S. case, we

Table 6.2. Preferences over support for a UN peacekeeping force in the United States and Mexico, 2004 and 2006

	Mexico		United States	
	2004 Coefficient (Std. Err.)	2006 Coefficient (Std. Err.)	2004 Coefficient (Std. Err.)	2006 Coefficient (Std. Err.)
Terror Threat	0.315++ (0.092)	0.317++ (0.077)	0.307++ (0.093)	0.315++ (0.092)
PAN	0.260** (0.093)	0.092 (0.087)		
PRI	0.052 (0.085)	−0.149 (0.101)		
PRD	0.044 (0.133)	−0.093 (0.105)		
Ideology			0.144** (0.032)	0.252** (0.032)
Education	0.085** (0.017)	0.030 (0.019)	0.035 (0.039)	−0.057** (0.026)
Female	−0.057 (0.071)	−0.034 (0.070)	−0.029 (0.087)	0.156* (0.081)
Income	−0.112** (0.031)	0.021 (0.017)	0.053* (0.029)	0.009 (0.011)
Constant	−0.422** (0.129)	−0.260** (0.123)	−0.217 (0.204)	−0.446* (0.191)
N	1331	1343	1133	1196
Chi^2	46.959	33.538	32.81	74.33
Chi^2 probability	0.000	0.000	0.000	0.000

Note: Coefficients in cells are the results of probit analyses, with robust standard errors. Significance thresholds are as follows: **$p < .05$ (two-tailed); *$p < .10$ (two-tailed); ++$p \leq .05$ (one-tailed); +$p \leq .10$ (one-tailed). We use one-tailed tests on Terror Threat as the hypotheses are unidirectional and report robust standard errors.

see that subjects in both conditions are fairly supportive of participating in a UN peacekeeping mission. In other words, we do not find any differences across the two conditions. Again, we will explore later in the chapter whether this result might be due in part to higher levels of anxiety in 2007. With the exception of this last result, we find fairly broad support for our argument that individuals exposed to terror threat become more supportive of general security engagement.

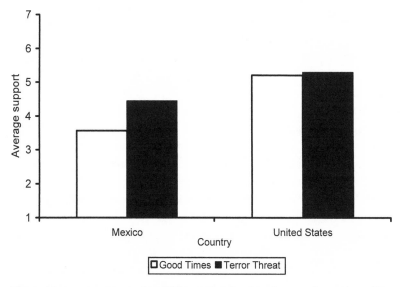

Figure 6.1. Average support for a UN peacekeeping force by experimental condition and country, MEX06s and US07s

While the peacekeeping questions tap into militant engagement, they only specify a multilateral endeavor. As we indicated earlier, it is only countries rich in resources that are most able to realistically consider both unilateral and multilateral approaches to international engagement. We therefore narrow our focus to the United States in order to look more closely at this issue. In our fall 2006 experiment, subjects were asked to indicate the extent to which they agree that the United States should work to pursue international problems with diplomacy or other such international efforts or resort to military force if diplomacy fails. Higher values on this seven-point scale, Unilateral Foreign Policy, indicate more militant responses. This question then pits nonmilitant endeavors involving more than one country against militant endeavors presumably by a single country. We find that individuals in the Terror Threat condition are more likely to prefer a unilateral militant approach when diplomacy fails relative to those in the Good Times condition (see Web Supplement A, table 6.a). It is worth noting that the results in this second experimental study are more in line with the above-reported results from the U.S. survey data.

Antiterrorism Engagement

We now explore how the threat of terrorism affects preferences over a range of militant and nonmilitant policies meant to directly combat the terror threat. In three of the four principal studies (the exception is the Mexico survey data), we have questions related more specifically to the issue of terrorism. The U.S. surveys have just one question that relates specifically to militant antiterrorism engagement. Respondents were asked if they think that the UN Security Council should (coded as "1") or should not (coded as "0") have the right to authorize the use of military force to stop a country from supporting terrorist groups. In both the U.S. and Mexico experiments, we make use of three questions for which subjects indicated their level of support on a seven-point scale for multinational efforts to combat international terrorism. More specifically, respondents were asked to what degree they support tougher international laws aimed at countries that harbor terrorists. They were likewise asked their preferences over sharing intelligence information with the United States (in our Mexico study) and with Mexico (in our U.S. study). Finally, they were asked about their willingness to contribute to a multinational military campaign against a terrorist target (Contribute to a Military Campaign). Higher values on each measure indicate a preference for multinational efforts in the fight against terrorism. These measures capture both militant and nonmilitant cooperative endeavors.

Turning first to the U.S. survey data, we find evidence that individuals who perceive a terror threat are more supportive of militant antiterrorism policies (see Web Supplement A, table 6.b.). Transforming these results into substantively meaningful effects, those who perceive a terror threat are 22.1 percentage points more supportive of allowing the UN Security Council to take military actions in order to combat international terrorism in the 2004 study and 24.3 percentage points more supportive in the 2006 study. In short, the U.S. survey data analyses provide clear support for becoming more supportive of international efforts to confront the terror threat.

To assess our expectations using our experiment-based data, in figure 6.2 we simply compare the average level of support for antiterrorism policies in the Terror Threat and Good Times conditions for both countries. For Mexico, we see that for all but one measure (tougher international laws) the average values in the Terror Threat group are higher than in the Good Times condition. These differences are also statistically meaningful. Thus, in Mexico, increasing concerns about a terrorist attack leads to greater preferences for sharing intelligence, a nonmilitant endeavor, and for contributing to a military campaign against a terrorist target, a militant endeavor. However, we should note that on average, Mexican subjects in the Terror Threat condition are still just shy of being supportive of a

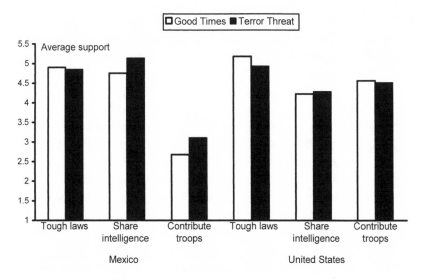

Figure 6.2. Average support for antiterrorism policies by experimental condition and country, MEX06s and US07s

military campaign (mean = 3.10 on the seven-point scale). So, while threatening conditions push Mexicans in our study relatively closer to militant internationalism, it does not necessarily lead them to fully embrace this policy dimension.

The results for the US07s study are on the right-hand side of figure 6.2. Contrary to the results in the survey, we do not find any meaningful differences between the Terror Threat and Good Times conditions. Once again, we note that a potential reason for the lack of results for international engagement may be that we are not distinguishing between different types of emotions. As we indicated earlier, Huddy and colleagues (2005) suggest that anxiety leads people to be less supportive of militant behavior, while anger makes them more supportive. In the U.S. survey data results, the meaningful findings for Terror Threat may have occurred because individuals in the sample were on average more angry than anxious about the threat. We have no way of knowing this since emotions questions were not asked on the survey. By the time of our experimental study in 2007, it could be that our student sample was particularly anxious, perhaps due to the war in Iraq, and the Terror Threat may have further heightened this anxiety, overwhelming the effects of any increased anger.

We happened to include a battery of emotions questions at the end of the U.S. 2007 experimental study, and as well on the fall 2006 U.S. study, and this allows us the opportunity to explore whether emotions might be an important part of the overall story. We do so in two ways. First, we compare anxiety levels, as well as other emotions, across time in order to see if there is any support for our speculation that such feelings were on the rise. If anxiety was on the rise in general, this might account for subjects' relative unwillingness to support engagement in times of terror threat more than in good times. Second, we conduct a more nuanced analysis of the entire emotions battery for 2007 and evaluate this in relation to preferences over international engagement.

While we cannot directly assess if our sample is particularly anxious relative to the rest of the population, we can offer evidence to suggest that the 2007 student sample is *more* anxious than a fall 2006 student sample (i.e., US06s). Though this is not a perfect indicator since we have different subjects, it can lend some empirical support to our claim. When examining the series of emotions questions in our fall 2006 and spring 2007 studies (using the PANAS battery, which we discussed in chapter 2), we find that anxiety and anger characterize one dimension, while positive emotions (proud, active, determined, and strong) comprise a second dimension.[12] Comparing these two emotions across our experimental conditions, both sets of emotions are higher among those in the Terror Threat condition relative to those in the Good Times condition, as expected. However, looking across studies, we do find evidence that the negative emotion factor is higher for the whole sample in 2007 (mean = .057) compared to 2006 (mean = −.53), while the positive emotion factor is higher in 2006 (mean = .20) compared to 2007 (mean = −.21).[13] The same pattern holds if we just look at those in the Terror Threat condition.[14] Thus, we have some support for our contention that overall anxiety levels were higher in the spring of 2007 relative to an earlier point in time. Furthermore, we see that while exposure to the Terror Threat condition in the fall of 2006 appears to have made subjects feel more proud and strong than anxious, the reverse pattern held by the spring of 2007.

While we do not find distinct dimensions for anger and anxiety to further test the claims of Huddy et al. (2005), we can look at the effect of these negative and positive emotions on our international engagement measures for 2007. When we run this type of analysis (see Web Supplement A, table 6.c), we find that those who exhibit positive emotions are more supportive of all of the antiterrorism engagement measures with the exception of creating tougher international laws. They are also more supportive of the prior engagement measures of being active in world affairs and contributing to a UN peacekeeping force. Meanwhile, we uncover no effects for negative emotions. These results seem consistent with the conditioning role that we might expect emotions to play in times of terror threat since the positive emotion factor captures feelings such as being proud, strong, and determined, rather than feelings such as joy and happiness.[15] This preliminary probe affirms that emotions play an important role in moderating the relationship between terrorist threat and preferences over international engagement. It also suggests that a fruitful avenue for future research is one that more carefully dissects and documents the exact nature of this conditioning role with respect to terrorist threat and, possibly, other types of threats.

Summary

The analyses thus far present a mostly consistent picture for the United States and Mexico. For both nations, perceiving the specter of a terrorist threat has important implications for foreign policy preferences. In both countries, in the face of a terror threat, individuals became more supportive of international efforts in general, more supportive of multilateral militant engagement, and more supportive of various counterterrorism policies. We have found these effects using several sources of data across both countries. While the U.S. experimental results were a bit weaker, once we took into account one's emotions, we found the same pattern among individuals who came to feel more proud and strong in relation to the terror threat. Another important finding was that the substantive impacts of perceptions of terror threat on support for international engagement were not very different across the two countries, even though the elite information environment was quite different.

It is worth, at this point, briefly revisiting the question of whether this type of coping strategy reflects instrumental or psychological processes. As in some other cases, the evidence seems to suggest that both are at play. Individuals, even in a context without elite cueing, adopt preferences clearly designed to help mitigate the terrorist threat. However, we also find that responses differ depending on one's emotional state, which suggests that something more psychological may also be at work.

Protecting at Home in the Face of Terrorist Threat?

We now turn to our second expectation concerning the tendency to prefer policies targeted at protecting the homeland under conditions of terror threat. For both countries, we examine preferences related to tightening the border, and in the U.S. case we also explore questions on homeland security spending and support for trading civil liberties for more security.

Preferences for Border Policy

The Mexico and U.S. surveys included two questions related to protection at home. Respondents in Mexico were asked if they support increasing the entry and exit requirements on people from other countries (Control Movement of People), as well as increasing controls on the movement of goods across its borders and into its ports and airports (Control Movement of Goods). Respondents in the United States were asked two variations on support for restricting immigration. The first question in the United States addressed support for reducing illegal immigration (Immigration #1), while the second examined support for increasing legal immigration (Immigration #2). As we have coded them, higher values on all four measures indicate support for more restrictions on the movement of goods and people. In the MEX06s and US07s experiment-based studies, we replicated the questions asked in the Mexico survey on the movement of goods and people, but increased the response options to a seven-point scale.

In both countries, we find substantial evidence that terrorist threat increases support for more restrictions on people and goods. For the surveys, given that we have two measures for each country and two years of data, we only present the effect of the Terror Threat indicator in each analysis in table 6.3 (the full results are in Web Supplement A, table 6.d.). Turning first to the Mexico survey results, our analyses show that Mexicans who perceive a terror threat are more supportive of increasing restrictions on the movement of people and goods in both the 2004 and 2006 study. These effects are also quite meaningful. For example, in the 2004 study, individuals who perceive a terror threat are 13.5 percentage points more supportive of restricting the movement of people and 14.9 percentage points more supportive of restricting the movement of goods in and out of the country, relative to those who did not perceive a terror threat. A similar pattern obtains for the case of the U.S. survey results. We find that individuals who perceive a grave terror threat are more supportive of restricting illegal and legal immigration.[16] In 2004, perceiving a grave threat moves an individual about .28 units (on a three-point scale) in favor of restricting illegal immigration and .12 units in favor of restricting "legal" immigration. Recall that in chapter 3, in an analysis of the ANES panel study, we found that individuals worried about terrorism became more supportive of restricting

Table 6.3. Support for measures to protect the homeland in the United States and Mexico, 2004 and 2006

		2004 Coefficient on Terror Threat (Standard Error)	2006 Coefficient on Terror Threat (Standard Error)
Mexico	Control Goods	0.494++ (0.103)	0.444++ (0.090)
	Control People	0.442++ (0.100)	0.418++ (0.090)
United States	Control People #1	0.284++ (0.045)	0.335++ (0.039)
	Control People #2	0.121++ (0.047)	0.174++ (0.062)

Note: Significance thresholds are as follows: **p < .05 (two-tailed); *p < .10 (two-tailed); ++p ≤ .05 (one-tailed); +p ≤ .10 (one-tailed). We use one-tailed tests on terror threat as the hypotheses are unidirectional and report robust standard errors. Probit analyses are used for Mexico since the variables are dichotomous, OLS is used for the United States since the measures are three-point scales. Full results are in Web Supplement A, table 6.d.

immigration levels and of spending to increase border patrol to prevent illegal immigrants from getting into the country (see figure 3.2). Thus, the findings across both sets of surveys are consistent.

These findings are also reinforced by the experimental results. In figure 6.3, we present average support for controlling the movement of people and goods by experimental condition for each country. Here we see that Mexicans in the Terror Threat condition are more supportive of policies of protection within (via controlling the movement of goods and people) relative to those in the Good Times condition, and average support among this group is rather high (5.85 and 5.06, respectively). These differences are statistically meaningful. In the U.S. study, average responses to both questions are higher in the Terror Threat condition and, moreover, for the question concerning the movement of people this latter difference is statistically reliable.

It should be very clear at this point that support for tightening up the border is a general response to the threat of international terrorism. We find support for this pattern of results in both experimental and survey data across both countries. It is important to note that these findings are thus consistent across residents of countries that vary with respect to the

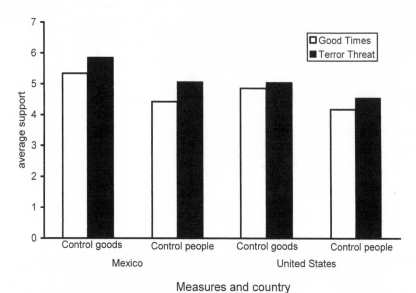

Figure 6.3. Average support for protecting the homeland by experimental condition and country, MEX06s and US07s

terror threat and elite rhetoric about the threat; despite these and other differences, individuals in the United States and in Mexico respond similarly with respect to their preferences for protecting the homeland. We now turn to examine preferences over more general security measures, which we are able to examine using data from some of our other U.S. experimental studies.

General Security

One issue we were interested in was how much individuals are willing to trade their civil liberties for more security. We therefore included a question, Civil Liberties, that asked respondents to place themselves on a seven-point scale ranging from "we should protect civil liberties at all costs" to "we should protect security at all costs." We were also interested in more general preferences toward spending on homeland security. We included a Homeland Security question, which asked respondents to place themselves on a seven-point scale ranging from "spend much less" to "spend much more" on homeland security. Since this question does not involve tradeoffs, we further asked people for their support for a tax increase in order to make improvements in homeland security. We examined this last question in chapter 5, in our analyses of self-sacrifice and we turn to it again because it taps preferences over protecting at home. These three questions — civil liberties, spending on homeland security, and taxation for homeland security — were asked in US05ns and the US05s studies, while the homeland security spending question was also asked in the US06s study.

We find support for our expectations across all three measures (for full results see Web Supplement A, tables 6.e, 6.f, and 6.g). First, for both studies in which the Civil Liberties question was asked, we find that individuals in the Terror Threat condition are more supportive of restricting civil liberties for more security. Exposure to the Terror Threat condition moves student subjects in the 2005 study about one-half a unit on the scale. Meanwhile, it appears that the Terror Threat condition also leads to preferences for more *spending* on homeland security, though the effect is only meaningful for the US06s study (the results for US05ns are close to significant, $p = .112$, one-tailed). Here, exposure to the Terror Threat condition moves subjects almost a full unit on the scale. A similar question also appeared on the ANES panel study. In analyses of those data, we also find that individuals who think future terrorist attacks are more likely are more supportive of increased spending on homeland security (see Web Supplement A, table 6.h). Finally, subjects in the Terror Threat condition in US05ns are more willing to increase *taxes* to improve homeland security.[17] Overall, then, the results from these additional analyses provide further support to our argument that individuals are more inclined to support policies to protect the homeland during times of terror threat.

To conclude this section, we note that we find substantial support for the second objective we proposed individuals would adopt in the face of terrorist threat: protecting at home. As with the first objective, we believe that the expression of these preferences likely reflects both instrumental and psychological processes. In many ways, tightening up the border and imposing more security in the face of a terror threat are quite rational responses. In fact, this has been a common response in times of war throughout U.S. history, at the least. However, the speed with which individuals come to adopt such preferences may also signal a deeper type of psychological motivation. Even many members of the U.S. Congress did not closely read the PATRIOT Act before voting it into law forty five days after 9/11! We remind the reader that it is beyond the scope of our study to provide a definite answer as to whether individuals — and/or members of Congress — react to the terrorist threat in the ways we have identified because they rationally assess these to be the most optimal strategies to adopt or because they feel a deep psychological need to alleviate negative feelings imposed by the threat. We hope, however, that we have identified the most plausible explanations in the case of this and our other coping strategies and we leave the rest for future work.

Conclusion

Do preferences for engaging abroad and protecting the homeland place democracy at risk? We believe there is a clear stress put on democracy with respect to some of the policies related to homeland protection. Many of the policies employed in the post-9/11 world curb our civil liberties. For example, the administration conducted warrantless wiretapping of citizens and noncitizens without FISA court approval until Congress stepped in to require FISA approval for wiretapping within the United States and for American citizens abroad. The government has argued that these restrictions on civil liberties are essential to win in the war against terror. Such temporary restrictions in times of war are common historically. For example, Lincoln suspended the writ of habeas corpus during the Civil War (though this power for the executive was declared unconstitutional by the Supreme Court in the *ex parte* Milligan decision after the conflict was over). An added aspect of this particular stress with respect to the war on terror is that there is no clear end in sight. Thus, at least some restrictions on our basic democratic rights may persist for an indefinite period of time.

With respect to preferences over international engagement, these may place more of an indirect stress on democracy. Preferences for unilateral, militant foreign policies may endanger the reputation of a country abroad. To the extent that the United States has pursued such a foreign policy in the war on terror, public opinion of the United States around the world appears to have declined. The increased animosity against the United States actually may help organizations like Al Qaeda recruit members, and this in turn may fuel a vicious cycle in which the threat of future terrorist attacks is increased, which increases politicians' and the public's support for restrictions on our liberties that may then remain in place for an extended period of time.[18]

In the next chapter, we tie together our arguments and findings for the three coping strategies. As we do so, we return to a deeper discussion of the implications of our work with respect to the extent to which times of terror threat place democracy at risk.

Conclusion

To a seemingly unprecedented degree, citizens in democratic nations are confronted with terrorist threat. A surge in the strength, visibility, and spread of international terrorism has left few corners of the world free from this menace. The threat of terrorism carries political relevance because individuals see politics through different lenses in times of crisis compared to good times. Our intention in this book has been to develop a better understanding of the ways in which conditions of terrorist threat affect citizens' evaluations, attitudes, and behaviors. Through novel experiment-based data collected in the United States and Mexico, combined with survey data, we have demonstrated that the terrain affected by terrorist threats is vast. We have added to scholarship in the fields of study addressed within this project and, in so doing, we have also raised new questions that help identify a research agenda for further scholarship.

In this concluding chapter, we draw our story to a close in the following manner. First, we summarize our argument and results. Second, we discuss the degree to which these findings suggest that terrorist threats may (or may not) place democracy at risk. Third, we raise the issue of elite engineering, that is, to what extent elites might purposefully and successfully manipulate the salience of a particular threat in order to gain some political purchase. Fourth, we address some lingering questions about the importance of country context and how it may (or may not) condition reactions to terrorism and other types (e.g., economic) of threat.

Individual Reactions to Terrorist Threats

Our argument is that individuals tend to cope with the negative emotions aroused by terrorist threat by using one or more of three politically relevant strategies. At the heart of collective crises, such as terrorist threats, is an individual's inability to resolve the situation on his or her own. A person might take actions to defend against a collective threat, but eliminating that threat altogether is beyond his or her means. Therefore, in order to restore feelings of security, efficacy, order, and calm, the individual pursues coping strategies aimed at one or more of three levels: fellow individuals; subnational or national leaders and government; and, the international arena. With respect to the first, some individuals become more distrusting, less tolerant, and more punitive in their attitudes toward and preferences over the treatment of other individuals. With respect to the second, individuals project additional leadership qualities onto a selected leader, weight strong leadership more heavily in their voting decisions, and express an increased willingness to protect and assist the selected leader. With respect to the third, individuals express preferences for a foreign policy marked by dual objectives: protecting the homeland while engaging abroad. In this section, we review the evidence we assembled in earlier chapters, which substantiates the use of these three coping strategies in times of terror threat (compared to times of relative prosperity and well-being).

Coping Strategy 1: Authoritarianism

In chapter 3 we focused on individuals' attitudes toward one another and, specifically, examined the relationships between threat and indicators of distrust, intolerance, punitiveness, and general authoritarian attitudes. Our principal findings are twofold. First, using survey data we identified links between terrorist threat and decreased social trust, decreased sympathy toward two out-groups (gays and immigrants), and tougher stances on crime. Second, we used experimental data both to examine whether individuals predisposed to authoritarianism express relatively more authoritarian attitudes in times of threat and to demonstrate a more concrete causal link. Using data from both the United States and Mexico, and student and nonstudent samples, we showed that conditions of terrorist threat (compared to good times) indeed activate the effect of authoritarian predispositions, leading those so disposed to express relatively higher levels of authoritarian attitudes. We demonstrated the robustness of this finding as it extended to specific measures of intolerance and punitiveness in Mexico and by comparing the effect of terrorist threat to economic threat. With respect to the first, we found that authoritarian predispositions exerted a much greater effect on intolerance toward disliked groups and punitiveness toward criminals for those exposed to conditions of terror threat as opposed to good times. We also found little evidence that economic threat functioned similarly to terrorist threat in the United States; however, in Mexico—a country in which economic crises at the time of our study may have been more vivid in individuals' memories—we found that the effect of economic threat at times mirrored that of terrorist threat.

Coping Strategy 2: The Exaltation of Leadership and Its Consequences

We examined the effect of terrorist threat on evaluations of leaders in chapters 4 and 5. Once again, we analyzed data from both the United States and Mexico, and for each case we examined both experiment-based and survey data. We found ample support for our expectation that in times of terror threat, individuals view alternative leaders in starker terms—they perceive a selected individual as a stronger (chapter 4) and more charismatic (chapter 5) leader while they perceive the rival candidate as weaker and less charismatic (compared to good times).

In chapter 4 we looked at perceptions of strong leadership using experimental data from the 2004 U.S. presidential election and the 2006 California gubernatorial election. In both studies, we found that exposure to terror threat increased evaluations of the Republican incumbent as a "strong leader" relative to the Democratic challenger. For the most part, analyses of ANES survey data mirrored these findings. In chapter 5 we showed a similar set of relationships with respect to perceptions of Bush's charisma in the 2004 study. In a follow-up study with nonstudents we demonstrated a similar projection of charisma for Bush in the terror threat condition, but only among those low to average in political sophistication. Meanwhile, we did not find any effects in that study for an economic threat.

We also explored the relationship between terrorist threat and perceptions of charisma using experiment-based data from Mexico. Again we found clear evidence that the terror threat condition, compared to times of well-being, caused individuals to perceive the relatively more conservative, incumbent party's candidate as more charismatic while perceiving his rival as significantly less charismatic. We were also able to use the Mexico experiment and novel survey data to examine whether other types of threat conditions have similar effects. First, in the case of the experiment, we observed that an economic threat similarly affected leadership evaluations, though the effects were a bit weaker than those registered for the terror threat.

Chapters 4 and 5 demonstrate that conditions of threat affect perceptions of the strength and charisma, respectively, of relevant political leaders. Each chapter then continued on to consider a different set of questions. In chapter 4 we began with the expectation that under times of terrorist threat, compared to times of relative well-being and prosperity, individuals will assign relatively greater weight to their evaluations of candidates' leadership traits in their voting decisions. We found strong support for this expectation in experimental and survey data from the 2004 U.S. presidential election, as well as experimental data from the 2006 California governor's race.

In the second half of chapter 5 we examined some of the political consequences of terrorist threat and charisma perceptions. We looked for such effects in three domains: blame reduction, self-sacrifice, and preferences for greater executive power. Using data from three experiment-based studies conducted in the United States, we found clear evidence that conditions of terrorist threat either directly and/or indirectly (via charisma) caused individuals to be less likely to blame George W. Bush for a variety of policy failures such as the CIA leak scandal, faulty intelligence with respect to Iraq, and lapses in homeland security. With respect to self-sacrifice, we demonstrated links among terror threat, perceptions of charisma, and willingness to engage in campaign-related activities on behalf of George W. Bush, though only for Republicans. However, all partisans exposed to the threat of terrorism experienced elevated perceptions of Bush's charisma that in turn led them to be more willing to sacrifice their own resources on behalf of policies clearly related to his policy agenda. Finally, for issues of executive power, we brought into the picture our data from Mexico, where we presented strong evidence linking terrorist threat and (just slightly weaker evidence linking) perceptions of charisma to preferences for a stronger executive. We then turned to data from a later study in the United States (2007), in which we demonstrated that conditions of terrorist threat at this juncture in time (a time in which Bush was experiencing very low levels of approval) caused individuals to prefer a *weakening* of the executive office. Finally, in this chapter we were able again to compare the effects of terrorist threat to the effects of economic threat. For the most part, in both the United States and Mexico cases, an economic threat was less consequential than a terrorist threat.

Coping Strategy 3: Dual Foreign Policy Objectives

In chapter 6 we documented the relationship between threat and foreign policy objectives. We found support for our argument that under conditions of terrorist threat, individuals come to prefer policies aimed at engaging abroad while protecting the homeland. This support came from, and was notably quite consistent across, a wide range of experimental and survey data from both the United States and Mexico.

We demonstrated with survey data that under times of terror threat, citizens in the United States and Mexico prefer higher levels of engagement abroad. The same data and experimental data from Mexico showed that people became more willing to engage in militant internationalism by contributing troops to a UN peacekeeping force, while subjects in the U.S. experiment (2006) became more supportive of a unilateral militant approach. Turning more specifically to the issue of terrorism, we found support for a range of militant and nonmilitant antiterrorism policies. Citizens in the U.S. study who thought terrorism was a grave threat (in the survey data) were more supportive of giving the UN Security Council the authority to stop a country from supporting terrorist groups. Meanwhile, in the experimental data from Mexico, individuals exposed to the terror threat condition were more supportive of sending troops to a multinational force against a terrorist target and in sharing intelligence information with the United States. The only case in which we did not find a direct effect of the terror threat condition on support for increased engagement was the U.S. 2007 experimental study, in which a more detailed analysis revealed that those who came to feel proud and strong following the terror threat treatment were more supportive of being active in the world, contributing to a UN peacekeeping force, and of a variety of antiterrorism policies.

We also looked at several different types of policies associated with protecting the homeland. In analyses of both experimental and survey data, we found that conditions of terror threat made individuals more likely to support stricter entrance and exit requirements on people and goods in Mexico, and on people in the United States. In other experimental studies, we demonstrated that subjects exposed to a terror threat were more supportive of increasing taxes for and general spending on homeland security.

They also became more supportive of policies aimed at obtaining higher levels of security, even at the expense of civil liberties.

Discussion

Conditions of terrorist threat clearly motivate individuals to adopt one or more coping strategies, in the ways described above. Do individuals react in similar ways to other types of threat? Collective crises of all types increase feelings of anxiety, worry, distress, hopelessness, and possibly even fear and anger. One might expect, then, that these coping mechanisms would have relevance beyond terror threats. Interestingly and as we noted above, where we examined economic threat alongside terror threat, we found only some evidence (and mostly in the case of Mexico) that individuals adopted the coping mechanisms we have outlined here to the same degree. Later in this conclusion we will discuss country context and offer some speculation into what might explain the relatively greater effects of economic threat in Mexico. Also in the case of Mexico, we were able to examine public security threat and political threat indicators and found evidence that they were tied to perceptions of charisma. Given that we did not examine these in the United States, we cannot say if these effects are country-specific and we leave this as an open question. We do anticipate, though, that in the United States and in other contexts we were unable to examine here, threats other than international terrorism motivate individuals to seek out and find strong and charismatic leaders, with similar political consequences to those we have described in this project.

At a minimum, we might expect other national security crises to have similar effects. In fact, considering all three coping mechanisms jointly—the increased expression of authoritarian and related attitudes, seeking out a strong leader, and the desire to protect at home—it is not hard to recall instances in which a more traditional national security crisis appeared to induce such shifts. An obvious example is found in World War II. One segment of the U.S. population, Japanese citizens and noncitizens, was singled out for internment on the West Coast. While this was a military policy to "protect the homeland," the policy originated from demand by state and local officials in California in response to fear of the ethnic Japanese among the public (Rehnquist 1998). With respect to evaluations of leaders, according to research by Berinsky (2009), FDR's advisors were well aware that the president benefited from the salience of World War II in his re-election bid. Thus, it seems at least probable that the effects of terrorist threats and more traditional national security threats mirror each other in some key ways. Nonetheless, the distinct nature of the terrorist threat carries additional implications for the exact nature of international engagement that is preferred and for the duration of the attitudinal shifts that are observed. We discuss the latter issue in the following section.

Democracy at Risk?

A concern running through this book is the following: Do our findings demonstrate that individuals' responses to terrorist threats place democracy at risk? On balance we feel that the answer is yes. However, the degree to which particular coping strategies pose a threat to democracy also varies. Moreover, some of the shifts in evaluations and behavior that we detect are arguably signs of a healthy democratic citizenry, one that responds to and attempts to help remedy a crisis situation. We nonetheless conclude that some of these shifts are quite disconcerting from the perspective of the *quality* of democracy and its practices. It is less likely that these shifts will cause regime disruption, but we can even here imagine a few scenarios in which these shifts could also be related to democratic durability.

Why might these shifts in the attitudes, evaluations, and behavior of individuals in times of terror threat be reason for alarm? To the extent that any given crisis carries with it threats to democratic quality, these arguably could be fleeting and therefore only cause a temporary and mostly social disruption. On the other hand, two factors might cause those effects to endure. One is general and the other is specific to the new terrorist threat. First, in some cases, temporary shifts in support for different types of policies might be captured in legislation, some of which may then persist on the books long past when attitudes have reverted to reflect better times. That said, under many cases, threat-induced policy shifts may be reversed once the threat recedes. As we have indicated earlier in the book, this is exactly what happened in the cases of civil liberty infringements during previous, traditional wars. This brings us to our second point. The threat of terrorism is different in one key respect from traditional wars: there is no clear end date. Complete and total victory over terrorism may arguably never be achieved. Threats from international terrorism are not likely to recede in the near future. Furthermore, how does one end a war against a tactic?[1] The "war on terrorism" is not a war against a particular group but, rather, a fight to eliminate the use of a particular and deadly strategy. In short, the threat of terrorism is not something that appears likely to end in our lifetimes. Citizens may continue to feel motivated, for years to come, to pursue attitudinal, evaluative, and behavioral shifts that alleviate feelings of insecurity, distress, fear, and anger. For the U.S. case, Geoffrey Stone nicely summarizes the potential danger represented by the terror threat relative to past conflicts:

> As we have seen, a saving "grace" of America's past excesses is that they were of "short" duration and that, once the crisis passes, the nation returned to equilibrium. A war of indefinite duration however, compounds the dangers both by extending the period during which civil liberties are "suspended" and by increasing the risk that "emergency" restrictions will become a permanent fixture of American life. (Stone 2004, 545)

In an attempt to offer a summary statement regarding the potential of the terrorist threat to endanger the quality of democracy, we evaluate this possibility with respect to each of our three coping strategies. As we pursue this discussion we stress three points: first, some of the shifts individuals experience in times of terrorist threat might actually be beneficial to the survival of the democratic system or, at the least, benign in terms of their effects on democratic quality; second, other shifts appear to have the clear potential, if left unchecked, to undermine democratic quality; and, third, under special circumstances, the stress on democracy posed by the terrorist threat may be sufficient to threaten the very durability of the democratic system. When we discuss democratic quality, we refer to the social fabric underlying the system (e.g., how citizens treat one another), the rights individuals are granted by the system, and the actual functioning of the system (e.g., types of leadership, accountability, and institutional practices).

Authoritarianism as a Threat to Democracy

In the case of our first coping strategy, increased distrust and authoritarian attitudes seem to pose a clear threat to democracy from the perspective of social harmony and, possibly, civil rights. It is also possible to argue that a certain level of increased distrust may help safeguard a country against actions by enemies. However, increased distrust alongside the broader attitudinal shifts documented in chapter 3 has the potential to disrupt social relations, as particular individuals and groups are marginalized and perhaps threatened by those seeking to protect the in-group, preserve the status quo, and find an outlet for negative emotions such as anger. In the introduction, we showed majority support in survey data for policies that would restrict the civil rights of Arab Americans. If these attitudinal shifts carry with them behavioral consequences, then the social fabric of the democracy is subject to greater rupture. Also in the introduction, we retold stories of attacks on Muslim-appearing individuals following the 9/11 attacks. Such behaviors are certainly extreme and hopefully rare manifestations of an authoritarian mood shift but they nonetheless are obviously well within the range of what is possible in the specter of a terrorist threat.

When authoritarian attitudes spill over beyond minor changes in how neighbors treat each other and beyond major but hopefully rare hate-based incidents and into policy, their effects may become more durable. Facing a citizenry that calls for order and security and which is relatively less sympathetic to out-groups, legislators might enact legislation aimed at restricting liberties more generally and benefits specifically to obvious out-groups (such as immigrants and gays). As we will discuss much more with respect to the third coping mechanism, a call for order and security may make individuals more willing to cede their own liberties for more security. They may be even more willing to do so for out-groups that appear particularly threatening, such as those with Arab and/or Muslim backgrounds. In our data, we observed that people became more supportive of restrictions against immigrants. The past several years have witnessed a crackdown on undocumented workers and the employers who hire them, often under the claim of national security, despite the fact that most of these individuals pose no significant security risk. Part of the reason is due to the reorganization of the government, such that the Department of Homeland Security now oversees the operations of Immigration and Customs Enforcement (ICE). However, even at the local level anti-immigrant policies have increased since 2001 (Ramakrishnan and Wong 2008). Furthermore, with the increasing use of propositions and initiatives, just about anyone can place policies against out-groups on the ballot (subject to meeting signature requirements). As one example, voters in Arizona passed an anti-immigrant proposition in 2004, and then another against employers who hire undocumented workers in 2006. With respect to gays, in 2004, there were anti–gay marriage initiatives in eleven states, all of which passed, and eight of which also banned civil unions. Most recently, in 2008, Californians passed Proposition 8, which changed the state constitution to eliminate the right of same-sex couples to marry. Recall that in our studies we observed a link between terror threat and negative feelings toward gays. While we cannot conclude with absolute certainty that the specter of another terrorist attack in the post-9/11 period is partly responsible for these initiatives, our data are certainly consistent with such an interpretation.

Finally, we would suggest that these issues have implications that stretch beyond the realm of domestic practices and policy. Put simply, authoritarian shifts may have consequences for the types of practices that are pursued abroad, by the military and other security groups acting on behalf of the threatened country. As we reported in chapter 3, in a 2006 national survey of the United States conducted by the CCFR, respondents were asked whether they approved of using torture to get information from suspected terrorists. Those who responded that they believed that international terrorism is a "critical threat" were more likely to approve of the use of torture, even after controlling for other likely predictors such as ideology, education, income, and gender.

The Exaltation of Strong Leaders as a Threat to Democracy

In contrast to the first case, the findings related to our second coping strategy present more of a mixed bag with respect to their implications for democracy. Projecting leadership qualities onto a select individual while downgrading leadership evaluations of his or her rival might simply be a benign coping mechanism, providing the populace with a sense of security (perhaps also mitigating against a need to utilize other coping strategies). On the other hand (subjecting this tendency to the toughest interpretation we can imagine), perceiving leaders in starker terms could contribute to polarization and related divisiveness among citizens championing different leaders. That said, on balance, this feature of the second coping strategy does not seem to pose a deep threat to democracy, when considered on its own.

However, the tendency to seek out and compel oneself to find a strong and charismatic leader arguably places stress on democracy when it is combined with several other consequences. In chapter 4 we showed that individuals weight relevant candidate traits (namely, strong leadership) more strongly in their voting decisions in times of terrorist threat. This practice has at least two interpretations from the perspective of democracy. In the first place, this could be a sign of a healthy democracy, if citizens (who are often depicted as underinformed and underengaged) actually awake to the changing environment at the onset of a threat and adapt their voting strategies accordingly. By placing into office an individual with strong leadership potential (though recall that some of this leadership potential rests on biased perceptions), voters might facilitate a quick resolution to the crisis. After that point, citizens presumably can and will revert to placing more weight on other standard vote choice ingredients, such as issues and party identification. In the second place, however, the downplaying of issues in favor of candidate personality traits might be detrimental to the extent that individuals are content to sit back and allow the leader to govern using whatever means necessary.

In chapter 5 we showed that a focus on strong leadership does not end with perceptions and vote choice, but also has implications for the evaluations and behaviors citizens are willing to make on behalf of leaders. In times of terror threat, individuals are more willing to sacrifice their own resources on behalf of a given leader, are less willing to blame that leader for mistakes, and are—in some cases at least—willing to cede extra institutional powers to that leader. Self-sacrifice might be thought of as a healthy enterprise in which citizens can engage in order to facilitate the resolution of the crisis. Advocates of an active public should take heart in the fact that citizens do show a willingness to contribute their own resources in times of threat. There remains, though, the possibility that such measures might threaten democracy to the extent that the leader's agenda contains policies that seek to undermine democratic institutions. Blame reduction and preferences for centralizing power in the executive seem more problematic at face value. We may need to give a leader who arises in times of crisis the benefit of the doubt and time in order to enact change (after all, FDR experimented with many policies that failed in trying to overcome the Great Depression). However, if individuals fail to blame the leader for policy mistakes at the next election and continue to vote for the "strong" leader, then voting decisions eventually become devoid of meaning and leaders devoid of responsibility for outcomes. If citizens do not hold leaders accountable, then the quality of democracy certainly suffers.

Finally, it may seem practical to give extra power to the executive, relative to other branches, in times of crisis. However, a willingness to shift the balance of power to the executive, in a context without a clear end in sight, may substantially alter democratic institutions. We observed such a shift in preferences in our study of Mexico in 2006. A silver lining shined through though in our final analyses in chapter 5, when we demonstrated that under some circumstances conditions of terrorist threat can cause individuals to prefer a *weaker* executive office. In the case of the United States in 2007, student subjects in our study appear to be acting against earlier tendencies in the U.S. public to cede power to the executive office in the aftermath of 9/11. This suggests that issues of timing and, possibly, institutional context combine to moderate the effect of terrorist threat on preferences over a strong executive; in at least some cases at some point in time citizens will step in to check the consolidation of power in the executive office. Of course, we only found this among a sample of students, and so we do not know whether these effects would obtain in the more general population. But as we mentioned in the introduction, the U.S. public has become increasingly critical of the policies of the Bush administration.

Dual Foreign Policy Objectives as a Threat to Democracy

The last coping strategy also presents a bit of a mixed bag with respect to the stress placed on democracy. For most types of international engagement, it does not appear that there are any direct stresses. Preferring that one's country is more active in the world in general and/or pursues selected nonmilitant cooperation (such as sharing intelligence on terrorist threats) and militant cooperation (such as a multilateral attack against a terrorist target) does not seem to pose an obvious threat to democracy. If anything, such multilateral actions may make democracies safer and more viable. Nonetheless, preferences for unilateral foreign policies could potentially place indirect stress on democracy. As the United States has pursued a more unilateral foreign policy in the war on terror, public opinion of the United States around the world has declined. As we pointed out in chapter 6, increased animosity against the United States actually may help organizations like Al Qaeda recruit members, which might increase the threat of future attacks, and thus the need for more policies to protect the homeland. These latter policies may place a heavy toll on democracy at home.

We found that policies related to homeland protection were supported by a broad cross-section of individuals in both the United States and in Mexico. Policies related to protecting the border may not place too much stress on democracy, *unless* (as might happen more often than not) such policies lead to unreasonable searches and detentions that are inconsistent with basic freedoms guaranteed to citizens and noncitizens alike. Empirical examples abound of other policies, implemented in the aftermath of terrorist attacks, which pose a clear danger to civil liberties. As we discussed in chapter 6, the USA PATRIOT Act passed with broad support in both chambers just forty-five days after 9/11. The bill gave federal officials much greater authority to track and intercept communications at home and abroad and gave law enforcement officers more power to detain and remove immigrants suspected of terrorist activities. In the United Kingdom, the Anti-Terrorism, Crime and Security Act (ATCSA 2001) gave the government the authority to indefinitely detain a person if the Home Secretary issues a certificate stating a reasonable belief that a person's presence in the United Kingdom is a risk to national security, and a reasonable suspicion that the person is a terrorist. A similar tightening of security laws has occurred in other countries hit by attacks, such as Spain and Indonesia. Even countries that have not been directly affected have enacted antiterror legislation, such as Australia and Belgium. To the extent that these new laws compromise democratic values and practices, and to the extent that they are likely to remain active for years to come, we suggest they pose a threat to democratic quality.

There is also the possibility that elites might act in an entrepreneurial way, using the threat of a terrorist attack in order to gain support for policies aimed at restricting rights and benefits or to target domestic insurgent groups. For example, a legislator who prefers increased government surveillance might find it politically useful to issue statements about the high likelihood of a terrorist attack in the near future, in order to activate authoritarian predispositions and, in particular, concerns about order and security among at least a receptive subset of the population. The current debate over wiretapping in the United States arguably shows traces of the use of the terror threat in order to garner public support for such activities. Countries have also used the language of international terrorism to crack down on domestic insurgent groups, such as with ETA in Spain and the ethnic Uighur community in China. The degree to which threats might be manipulated, and restrictive policies pursued, may depend on the strength of the democracy. Where the media remains fully independent and where interest groups mobilize freely to safeguard civil liberties, purely entrepreneurial activities and their effects may remain relatively minor. Where the executive has a greater ability to use the media to build up the perception of threat and has the ability to silence government critics, authoritarianism may have a greater and longer imprint on a society.

Executive actions that threaten civil liberties during times of war are quite common (Rehnquist 1998). Considering just the U.S. case as an example, as we have already discussed, Lincoln suspended the writ of habeas corpus during the Civil War. Woodrow Wilson received broad authority from Congress to censor communication during World War I. During World War II, FDR tried Nazi saboteurs who had landed on U.S. soil, even those who were U.S. citizens, in military tribunals. Furthermore, the ethnic Japanese, both citizen and noncitizen alike, were interned on the West Coast, while Hawaii was subject to martial law. While there has been some shift over time in executives seeking authority from Congress for such actions, the legislature providing such authority to do so during a time when there is no foreseeable end to the threat seems to place even more stress on democratic practices and citizen rights. As citizens come to support security over civil liberty in the war on terror, what happens to support for the foundations of democracy? As we noted in the introduction, it is Benjamin Franklin who stated, "They that can give up essential liberty to obtain a little temporary safety deserve neither liberty nor safety." Of course, we also discussed the nuances in this quote. It may be perfectly reasonable to give up some liberties for more security in times of war. However, with no clear end in sight to these policies that seek to protect the homeland, a country could arguably risk a withering away of support for basic democratic values, which may result in a significant diminishing of the quality of the democratic state in which we reside.

Discussion

Even if some consequences of the three coping strategies have the potential to negatively affect democratic quality, should we really expect that any of these effects are widely expressed and/or long-lasting? In the experiment-based studies we analyzed here, subjects were exposed to relatively small bits of information. Our audiovisual presentations were just about a minute and a half in length. Our newspaper articles were about one page in length. The brevity of our treatments, presented in an artificial laboratory setting, gives us increased confidence in the generalizability of our results. When the threat of terrorist attacks is heightened, for example, individuals are likely bombarded with information about the threat, from politicians, all forms of the media, and in conversations with family and friends. Thus, we assume that our experiments present a "least likely" scenario for finding differences in behaviors across terror threat and good times conditions. That said, while we have significant confidence in the results we find, we lack leverage on the question of duration. How long might these effects persist? Based on our experiments, we can only say that—when just a small dose of threat is applied—the effects last through what were often quite lengthy surveys. If the duration of effects is related to the amount of information about the threat, as seems plausible, then we expect that the effects of terrorist threats on citizen attitudes, evaluations, and behavior in the real world are not fleeting.

We have mentioned already two additional reasons why the effects of terror threats might persist beyond the short-term. The first concerns legislation, which might persist well after attitudes revert to normal. The second is that, in contrast to traditional wars or other security crises, terrorism has no definite end. Since 9/11 and arguably before, the United States has been operating under the threat of terrorist attacks. Certainly, the salience of that threat has shifted over time. But, the basic plausibility of that threat has remained, and remains, a feature of modern political life. In the words of Vice President Dick Cheney, it reflects the "new normalcy." Given the nature of the new terrorism and the difficulty in combating it, a true "good times" scenario, one devoid of terror threat, is unlikely to surface in the foreseeable future. Thus, individuals may need to employ one or more of the coping mechanisms we have identified above for an indefinite period of time. But we also recognize two important factors. First, as we said, the salience of the threat may ebb and flow. Second, it is not clear whether the specter of a relatively new threat has different effects on citizens' attitudes, evaluations, and behaviors than one to which citizens have become accustomed. Arguably, if a crisis is defined by a change or expected change in the status quo, then a situation in which threat is constant is not a crisis.

In conclusion, we assert that some, but not all, of the responses we examine to terror threats place democratic quality *at risk*. Increased authoritarian attitudes, increased preferences for policies that privilege security and order over freedom, and a tendency to (semi-) blindly follow and support strong leaders (even if they make policy mistakes) are attitudinal shifts that are, at the least, inconsistent with the democratic ideal. The extent to which they *injure* democracy in irreparable ways is more debatable. Indeed, we assume that the extent to which democracy is injured may depend on factors that lie mostly outside the scope of this study, including the duration of the threat, the depth and duration of its attitudinal consequences, the extent to which attitude shifts are captured in legislation, and the initial strength of the democracy (on this latter point, see more below).

Engineering Threats for Political Purposes

In the above sections, we have alluded to political elites acting as entrepreneurs with respect to the framing of threats and we noted that threats may surge and recede over time. These factors help introduce the following question: To what extent might political elites play a role in crisis creation? We think the answer is that elites can certainly play a role, but that a political payoff is not guaranteed.

First we note that elite manipulation is not a necessary factor behind the effects that we have detected in this manuscript. The terror threat treatments in our experimental conditions always omitted reference to any particular administration. Further, we found effects for threats regardless of the level of existing political debate on the issue. Thus, we found effects for the terror threat treatment in the 2006 California gubernatorial election, in which terrorist threat was not particularly salient, and in a 2006 study of

Mexico, a country that has not experienced a direct attack by international terrorists.

Nonetheless, we are cynical enough to believe that enterprising elites who foresee certain political payoffs *might* attempt to manipulate the threat context. We see at least three strategies in this regard. First, one can make a threat more salient than it might otherwise be. Thus, for example, Mueller (2006) argues that political elites in the United States (as well as those in other positions likely to benefit) have generated a climate of crisis surrounding the possibility of another terrorist attack when Mueller argues that possibility is, in fact, quite low. Another example of such apparent engineering is provided by Andrés Manuel López Obrador, the second-place candidate in the 2006 Mexican presidential election. In the aftermath of the close election, López Obrador cried foul and managed to fuel a political crisis, focused on the legitimacy of the electoral count, that—as our survey data analysis in chapter 5 demonstrates—was associated with increased perceptions of his charisma (among those who perceived a crisis in this area).

Second, elites may select to play up a series of threats sequentially in order to maintain an environment of anxiety, distress, and fear among their citizenry. Arguably a quintessential example of such behavior is provided by the current president of Venezuela, Hugo Chávez, who took office in the midst of an economic and political crisis in Venezuela. Since then he has cycled through a variety of threats, including pervasive corruption, diplomatic conflicts with his neighbors (particularly Colombia), and alleged assassination and invasion plans by the United States. Leaving aside the validity of these threats, with each instance Chávez has successfully convinced the public (or at least key sectors of the population) that he alone is capable of resolving the crisis posed by that threat. Not only is support for Chávez indicated by his victories at the polls but it is also evidenced in the ease with which he has consolidated power in the executive office.

Finally, in the aftermath of a crisis, a leader can use the fact that he was "in the right place at the right time" to his advantage. For example, while Rudy Giuliani was known as tough on crime in New York City prior to 9/11, stock in his leadership skills skyrocketed after the 9/11 attacks. Overnight, Giuliani became a household name across the United States and abroad. Our analyses suggest that since he was the incumbent mayor during an externally provoked attack, he received a big boost in leadership evaluations (see again the figure from the introduction). To be fair to Giuliani, we should note that some of this boost in leadership perceptions likely came about because of his decisive and effective leadership in the wake of 9/11.

But, if we are correct that conditions of terrorist threat cause individuals to increase their perceptions of the strength and charisma of certain leaders, then it is reasonable to conclude that at least some of this boost is attributable to our second coping strategy. Either way, the boost carried with it some clear benefits for Giuliani. After he left office, Giuliani started a consulting firm to advise on crisis management, further developing his reputation in this area. It is no wonder that he then ran for the Republican presidential nod on a platform of strong leadership in an age of terrorism. While certainly not a laughing matter, the facetious online newspaper *The Onion* most aptly described his candidacy in a headline: "Giuliani to Run for President of 9/11."[2]

All this said, we advise some words of caution for those entrepreneurs (or political consultants) among our readership, who might decide to embark on a plan of crisis creation. First, we believe that such activity can have serious, negative consequences for democracy. This much should be clear from our earlier discussion. We further believe that such activities do not carry a guaranteed payoff. In the first place, and perhaps most obviously, the threat a political elite attempts to manipulate must be plausible. Thus, the terrorist threat is credible given the sheer number of international terrorist attacks, as well as statements issued by Al Qaeda and others expressing an intent to engage in future attacks (even if some argue that the threat is overstated). As another example, discussion in Eisenstadt and Poiré (2006) indicates that the accusations made by López Obrador, which helped generate a political crisis in the aftermath of the 2006 Mexican presidential election, were relatively more plausible given certain existing weaknesses in the electoral system and institutions.

In the second place, it is critical that the elite be able—at some point—to resolve the threat. While increased charisma, and the presence of the threat itself, may enable leaders to avert blame for poor output in the short- or even medium-run, such a scenario is unlikely to last. As the costs of combating the threat increase or reach some intolerable threshold (in terms of causality levels in wartime, for example) individuals may withdraw support for incumbents.[3] Absent costs, if elites fail to provide a solution to the threat, the public's patience may still wear thin. We have already documented a negative relationship between conditions of terrorist threat and support for a strong executive in the United States in 2007. As another example, as of the fall of 2007, there were signs that Venezuelans were growing frustrated with respect to Hugo Chávez's (in)ability to deliver on economic promises made during and since his initial campaign for office nearly ten years ago. On December 2, 2007, the voting public defeated his proposed constitutional reforms by a two-percentage-point margin. Prior to the vote, a service industry worker was reported saying: "Chávez is delirious if he thinks we're going to follow him like sheep. . . . If this government cannot give me milk or asphalt for our roads, how is it going to give my mother a pension?"[4] In short, politicians hoping to take advantage of a crisis scenario must be careful to resolve or mitigate the threat before the costs become unbearable to the public, even one attempting to perceive its leader in the best possible light.

As a third issue, we note that politicians sometimes mishandle crisis conditions, which can cause the threat to backfire and the public to act in ways not directly predicted in the studies we have presented here. The 2004 bombings in Madrid provide a good example. On March 11, 2004—three days before Spain's general elections—bombs went off in four commuter trains in Madrid. The 3/11 terrorist attack killed 191 individuals and wounded over 2,000 more. It was later determined that the attacks were conducted by a group of individuals acting on behalf of, or at least inspired by, Al Qaeda. The political repercussions of the attack were immediate and broad. The effect most pertinent to this discussion is that, whereas the incumbent administration was heavily favored prior to the attacks, public opinion quickly shifted in favor of the opposition. In an election marked by unprecedented levels of voter turnout, the incumbent party soundly lost the election. Why? One important factor appears to be perceptions that the administration mishandled the crisis, in particular, by immediately and mistakenly attempting to place the blame on the domestic terrorist group, ETA.[5]

Even in cases in which nature is the clear culprit, leaders can still botch the handling of a crisis. The snail's pace response by the federal government to the costliest and one of the most deadly hurricane disasters in U.S. history, Hurricane Katrina, caused George W. Bush's approval ratings to plummet to historic lows. The administration learned its lesson from Katrina and, consequently, Bush was on the ground immediately in southern California during the firestorms that wreaked havoc in September of 2007. A related possibility is that threats could backfire, or have consequences that are different from those we would predict, if a leader takes ownership of a given threat domain and then fails at preventing the realization of that threat. Thus, for example, we suspect that George W. Bush toward the end of his two terms in office was more vulnerable to public opinion shifts in the event of another large terrorist attack because of the fact that, in the aftermath of 9/11, he staked himself and his reputation as the nation's protector.

Finally, a leader's baseline level of support and popularity may matter. While we argued in chapter 1 that in the case of an externally provoked dramatic foreign policy event, the incumbent will receive a boost in leadership evaluations (and likely approval), this may not hold under all conditions. For example, if an incumbent political figure is already registering very low levels of popular approval, then that individual may not receive a boost from a dramatic foreign policy event. Under such conditions, the media, other elites, and the public in general may be more likely to critique the leader's inability to handle the new threat context, rather than praise it.[6]

The Importance of Country Context

One of the surprising features of our findings is the degree of continuity in reactions to terrorist threat that we find in the United States and Mexico. In the case of the United States, we have an advanced industrial society, with an established history of party competition, and one that has experienced direct attacks by international terrorist groups. In the case of Mexico, we have a country that economically is less developed, politically only recently transitioned to competitive party politics, and that has been threatened and indirectly affected by international terrorism but not directly attacked. Despite these differences, citizens of both countries react in remarkably similar ways across the range of measures that we explored. This fact attests to the robustness of our results. However, it also begs the question: does country context matter?

We believe it may, to some extent. First, and as we also noted elsewhere, it may be that the strength of a democracy plays an important role in mitigating the otherwise potentially damaging effects a terrorist threat has on democratic values and institutions. In fact, it may be country context that determines whether the stress on democracy is a matter of quality (as we have concentrated on) or a matter of regime survival. In the introduction we discussed an example of a fragile democracy in which the combination of terrorist threat alongside economic and institutional crises led to a shift away from democracy as a regime type; in this case, the charismatic Peruvian president Alberto Fujimori ascended to power in the midst of all three of these crisis conditions and succeeded, at least temporarily, in shutting down congress and other offices within the once-democratic state. Though simply an anecdote for our purposes, this case suggests that country context may critically influence whether a terrorist threat merely results in a slight decline in democratic quality or helps bring about a rupture in the system itself. In addition to the presence of other crises simultaneous to the terrorist threat, we can think of several other features that may matter with respect to the harm imposed on democracy.

Recent research demonstrates that the presence of a prime that references democratic values might be able to counteract certain negative tendencies associated with reminding individuals of the vulnerability of their own mortality.[7] This research suggests that to the extent to which there exist voices, for example, promoting tolerance and/or opposing the consolidation of power in the executive office within the context of a terrorist threat, these might offset some of the findings we have detailed within this work. We would expect such voices to be stronger where democracy is more deeply rooted and where, as a consequence, the media provides a venue for contrasting opinions and special interest groups promoting civil liberties and other democratic values and practices operate freely. Of course, such voices may be slow to surface, even in an established democracy. We also expect that the strength of democracy might matter in terms of helping to define the range of options that citizens consider attractive; thus, in a country with a longer history of checks and balances, citizens may not consider extensive consolidation of power in the executive office as a realistic or appealing option, nor may rival elites at other levels of office allow it. If such allowances are made, they may only last for the duration of the threat.

Second, country context might help determine which threats are not only plausible but also which threats are most disconcerting. In many cases, when we were able to make comparisons across two threats, we found that the terror threat condition had a relatively stronger effect than the economic threat condition. However, on balance, we found that the latter mattered relatively more in Mexico than in the United States. It may be that the extent of damage implied by an economic crisis in Mexico is greater for at least two reasons. First, the country's relatively less extensive social welfare safety net might make individuals more concerned about an impending economic crisis. Second, given that Mexico has experienced a greater number of economic crises in recent times, and of greater severity (compared to the United States), the threat of an economic recession might carry greater weight. However, it could also be that economic issues were simply not as salient in the United States at the time of our studies. As we are writing this conclusion, home foreclosures have skyrocketed, major companies such as Lehman Brothers have collapsed, and the Dow Jones industrial average lost more points one day in September of 2008 than it did the first day the market opened after 9/11. Needless to say, experts are predicting that the current severe economic recession in the United States will be one of the most devastating in U.S. history. In this changed context, we may find stronger effects for an economic threat in the United States. In fact, we already see signs that in the face of this very significant and increasingly tangible economic threat, the U.S. public is accepting of a greater centralization of power. Our theoretical framework would lead us to expect the public to pin their hopes on individuals seen as outside the sphere of responsibility for this crisis, on individuals with personal experiences in the area of crisis, and on those whose popularity is not suffering already. While we are drafting this conclusion, the U.S. public, by a substantial margin, elected Democratic challenger and first-term senator Barack Obama president of the United States. They have also acquiesced to a significant expansion of government intervention in the economy under the direction of the secretary of the treasury. And the New York City council has granted Mayor Michael Bloomberg, known for his financial acumen and popularity among New Yorkers, the right to run for a previously prohibited third term in that executive office. While neither of these maneuvers has been without controversy, they have nonetheless proceeded.

Not only does the salience and vividness of the threat matter, but existing institutions and norms likely also influence the effects of threat on a given country and its citizens. As another point of comparison outside the scope of our study, the aftermath of the 2000 presidential election in the United States was much less contentious than the aftermath of the 2006 presidential election in Mexico, even though the race was arguably a bit closer in the former case (and was essentially determined by the U.S. Supreme Court, while the electoral tribunal in Mexico deemed that the election was fair). Whereas some groups in the United States protested the outcome, Al Gore accepted the decision of the Court and did not lead any protests. This is in stark contrast to the behavior of López Obrador, who led massive protests after the election. Again, country differences—in this case political norms and institutions—may help explain why the political crisis was much more acute in the Mexican context.

Finally, it may be that institutional context matters broadly in terms of whether the country's political system has experienced stability in its recent history or has experienced, at the opposite end of the spectrum, a near constant state of crisis. As we alluded to before, a constant state of crisis carries a bit of an oxymoronic connotation to it—a crisis is a significant turn away from the status quo. Our research, which compares times of threat to good times, says admittedly little about situations where the status quo is characterized by a continuous stream of repeated and severe negative events. We hope this issue is taken up in future scholarship.

Conclusion

The effects that terrorist threats have on political attitudes, evaluations, and behavior are extensive. We have strong evidence that individuals across two democratic nations employ at least three coping strategies under times of terror threat relative to times of well-being and prosperity. Furthermore, many of these results obtained in experimental settings in which subjects were only exposed to a treatment that was short in duration. The magnitude of the effects we find is likely to be much larger in real scenarios given exposure to repeated information about future threats or in the aftermath of a terrorist attack. While some of these shifts in attitudes, evaluations, and behavior may be the sign of a healthy citizenry that adapts to times of crisis, we hold that on balance these shifts place significant stress on democratic nations.

While we have shed light on individual responses to terrorism, we also hope that we have raised interesting questions for future research. As we mentioned, one question our study cannot answer is how long these effects endure. We also lack significant leverage on a related question: are the stresses put on democracy temporary, or might they have more permanent and lasting effects? Second, we did not look explicitly at how elites might use threats for their own political purposes. Under what conditions might such strategies be effective? In our experiments, we focused on threats removed from any framing by political elites; we only began to discuss the possibility of elite engineering in any detail in this concluding chapter. We further have not examined the factors that might reduce the stress placed on democracies under times of terrorist threat. For example, what role might the media and interest groups play in reminding citizens of democratic values? Will such reminders be effective in the face of terrorist threats? Is the degree of stress related to the institutional context of a given country? Are there other types of threats that might lead to similar strains on democratic nations? And, to raise an issue absent from any earlier discussions: to what extent might we find any of the three coping mechanisms addressed in this project employed in nondemocratic contexts? With respect to the use of our coping strategies, we did not directly assess whether or not people came to feel fewer negative emotions given the use of these strategies of coping with threat. Finally, to return to an issue that has been present all along but not explicitly tested: can we determine conclusively the extent to which the strategies for which we have evidence are purely instrumental, purely psychological, or a mixture of both (as we have tended to argue more often than not)? In conclusion, we hope that we have persuaded the reader of the importance of studying political behavior in times of terrorist threat, convincingly demonstrated the many effects that terrorist threat can have on individuals, and identified numerous paths down which future research in this issue area might travel.

Appendix

Question Wordings and Codings

Note: All questions used on studies in Mexico are presented here in English, as the authors' translations. Original Spanish versions are available upon request.

Chapter 2

1. Worry about Terrorism—All Experiments
    Wording: How worried are you that in the near future there will be terrorist attacks in this country?
        Four-point scale—US04s, MEX06s, US07s
        Seven-point scale—US05s, US05ns, US06s
    Coding: Pooled data rescaled to run from 0 to 1, with higher values indicating more worry.

2. PANAS Battery—US06s, MEX06s, US07s
    Wording: The following scale consists of a number of words and phrases that describe different feelings and emotions. Read each item and then mark the appropriate answer in the space next to that word. Indicate to what extent you are feeling this way right now.
        1. Very slightly or not at all
        2. A little
        3. Moderately
        4. Quite a bit
        5. Extremely
    Individual Items: Afraid, Scared, Nervous, Jittery, Irritable, Hostile,

Guilty, Ashamed, Upset, Distressed, Active, Alert, Attentive,
Determined, Enthusiastic, Excited, Inspired, Interested, Proud,
Strong.

Coding: Four factors derived from principal components factor analysis,
where higher values indicate higher levels of related emotions. (Also
see Web Supplement A, table 2.b.)

3. Worry about the Economy — US05ns, US05s, MEX06s, US07s
   Wording: How worried are you about the current state of the national
   economy?

       Four-point scale — MEX06s, US07s
       Seven-point scale — US05s, US05ns

   Coding: Pooled data rescaled to run from 0 to 1, with higher values
   indicating more worry.

Chapter 3

1. Key Variables from the ANES Panel Study 2000–2004
   A. Social Trust
      Social Distrust 1: Generally speaking, would you say that most people
      can be trusted, or that you can't be too careful in dealing with
      people? (P001475, P025101).

      Social Distrust 2: Do you think most people would try to take advantage
      of you if they got the chance or would they try to be fair? (P001476,
      P025102).

      Social Distrust 3: Would you say that most of the time people try to be
      helpful, or that they are just looking out for themselves? (P001477,
      P025103).

      Coding: All three questions are dichotomous and coded so that "1"
      means distrust.
   B. Neighborhood Trust
      Neighbor Trust 1: Next we have some questions about the people you
      regularly see in your neighborhood. In general, with these people
      in mind, would you say that they are just looking out for themselves
      all of the time, most of the time, some of the time, hardly ever, or
      never? (P001737, P045169)

      Neighbor Trust 2: Would you say those people you see regularly in your
      neighborhood try to take advantage of others all of the time, most
      of the time, some of the time, hardly ever, or never? (P001738,
      P045169)

Neighbor Trust 3: Again, thinking about those people you see in your neighborhood, would you say they treat others with respect all of the time, most of the time, some of the time, hardly ever, or never? (P001739, P045171)

Neighbor Trust 4: Would you say that honest describes the people in your neighborhood extremely well, quite well, not too well, or not well at all? (P001740, P045172).

Coding: All four questions are coded so that higher values indicate more trust. Questions 1–3 are on five-point scales (coded 1–5) and question 4 is on a four-point scale (coded 1–4).

C. Feelings toward Gays

How would you rate [on the feeling thermometer] gay men and lesbians, that is, homosexuals? (P001321, P025067, P045035)

Coding: Scale runs from 0 to 100, where higher values indicate warmer feelings.

D. Spending on Policing the Border

Should federal spending on tightening border security to prevent illegal immigration be increased, decreased, or kept about the same? (P000686, P025118x, P045078)

Coding: Three-point scale (1–3) in which higher values mean spend more.

E. Legal Immigration

Do you think the number of immigrants from foreign countries who are permitted to come to the United States to live should be increased, decreased, or left the same as it is now? A little or a lot? (P000510, P045109)

Coding: Five-point scale (1–5) in which higher values means decrease numbers.

F. Spending on Crime

What about dealing with crime? Should federal spending on dealing with crime be increased, decreased, or kept about the same? (P000684, P025109x, P025109x)

Coding: Three-point scale (1–3) in which higher values mean spend more.

G. Terror Threat

How likely do you think it is that the U.S. will suffer an attack as serious as the ones in New York and Washington sometime in the next twelve months? Would you say very likely, somewhat likely, somewhat unlikely, or very unlikely?

Coding: Four-point scale (1–4), in which higher values mean more likely.

2. Survey Data Controls, ANES Panel Study 2000–2004
   A. Party Identification
      Wording: Generally speaking, do you think of yourself as a Republican, a Democrat, an Independent, or what? Would you call yourself a strong Democrat/Republican or a not very strong Democrat/Republican? Do you think of yourself as closer to the Republican Party or to the Democratic Party?
      Coding: Seven-point scale with higher values indicating a more Republican identification.
   B. Ideology
      Wording: We hear a lot of talk these days about liberals and conservatives. Here is a seven-point scale on which the political views that people might hold are arranged from extremely liberal to extremely conservative. Where would you place yourself on this scale, or haven't you thought much about this?
      Coding: Seven-point scale, where higher values indicate a more conservative ideology.
   C. Education
      Wording: What is the highest grade of school or year of college you have completed? Did you get a high school diploma or pass a high school equivalency test? What is the highest degree that you have earned?
      Coding: Seven-point scale with higher values indicating a higher level of education.
   D. Income
      Wording: Tell me which category best describes your household income in 1999 before taxes. This figure should include salaries, wages, pensions, dividends, interest, and all other income.
      Coding: Twenty-one-point scale with higher values indicating a greater level of income.
   E. Female
      Wording: Gender of respondent
      Coding: Dummy variable coded as a "1" if the respondent is a female and "0" otherwise.
   F. Age
      Coding: Age of respondent
   G. Race and Ethnicity: Asian, Black, Latino, White, Mixed Race
      Wording: What racial or ethnic group best describes you?
      Coding: Dummy variable coded as "1" for each category above.

3. Key Variables, US CCFR, 2006
   A. Torture
      Wording: Most countries have agreed to rules that prohibit torturing prisoners to extract information. Which comes closer to your point of view?
      a. Terrorists pose such an extreme threat that governments should now be allowed to use torture if it may gain information that saves innocent lives.
      b. Rules against torture should be maintained because torture is morally wrong and weakening these rules may lead to the torture of U.S. soldiers who are held prisoner abroad.
      c. Not sure/Decline
      Coding: Dummy variable, where 1 = Option a above.
   B. Terror Threat Indicator
      Wording: Below is a list of possible threats to the vital interest of the United States in the next ten years. For each one, please select whether you see this as a critical threat, an important but not critical threat, or not an important threat at all.
      1. International Terrorism
      Coding: Dummy variable, where 1 = critical threat.

4. Control Variables, U.S. CCFR, 2006
   A. Ideology
      Wording: In general, do you think of yourself as:
      a. Extremely Liberal
      b. Slightly Liberal
      c. Moderate
      d. Slightly Conservative
      e. Extremely Conservative
      f. Not Sure
      Coding: Five-point variable coded such that higher values indicate a more liberal ideology.
   B. Education
      Wording: What is the highest degree or level of education that you have completed?
      Coding: Four-point scale with higher values indicating higher education.
   C. Income
      Wording: What is your household income?
      Coding: Nineteen-point scale with higher values indicating a higher level of income.

D. Female

Wording: Gender of respondent

Coding: Dummy variable coded as a 1 if the respondent is a female and 0 otherwise.

5. Authoritarian Predispositions

A. Child-Rearing Battery — US05ns, US05s, and MEX06s

Wording: We have some questions about the qualities that people think we should try to encourage in children. For each pair of qualities, please mark which one of the two you think is more important for a child to have.

    a. A child obeys his parents v. a child is responsible for his or her own actions

    b. A child has respect for his elders v. a child thinks for him- or herself

    c. A child has good manners v. a child has good sense and sound judgment

Coding: Factor derived from principal components factor analysis, where higher values indicate higher levels of authoritarian predispositions.

B. Word Choice — MEX06s

Wording: For each of the following pairs of words, please indicate which one appeals to you more. Even if both words seem appealing or neither is very appealing, just pick the one that sounds better to you.

    a. obey or question

    b. rules or progress

    c. obedience or curiosity

Coding: Additive index, combined with the child-rearing battery, where higher values indicate higher levels of authoritarian predispositions [see n. in chapter 3 on treatment of missing values].

6. Authoritarian Attitudes (Twelve Items Extracted from the Right Wing Authoritarianism Scale)

Wording: We will now present you with some statements. Please answer the following questions according to the scale below [scale goes from 1 = Strongly Agree, 7 = Strongly Disagree]:

    1. Life imprisonment is justified for certain crimes.

    2. It is important to protect the rights of radicals and deviants in all ways.

    3. There are many radical, immoral people in our country today,

who are trying to ruin it for their own godless purposes, whom the authorities should put out of action.

4. There is no "ONE right way" to live life; everybody has to create his or her own way.

5. Our country needs free thinkers who will have the courage to defy traditional ways, even if this upsets many people.

6. It would be best for everyone if the proper authorities censored magazines so that people could not get their hands on trashy and disgusting material.

7. It is wonderful that young people today have greater freedom to protest against things they don't like, and to make their own "rules" to govern their behavior.

8. What our country really needs, instead of more "civil rights," is a good stiff dose of law and order.

9. Some of the best people in our country are those who are challenging our government, criticizing religion, and ignoring the "normal way" things are supposed to be done.

10. Once our government leaders give us the "go ahead," it will be the duty of every patriotic citizen to help stomp out the rot that is poisoning our country from within.

11. We should treat protesters and radicals with open arms and open minds, since new ideas are often the lifeblood of progressive change.

12. The facts on crime, sexual immorality, and the recent public disorders all show we have to crack down harder on deviant groups and troublemakers if we are going to save our moral standards and preserve law and order.

Coding: Additive index, where higher values indicate greater levels of authoritarian attitudes.

7. Related Preferences (MEX06s)

A. Crime

Wording: Which of the following statements comes closest to your own views?

"In dealing with the problem of street crime, it is important for police to protect the rights of those accused of committing a crime, even if it gets in the way of stopping these crimes."

"In dealing with the problem of street crime, it is important for police to do whatever it takes to stop these crimes, even if this violates the rights of those accused of committing a crime."

Coding: Dummy variable, where 1 = important for police to protect rights.

B. Intolerance Battery

   Wording: With respect to the group you marked above, please answer
   how much you agree or disagree which the statements that follow,
   according to the scale below [scale goes from 1 = Strongly Agree to
   7 = Strongly Disagree]:

   a. Group X should be allowed to make a speech in my city.
   b. Group X should be allowed to protest against the government.
   c. Group X should be allowed to hold a rally.
   d. Group X should be allowed to run for office.
   e. Group X should be allowed to teach in public schools.

   Coding: Additive seven-point scale, where higher values indicate more
   support.

8. Additional Questions in Experiments (Controls)

   A. Ideology (US05ns, US05s, MEX06s)

      Wording: We hear a lot of talk these days about liberals and conserva-
      tives. Here is a seven-point scale on which the political views that
      people might hold are arranged from extremely liberal to extremely
      conservative. Where would you place yourself on this scale, or
      haven't you thought much about this?

      Coding: Seven-point scale, where higher values indicate a more conser-
      vative ideology.

   B. Education (US05ns)

      Coding: Nine-point scale where higher values indicate more education.

   C. Party Identification (MEX06s)

      Wording: In general, do you consider yourself a priísta, panista, or
      perredista?

      Coding: A series of dummy variables for each party, with Other and
      None combined as the baseline (comparison) category.

   D. Political Interest (MEX06s)

      Wording: How interested are you in national politics?

      Coding: Three-point scale, where higher values mean more interest.

Chapter 4
Perceptions of Leadership Analyses

1. Leadership Question (US04s, US06s, and ANES Panel Study)

   Wording: Think about Y. In your opinion, does the phrase "he provides
   strong leadership," describe Y extremely well, quite well, not too
   well, or not at all?

Coding: Four point scale where higher values indicate greater perceptions of strong leadership.

2. Other Trait Questions
   A. Moral
      Wording: In your opinion, does the phrase, "he is moral," describe Person Y extremely well, quite well, not too well, or not at all?
      Coding: Four point scale where higher values indicate greater perceptions of "he is moral."
   B. Intelligent
      Wording: In your opinion, does the phrase, "he is intelligent," describe Person Y extremely well, quite well, not too well, or not at all?
      Coding: Four point scale where higher values indicate greater perceptions of "he is intelligent."
   C. Cares about People
      Wording: In your opinion, does the phrase, "he really cares about people like you," describe Person Y extremely well, quite well, not too well, or not at all?
      Coding: Four-point scale where higher values indicate greater perceptions of cares about people.
   D. Honest
      Wording: In your opinion, does the phrase, "he is honest," describe Person Y extremely well, quite well, not too well, or not at all?
      Coding: Four-point scale where higher values indicate greater perceptions of "he is honest."

3. Additional Measures—Experiments
   A. Party Identification (US04s, US06s)
      Wording: Generally speaking, do you think of yourself as a Republican, a Democrat, an Independent, or what?
      Coding: Dummy variables, where Independent or Other response is the baseline (comparison) category.
   B. Female (US04s)
      Wording: What is your gender?
      Coding: Dummy variable where 1 = female.
   C. Political Interest (US06s)
      Wording: Same as chapter 3, section 8, D.
      Coding: 3-point scale, where higher values mean more interest.
   D. Ideology (US06s)
      Wording: Same as chapter 3, section 8.A.

Coding: Seven-point scale, where higher values indicate a more conservative ideology.

4. Controls—ANES Panel Study
   Same as chapter 3, section 2, with additional measures/changes below.
   A. Partisan Identification
      Wording: Same as chapter 3, section 2.A.
      Coding: Dummy variables, where Independent or Other response is the baseline (comparison) category.
   B. Ideology
   Same as chapter 4, section 3.D, above.

Vote Choice Analyses

5. Vote Choice
   A. Vote Bush (US04s)
      Wording: Who do you think you will vote for in the election for president this coming November?
      Coding: Dummy Variable, 1 = Vote for Bush, 0 otherwise.
   B. Vote Schwarzenegger (US06s)
      Wording: Who do you think you will vote for in the election for governor this coming November?
      Coding: Dummy Variable, 1 = Vote for Schwarzenegger, 0 otherwise.
   C. Vote Bush, ANES Panel Data
      Wording: How about the election for president? Did you vote for a candidate for PRESIDENT? Who did you vote for?
      Coding: Dummy Variable, 1 = Vote for Bush, 0 otherwise.

6. Additional Experiment Measures
   A. Partisan Identification (US04s and US06s)
      Wording: Generally speaking, do you think of yourself as a Republican, a Democrat, an Independent, or what? Would you call yourself a strong Democrat/Republican or a not very strong Democrat/Republican? Do you think of yourself as closer to the Republican Party or to the Democratic Party?
      Coding: Seven-point scale with higher values indicating a more Republican identification.
   B. Issues (US04s)
      Wording: Would you say that compared to one year ago, the economy has gotten better, stayed the same, or gotten worse?

Wording: Would you say that compared to one year ago, the nation's security has gotten better, stayed the same, or gotten worse?

Wording: Some people think the government should provide fewer services, even in areas such as health and education in order to reduce spending. Still others feel it is important for the government to provide many more services even if it means an increase in spending. How about you? On a scale of 1 to 7, where a 1 indicates that the government should provide fewer services and a 7 indicates that government should provide many more services, where would you place yourself, or haven't you thought much about this? 8 = haven't thought much about this.

Wording: Some people believe we should spend much less money for defense. Others feel that defense spending should be greatly increased. How about you? On a scale where a 1 indicates spending much less on defense and a 7 indicates spending more, where would you place yourself, or haven't you thought much about this? 8 = haven't thought much about this.

Coding: Factor derived from principal components factor analysis, where higher values indicate higher levels of conservative opinions and better evaluations.

C. Issues (US06s)

Wording: Thinking about the next twelve months, do you expect California's security to get much better, better, somewhat better, stay about the same, or get somewhat worse, worse, or much worse?

Wording: Thinking about the next twelve months, do you expect California's economy to get much better, better, somewhat better, stay about the same, or get somewhat worse, worse, or much worse?

Wording: Some people believe California should spend much less money for homeland security. Others feel that homeland security spending should be greatly increased. How about you? On a scale where a 1 indicates spending much less on homeland security and a 7 indicates spending more, where would you place yourself, or haven't you thought much about this?

Wording: Some people think the state government should provide fewer services, even in areas such as health and education in order to reduce spending. Still others feel it is important for the state government to provide many more services even if it means an increase in spending. How about you? On a scale of 1 to 7, where a 1 indicates that the state government should provide fewer services and a 7 indicates that state government should provide many more services, where would you place yourself, or haven't you thought much about this?

Coding: Factor derived from principal components factor analysis, where higher values indicate higher levels of conservative opinions and better evaluations.

Chapter 5
Effect of Threat on Charisma

1. Charisma Battery (US04s, US05ns, MEX06s, Mexico Survey)

   Wording: Considering Y, how in agreement or disagreement are you with the following?

   Please choose from the following answer choices, for each statement [scale is agree/disagree, 1-6 for US04s, US05ns, and MEX06s; and 1-4 for Mexico Survey]:
   - Instills pride in being associated with him.
   - Goes beyond his own self-interest for the good of the group.
   - His actions build my respect for him.
   - Displays a sense of power and confidence.
   - Talks to us about his most important values and beliefs.
   - Specifies the importance of having a strong sense of purpose.
   - Considers the moral and ethical consequences of his decisions.
   - Emphasizes the importance of having a collective sense of mission.
   - Talks optimistically about the future.
   - Talks enthusiastically about what needs to be accomplished.
   - Articulates a compelling vision of the future.
   - Expresses his confidence that we will achieve our goals.

   Coding: Additive scale, where higher values indicate greater perceptions of charisma.

2. Experiments-Control Measures

   A. US04s: Female and Partisan Dummies identified in chapter 4.

   B. US05ns: Education and Political Information identified in chapter 2.

   C. MEX06s: Political Interest, Ideology, and Partisan Dummies identified in chapter 3.

3. Mexico CIDE Survey—Threat and Control Measures

   A. Economy (P29)

   Wording: Thinking about Mexico's economic situation these days, would you say that the economic situation is very good, good, bad, or very bad?

Coding: Five-point scale, where higher values mean worse evaluations.

B. Election (P76)

Wording: In some countries, people think that their elections are clean. In others countries, that the elections are not clean. Using a scale where 1 means that the elections were NOT clean and 5 that they WERE clean, where would you place the last elections?

Coding: Five-point scale, where higher values mean greater perceptions of fraud.

C. Poverty (P35_5; asked of half the sample only)

Wording: In the last year, would you say that poverty has increased or diminished?

Coding: Three-point scale, where higher values mean increased.

D. Unemployment (P35_1; asked of half the sample only)

Wording: In the last year, would you say that unemployment has increased or diminished?

Coding: Three-point scale, where higher values mean increased.

E. Public Security (P2, Most Important Problem Question)

Wording: Thinking of the country in general, what do you believe is the most important political problem confronting Mexico these days?

Coding: Dummy variable, coded "1" if respondent mentioned a public security issue, such as insecurity, political assassinations, drug trafficking, violence, kidnappings, and guerrilla conflict, as one of the most important problem facing Mexico.

F. Ideology

Wording: Using the scale that appears on the card (showed to respondent), where 0 means liberal and 10 conservative, where would you place yourself?

Coding: Eleven-point scale, where higher values mean more conservative.

G. Efficacy (P5)

Wording: Some people think that their vote does not influence what happens in the country. Others think the opposite. Using a scale where 1 is that the vote does NOT influence much of what happens in the country and 5 indicates that the vote makes a big difference, where would you place yourself?

Coding: Five-point scale, where higher values indicate greater efficacy.

H. Church (PS24)

Wording: With what frequency do you attend church or temple? [only asked of those who gave a denomination, in response to a previous question]

Coding: Six-point scale, where higher values indicate greater attendance.

I. Age (PS2)

    Wording: How old are you?

    Coding: Ordinal variable.

J. Education (PS3)

    Wording: What is the highest level of education that you completed?

    Coding: Nine-point scale, where higher values mean more education.

K. Male (PS1)

    Wording: Interview-coded.

    Coding: Dummy variable where "1" indicates male.

L. Union (PS11)

    Wording: Do you belong to a union, labor organization, or labor association?

    Coding: Dummy variable coded "1" if the respondent answers yes.

M. Government Employee (govemp) (PS9)

    Wording: In what type of institution, organization, or business do you work?

    Coding: Dummy variable coded "1" if respondent selected 1 = Government (Federal, State, or Municipal)

N. Indigenous / White (PS22)

    Coding: Racial/ethnicity dummy variables; baseline is mestizo

O. Region (Edo)

    Coding: Dummy variables for North, South, Center, CenterWest, Mexico City.

P. Party ID (P20, P20A_1, P20a_2, P20a_3)

    Wording: Independent of which party you voted for in the past election, in general, do you sympathize with a particular political party? If "1" (yes) . . . which party?

    Coding: Dummy variables for the three main parties, with Other and None combined as the baseline (comparison) category.

Protecting and Assisting Charismatic Leaders

4. Blame Attribution

    A. Failures in Iraq, US04s

        Wording: Recent reports from the Senate intelligence committee indicate that the CIA provided faulty information on the presence of weapons of mass destruction in Iraq, which was one of Bush's main justifications for the war. On scale from 1 to 5, where 5 is very responsible and 1 is not at all responsible, to what extent do you think that President Bush is responsible for U.S. failures in Iraq?

Coding: Five-point scale, where higher values indicate more blame.

B. Blame Attribution, US05ns and US05s

Wording:

    a. In your opinion, which of the following actors is MOST responsible for current problems in Iraq?

    b. In your opinion, which of the following actors is MOST responsible for current problems in the U.S. economy?

    c. In your opinion, which of the following actors is MOST responsible for current problems with the environment in the U.S.?

    d. Recently credible reports have confirmed that government sources leaked information that compromised a CIA agent's identity, endangering the agent and her family. In your opinion, which of the following actors is MOST responsible for this scandal?

    e. In your opinion, which of the following actors is MOST responsible for current weaknesses in Homeland Security?

    f. In your opinion, which of the following actors is MOST responsible for failures associated with the response to Hurricane Katrina? [only asked in US05s]

Coding: For each question, a dummy variable assigns a value of "1" to answers of "Bush."

5. Self-Sacrifice

A. Campaign Related Activities, US04s

Wording: Please indicate which of the following activities (you can check as few as zero and as many as four) you would be willing to do for candidate George W. Bush.

    a. Make phone calls to get out the vote for this candidate.

    b. Attend a rally organized for this candidate.

    c. Take time to drive supporters of this candidate to the polls on election day.

    d. Contribute money to this candidate's campaign.

Coding: Additive scale (a count of yes responses), where higher values mean more sacrifice.

B. Self-Sacrifice on Policies, US05ns and US05s

Wording: Please indicate your level of support for the following policy changes on behalf of the country [scale goes from 1 = Strongly Oppose to 7 = Strongly Support]:

    a. A personal income tax increase for Homeland Security.

    b. A personal income tax increase for the mission in Iraq.

    c. A personal income tax increase for Social Security.

    d. A personal income tax increase for welfare programs.

    e. A personal income tax increase for education.

    f. A personal income tax increase for the environment.

Coding: For each variable, a seven-point scale where higher values indicate more support.

6. Preferences over a Strong Executive (MEX06 and US07s)

    A. Strong Executive

    Wording: With which phrase do you most agree: the president of the republic should be more powerful than the congress or the congress should be more powerful than the president?

    Coding: A dummy variable where "1" indicates president should be more powerful.

    B. Presidential Powers

    Wording: I am going to read you some actions that the president might take in foreign policy matters. Please tell me for each option, what is better, that the president takes action without needing congressional approval or that Congress gives its approval before the president acts.

       · Declaring war

       · Negotiating treaties and international agreements

       · Traveling abroad

       · Make important decisions in international organizations

    Coding: A count of how many activities the president should be able to do without congressional approval.

Chapter 6

1. Terror Threat Indicator-Mexico and U.S. Surveys

    A. Mexico CCFR Survey 2004 and 2006

    Wording: I am going to read you a list of things that may or may not affect Mexico's most important interests in the next ten years. Tell me if you consider (option) as a grave threat, an important but not grave threat, or a threat of little importance for Mexico.

       1. International Terrorism

    Coding: Dummy variable, where "1" = grave threat.

B. U.S. CCFR Survey 2004 and 2006
Same as for chapter 3, section 3.B.

2. Active in World Affairs—U.S. CCFR Survey 2004 and 2006, Mexico
CCFR Survey 2004 and 2006, US07s and MEX06s
> *Wording:* Do you think it will be best for the future of the country if we
> take an active part in world affairs or if we stay out of world affairs?
> *Coding:* Dummy variable coded as a "1" if respondents say it is best for
> their country to be "active in world affairs."

3. Controls for U.S. CCFR Survey 2004 and 2006
Same as chapter 3, section 4.

4. Controls for Mexico CCFR Survey 2004 and 2006
A. Party Identification
> *Wording:* Independently of the party you voted for, do you normally
> consider yourself to be a PANista, PRIista, PRDista, Verde Ecolo-
> gista, o some other party?
> *Coding:* Dummy variables equal to "1" for PAN, PRI, and PRD, and "0"
> otherwise.

B. Education
> *Wording:* What is the highest level of education that you have com-
> pleted?
> *Coding:* Nine-point scale with higher values indicating a higher level of
> education.

C. Income
> *Wording:* Adding all the earnings (net) of the members of your house-
> hold that work, what is your family's income range?
> *Coding:* Nine-point scale with higher values indicating a higher level of
> income.

D. Female
> *Wording:* Gender of respondent.
> *Coding:* Dummy variable coded as a "1" if the respondent is a female and
> "0" otherwise.

5. Security Engagement
A. UN Peacekeeping (Mexico CCFR Survey 2004 and 2006)
> *Wording:* If the United Nations asks member countries to send a
> military or police peacekeeping force to some part of the world,
> what are known as "blue helmets," do you think that Mexico should
> participate in the peacekeeping force or should it leave this type of
> activity to other countries?

Coding: Dummy variable coded as a "1" if respondent thinks that Mexico should participate and "0" otherwise.

B. UN Peacekeeping (U.S. CCFR Survey 2004 and 2006)

Wording: Thinking about specific steps that could be taken to strengthen the United Nations, here are some options that have been proposed. For each one, select if you would favor or oppose this step. Having a standing UN peacekeeping force selected, trained and commanded by the United Nations.

Coding: Dummy variable coded as a "1" if respondents favors having a standing UN force and "0" otherwise.

C. UN Peacekeeping (US07s and MEX06s)

Wording: If the United Nations asks member countries to participate in an international peacekeeping force being sent to some parts of the world, to what extent do you agree or disagree that Mexico [the U.S.] should participate in this kind of peacekeeping force?

Coding: Seven-point scale in which higher values mean more willingness to engage in this cooperative, security-related endeavor.

D. Unilateral Foreign Policy (US06s)

Wording: Some people believe the United States should solve international problems by using diplomacy and other forms of international pressure and use military force only if absolutely necessary. Others believe diplomacy and pressure often fail and the U.S. must be ready to use military force. How about you? On a scale of 1 to 7, where a 1 indicates that we should exhaust diplomacy and a 7 indicates that we should be ready to use military force, where would you place yourself, or haven't you thought much about this?

Coding: Seven-point scale, higher values mean use military force.

Note: The coding for the control variables of ideology and interest were identified in chapter 4. Higher values indicate more conservative and more interested.

6. Antiterrorism Engagement

A. Support a Military Campaign (US CCFR Survey 2004 and 2006)

Wording: Do you think that the UN Security Council should or should not have the right to authorize the use of military force for each of the following purposes: To stop a country from supporting terrorist groups.

Coding: Dummy variable coded as a "1" should have the right to authorize troops and "0" otherwise.

B. Terrorism Policy Battery (US07s and MEX06s)

Wording: In order to combat international terrorism, do you support or oppose the following policies:

- Support tougher international laws against countries that harbor terrorists
- Share intelligence information with the United States [Mexico]
- Contribute to a multi-country military campaign against a terrorist target

Coding: Seven-point scale where higher values on both measures indicate support for fighting terrorism in these ways.

7. Protection at Home—Control Movement of People and Goods
   A. Control People (Mexico CCFR 2004 and 2006)

   Wording: In order to combat international terrorism, do you believe that Mexico should or should not increase the entry and exit requirements on people from other countries?

   Coding: Dummy variable coded as a "1" if respondents supported increasing entry and exit requirements and "0" otherwise.

   B. Control Goods (Mexico CCFR 2004 and 2006)

   Wording: In order to combat international terrorism, do you believe that Mexico should or should not increase controls on the movement of goods across its borders and into its ports and airports?

   Coding: Dummy variable coded as a "1" if respondents supported controlling the movement of goods and "0" otherwise.

   C. Immigration #1 (US CCFR Survey 2004 and 2006)

   Wording: Below is a list of possible foreign policy goals that the United States might have. For each one please select whether you think that it should be a very important foreign policy goal of the United States, a somewhat important foreign policy goal, or not an important goal at all? Controlling and reducing illegal immigration.

   Coding: Three-point variable coded such that higher values indicate greater support for controlling immigration.

   D. Immigration #2 (US CCFR Survey 2004 and 2006)

   Wording: Should legal immigration into the United States be kept at its present level, increased, or decreased?

   Coding: Three-point variable coded such that higher values indicate greater support for decreasing immigration.

   E. Protect-at-Home Battery (US07s and MEX06s)

   Wording: In order to combat international terrorism, do you support or oppose the following policies:

Increase controls on the movement of goods through Mexico's [U.S.'] border, ports, and airports

Increase Mexico's [U.S.'] entrance and exit requirements for people from other countries

Coding: Seven-point scale where higher values on both measures indicate a stronger preference for controlling and protecting the homefront in these ways.

8. Other Protect-at-Home Measures

A. Civil Liberties — Security Trade-off (US05ns, US05s)

Wording: Some people think it is important to protect the nation's security even if it means giving up some civil liberties, like having to carry a national identification card or having phone calls monitored. Others feel that we should preserve our civil liberties above all, even if it means risking the nation's security. How about you? On a scale of 1 to 7, where a 1 indicates that we should protect the nation's security at all costs and a 7 indicates that we should protect civil liberties at all costs, where would you place yourself, or haven't you thought much about this? 8 = haven't thought much about this.

Coding: Seven-point scale, where higher values indicate a preference for more security.

Note: The control variables for these studies were identified in chapter 3.

B. Homeland Security Spending (US05ns, US05s, US06s)

Wording: Some people believe we should spend much less money for homeland security. Others feel that homeland security spending should be greatly increased. How about you? On a scale where a 1 indicates spending much less on homeland security and a 7 indicates spending more, where would you place yourself, or haven't you thought much about this? 8 = haven't thought much about this.

Coding: Seven-point scale, where higher values indicate a preference for spending more.

Note: The control variables for these studies were identified in chapter 3.

C. Homeland Security Spending (ANES Panel Study)

Wording: Should federal spending on homeland security be increased, decreased, or kept about the same?

Coding: Four-point scale with higher values indicating support for increased spending.

Note: The coding for the control variables in the ANES panel study were identified in chapter 3.

D. Homeland Security Tax (US05ns and US05s)

    Wording: Please indicate your level of support for the following policy changes on behalf of the country [scale goes from 1 = Strongly Oppose to 7 = Strongly Support]: A personal income tax increase for Homeland Security.

    Coding: Seven-point scale where higher values indicate more support.

Notes

For Web Supplements A, B, and C, see http://www.press.uchicago.edu/books/merolla.

Introduction

1. Navy Department Library, "A Navy Department Library Research Guide," http://www.history.navy.mil/library/guides/terrorism.htm#definition (accessed May 28, 2008).

2. International incidents include events in which the perpetrators go abroad to strike their targets, select domestic targets associated with a foreign state, or create an international incident by attacking airline passengers or equipment. The latest year of data available is 2006.

3. On the World Trade Center attack, see "Man Indicted in Trade Center Attack," *Washington Post*, April 9, 1993, A6.

4. "September 11: For the Record," *USA Today Online*, September 11, 2002, http://www.usatoday.com/news/sept11/2002-09-10-for-the-record_x.htm (accessed November 30, 2007); "Low Birth Weights Linked to 9/11," *BBC News Online*, October 10, 2007, http://news.bbc.co.uk/2/hi/health/7037842.stm (accessed November 30, 2007); Dan Barry, "A Nation Challenged: The Mood; Denying Fear, but Embracing Nagging Doubts," *New York Times*, October 9, 2001, Lexis-Nexis Academic: Major U.S. and World Publications (accessed November 17, 2007); Suleman Din, "New Yorkers Left Fearful and Cynical," November 12, 2001, *The Gazette*, Lexis-Nexis Academic: Major U.S. and World Publications (accessed November 17, 2007); Robin Toner and Marjorie Connelly, "9/11 Polls Find Lingering Fears in New York City," *New York Times*, September 7, 2006, Lexis-Nexis Academic: Major U.S. and World Publications (accessed November 17, 2007).

5. Survey data collected by various organizations from September of 2002 to August of 2004 show that the percent of individuals who were "somewhat worried" stayed fairly constant between about 40 and 50%. The percent of individuals who were "very worried" fluctuated more, but was still high, ranging from about 15 to 30%.

Time series data containing evaluations of the likelihood of an attack on U.S. soil in the coming weeks are available from September of 2001 to July of 2007. The percent who thought an attack was very likely hovers around 15%, with a peak in 2001 of 41%. The percent who thought an attack was somewhat likely fluctuated between lows of 30% and highs of 50% throughout the series.

6. These are nonrival strategies, meaning that an individual might select just one of them or, just as easily, a combination.

7. Question wording varies across survey organizations. Some studies ask about Arabs and/or Arab Americans, while others ask about Muslims and Muslim Americans. The former set of labels refers to an ethnicity, while the latter references a religious group.

8. These are results from a *Newsweek* poll in July of 2007.

9. Gallup Poll, "Terrorism in the United States," 2007, http://www.galluppoll.com/content/default.aspx?ci=4909 (accessed August 4, 2007).

10. Sources for these media stories and quotes include the following: Greg Roberts and Lee Glendinning, "Muslims Try to Quell Anger after Mosque Destroyed," September 24, 2001, *Sydney Morning Herald*, and Elizabeth Judge, "Islamic School Forced to Close after Parents and Teachers Are Abused," September 14, 2001, *The Times*, both accessed from Lexis-Nexis Academic: Major U.S. and World Publications, November 17, 2007.

11. FBI data on anti-Islamic hate incidents is found at http://www.fbi.gov/ucr/hc2005/abouthc.htm (accessed October 16, 2007).

12. The results for the Patriot Act and wiretapping are from Gallup data in 2005 and 2006.

13. Order from President Lincoln to General Winfield Scott. April 27, 1861.

14. In looking at specific emotions, Valentino et al. (2006) find that anger makes people more likely to participate, though they do not deny a role for anxiety or enthusiasm. Radcliff (1992) does not examine emotions directly, but does show that a specific type of threat, economic decline, can increase participation (principally in developing countries).

15. Such a process of denying rights to certain groups has certainly occurred if we look back to examples of war in U.S. history (we need only think of Japanese internment camps). These rights have been reinstated after the threat recedes.

Chapter 1

1. These definitions are taken from *Merriam-Webster Online*, http://www.merriam-webster.com (accessed July 3, 2007).

2. Harris (reported in Mueller 2006, 2) has calculated the average person's life-long odds of being killed by an international terrorist attack, in the post-9/11 world, as roughly equivalent to the odds of being killed by an extraterrestrial rock hitting the earth's surface. Yet citizens in today's world appear much more concerned about the former than the latter.

3. And, in fact, surveys conducted in the days and months post-9/11 substantiate that those in the area around New York City were more likely to report symptoms consistent with posttraumatic stress disorder and/or general stress (Schlenger et al. 2002; Schuster et al. 2001).

4. On how intentionality, morality, and other factors affect how the public per-

ceives risk, see, for example, the discussion in Rogers et al. (2007) and the work cited within. With respect to elite engineering, Mueller (2006) argues that various special interests and political actors benefiting from counterterrorism rhetoric and efforts contribute to exaggerations of the terrorist threat (but see Allison 2004).

5. Research shows that the experience of a terrorist attack causes an increase in anxiety even among those not geographically proximate to the event. Schuster et al. (2001) analyze data from a national survey fielded in the week following 9/11; they report that 44% of respondents experienced "at least one of five substantial stress symptoms" after the event.

6. Lazarus (1991a, 1991b) has identified a battery of negative emotions, including anger, fear, shame, sadness, jealousy, and disgust. While we do not address it specifically, collective crises might also evoke feelings of sadness, particularly when the losses associated with such crises are made salient. Shame and jealousy seem less likely to arise in times of collective crises; however, we cannot *a priori* rule out these potential emotional responses.

7. We limit our focus to coping strategies with direct political relevance. Other strategies might be employed regardless of the level of crisis. For example, an afternoon shopping spree and drowning one's sorrow in a bottle of good wine might be considered relevant coping techniques for individual-level crises; in fact, scholarship has shown that commercial activity and alcohol consumption increased among certain segments of the population post-9/11 (see the discussion in Pyszczynski, Solomon, and Greenberg 2002).

8. "President Discusses War on Terrorism in Address to Nation," World Congress Center, Atlanta, Georgia on November 8, 2001, http://www.whitehouse.gov/news/releases/2001/11/20011108-13.html (accessed July 2, 2008).

9. Trust in the national government may instead increase given that terrorism is perceived as an external threat and so individuals rally around the incumbent leaders.

10. We explicitly fold the notion of intolerance under the general umbrella of authoritarianism, while recognizing that studies of both intolerance and tolerance often treat these phenomena as distinct from each other and broader concepts (for excellent reviews of the literature on tolerance and intolerance, see Gibson 2006, 2007).

11. See also Rokeach (1960), who argues that threatening environmental conditions can increase anxiety, which in turn can increase expressed dogmatism.

12. See, for example, aggregate work by Doty, Peterson, and Winter (1991), Jorgenson (1975), and Sales (1972, 1973), among others. On survey data, see for example Altemeyer (1988) and Sales and Friend (1973).

13. This conception of authoritarianism, which draws heavily from Feldman and Stenner (1997) and Stenner (2005), is somewhat narrower than operationalizations such as that advanced by Altemeyer (1988), which combines predispositions and attitudes. For example, in his measures of authoritarianism, Altemeyer (1988) includes tendencies toward conventionalism or protection of traditional values, ideas, and practices. At the same time, our conception of authoritarianism is relatively broad in a different sense, in that we assume that it can be manifest (and accordingly examine it) as both a stable personality trait and expressed opinions and behavior. The notion that there exist authoritarian predispositions, in the works cited here, and in our own work is greatly inspired by classic work on the authoritarian personality by Adorno et al. (1950).

14. For example, Feldman and Stenner (1997) and Stenner (2005) use survey data from multiple sources to document how, across different types of threat, individuals high in authoritarian predispositions are relatively more likely to express authoritarian attitudes. This research further suggests that not only do those predisposed toward authoritarianism become more authoritarian, but those predisposed toward libertarian (nonauthoritarian) ways become more liberal in the face of threat. However, Hetherington and Weiler (forthcoming) turn this argument on its head and claim that it is those with more liberal dispositions who become more authoritarian in times of threat and then return to that less authoritarian baseline once the threat subsides. They find support for their arguments looking at three measures of threat (gay rights, immigration, and response to terrorism).

15. At the individual level, issue-based voting is conditioned by certainty, political sophistication, interest, media exposure, trust, and risk propensity (e.g., Alvarez 1997; Gomez and Wilson 2001; Krause 1997; Morgenstern and Zechmeister 2001; Mutz 1992; Sniderman, Brody, and Tetlock 1991). At the contextual level, issue-based voting is conditioned by the salience of issues, the intensity of the campaign, whether candidates offer clearly distinct choices, and the presence of institutions that clarify decision-making responsibility for the voter (e.g., Abramson, Aldrich, and Rohde 2002; Anderson 2000; Cheibub and Przeworski 1999; Kahn and Kenney 1997; Nie, Verba, and Petrocik 1976; Page and Brody 1972; Pomper 1972; Powell and Whitten 1993).

16. These studies find that less sophisticated voters rely more on personal factors (Glass 1985; Miller, Wattenberg, and Malanchuk 1986) and less on issue-based considerations compared to high sophisticates (Aldrich, Gronke, and Grynaviski 2003; Glass 1985).

17. Prospect theory also provides reason to believe that, in crisis conditions, voters will place greater than usual weight on candidate traits. This theory holds that in the context of losses/crises (in contrast to contexts of gain/prosperity), individuals will be more inclined to be risk acceptant (Kahneman and Tversky 1979); they might, then, be willing to discount predispositions (such as party identification) in favor of new information. Empirically, there is evidence suggesting that, in times of crisis, individuals place relatively greater weight on leadership traits than on standard vote choice inputs (see, for example, work on *Fujimorismo* by Roberts 1995; Roberts and Arce 1998; and work on *Chavismo* by Weyland 2003).

18. This, of course, places charismatic leaders who arise in times of crisis in something of a bind. If they resolve the crisis, their image may suffer as their once-elevated status is returned to normal. If they fail to resolve the crisis, eventually, individuals may withdraw support. One creative solution that some political entrepreneurs have discovered is to "invent" new crises once the original crisis is resolved. It is an open question just how long such a strategy can be pursued before citizens withdraw the protective Teflon shield.

19. Other scholars argue and find that charismatic leaders are perceived as providing service to their followers, which becomes inspiring to followers and induces them to serve their organization (see Bligh, Kohles, and Meindl 2004; House, Spangler, and Woycke 1991; Kirkpatrick and Locke 1996; Shamir, Zakay, Breinin, and Popper 1998).

20. By self-sacrificial behavior, we mean behaviors traditionally associated with col-

lective action problems. It is often collectively rational, but not individually rational, for individuals to provide service to the collective.

21. Dana Blanton, "01/12/06 Fox News Poll: Homeland Security and Wiretapping," January 12, 2006, www.foxnews.com (accessed December 18, 2008).

22. In these cases, citizens ceded even greater authority to the executive. For example, Lincoln suspended the writ of habeas corpus during the Civil War and authorized the use of military tribunals, all before Congress had acted. During World War II FDR authorized the internment of Japanese citizens and noncitizens living on the West Coast.

23. While most scholars focus on the political leaders and institutional settings in which these phenomena arise, few studies investigate the degree to which citizens support, and even call for, such shifting of power in times of crisis. Yet national plebiscites supporting many of these institutional rearrangements, not to mention the election and re-election of these leaders, strongly suggests that the public mood becomes increasingly supportive of a centralized, strong executive in times of crisis.

24. Sandler (2005) labels the first a defensive strategy. Some of what we label "engage abroad" overlaps with his discussion of proactive policies, such as sharing intelligence or freezing terrorist assets.

25. In fact, such international cooperation on the terrorism issue is not unique to the post 9/11 world; rather, it has been a staple of U.S. antiterror policy. As Crenshaw (2003) points out: "International cooperation, whether bilateral or multilateral, regional or global, has been a centerpiece of American counterterrorism policy since the early 1970s. Although less visible, the pursuit of cooperation in international politics has become much more common than the unilateral resort to military force. . . . There is general agreement [in the literature] that cooperation is necessary and desirable in combating terrorism" (18).

26. Studies showing that Americans are more likely to support overseas military action as the perceived threat posed by a foreign aggressor increases include Herrmann and Tetlock (1999), Jentleson (1992), and, Jentleson and Britton (1998). While many of these studies focus on one point in time, Chanley (1999) using a time-series design finds that support for militant internationalism increases as people perceive military issues as more important. This relationship between increased threat and support for militant action has also been found in other countries, such as Israel (Arian 1989; Friedland and Merari 1985; Gordon and Arian 2001). It is relevant to point out that international cooperation is found to be less likely when military issues are perceived as the most important problems. For instance, Chanley's time-series analysis of public opinion data (1999) showed that cooperative internationalism (referred to as "general internationalism") is less likely when security is an issue.

27. TMT proponents might say that their stimuli capture the key feature of the environment we are interested in, specifically fear of mortality. However, as indicated here, the context we present to our subjects is richer than that studied by scholars of TMT; it is intended to elicit emotional responses, sociotropic as well as egoistic concerns, and anxiety with respect to an imminent, not a distant future or past, event. As also noted in the text, but worth repeating here, these distinctions are important in part because these other aspects of threat (e.g., emotional responses that are not treated by TMT scholars) are present in other threatening situations. This suggests the possibility that terrorism shares same fundamental similarities to

other threat conditions and individual reactions to these threats may reflect these similarities.

28. Note that we do not directly test whether the coping strategies have the presumed effects with respect to allaying anxiety, decreasing negative feelings, and restoring positive emotions. While we test (in selected cases) for shifts in emotions given exposure to the threat, we do not directly test whether the use of the coping strategies is responsible for these changed feelings. We believe this is a fruitful area for future research and we return to this issue in the book's conclusion.

Chapter 2

1. This discussion is drawn from a section of an article we coauthored with Laura B. Stephenson, "La Aplicación de los Métodos Experimentales en el Estudio de los Atajos Informativos en México." *Política y Gobierno* 14, no. 1 (2007): 117–42. Some segments of the discussion are further drawn from an article coauthored with Cindy D. Kam and Jennifer R. Wilking, "Beyond the 'Narrow Database': Another Convenience Sample for Experimental Research," *Political Behavior* 29, no. 4 (2007): 415–40.

2. It is worth reminding critics of experiments who harp on issues of generalizability of a key fact: all observation-based studies are subject to the concern that inferences based on a particular sample of individuals may not translate across other people, contexts, and/or time. This point is eloquently made in work by Morton and Williams (2006) and a gentle reminder of the point is raised in Kam, Wilking, and Zechmeister (2007).

3. An alternative to this between-subjects design would be a pre-test/post-test design. This would entail first asking subjects the key variables of interest, exposing them to a treatment, and then in a post-test measuring the key variables of interest again. One would then see if the treatment "worked" by determining whether subjects' responses shifted upon exposure to the different treatments.

4. Our research subjects were debriefed after each study and were told that the information they were presented with was created by the researchers for the purpose of the study, drawing on mostly real (but not entirely real) information. So, for example, in our 2004 study, we created a sentence stating "U.S. security officials are bracing for a series of attacks at least twice this magnitude, and likely greater." The CIA did not directly issue a warning that "al Qaeda has people in the United States on the verge of mounting a large-scale terrorist attack." However, various news sources reported on the threat of large-scale future attacks.

5. An example is provided by Nelson and Oxley's 1999 study of issue framing (among student subjects), in which they vary several components of the treatment (photograph, headline, quotations within the text) across two groups (e.g., environmental frame vs. economic frame). Nelson and Oxley argue that this type of approach is justified by a desire to increase external validity: "we have opted for greater experimental impact at the expense of some precision" (1046). The decision to avoid equivalent wording and content has two purposes in our study: first, to increase external validity by mirroring actual news stories; second, to insure that those receiving the Good Times condition were not primed to consider terrorist threat (which a treatment specifically discussing a lack of terrorist threat runs the risk of doing).

6. We used a series of focus groups to pretest the audiovisual presentations and made some minor changes as a result, prior to fielding the versions described here.

The pilot tests helped confirm that individuals reacted to the images and narration in the expected way, for example viewing the Terror Threat presentation as anxiety-provoking while perceiving the images and information in the Good Times audiovisual as positive and uplifting.

7. In order to present the news articles in as convincing a format as possible, we typically included conventional-looking bylines (e.g., Andrew Tardaca, Times Staff Writer, DATE) and conventional-looking Web links to the supposed article.

8. We also collected data on a levee threat in the study fielded during California's 2006 gubernatorial election. We do not explicitly examine these data in this work because we did not find any significant effects on the dependent variables we are interested in. The signs were often in the expected direction for leadership evaluations (negative), but were not statistically reliable.

9. A sample of individuals (N = 1500) from the local populations was purchased from a marketing company; employees from the campus population were sampled (N = 750) using a campus directory and drawing the first and last names of eligible participants for each letter of the alphabet until the sample was complete. Both target populations were recruited using mailings and a total of 342 subjects contacted the PIs to participate in the study (for more details see Kam, Wilking, and Zechmeister 2007).

10. This was equivalent to just over seven U.S. dollars at the time of the study.

11. Our research approach mirrors numerous studies that compare responses across a negative and a positive situation (e.g., tone of advertisements, different frames; see, for example, Druckman 2001; Geer and Geer 2003; Nelson, Clawson, and Oxley 1997; Nelson and Oxley 1999). Our conclusions are thus based on comparisons across these two situations, threat and good times (and not on any one of these situations in isolation).

12. This was the result of a programming error and was not intentional.

13. We occasionally use the term *status quo* to describe the control condition in recognition of the fact that the subjects participating in our studies came to the lab in a particular information context in which the threat of terrorism was moderately salient. The software used to program and run the U.S.-based studies was Inquisit v2.0.

14. All of the studies had IRB approval and the specific approval of the hosting department/institution.

15. In some studies, subjects responded on a four-point scale, while in others subjects responded on a seven-point scale. For ease of presentation and for comparison purposes, we pool the data and rescale the measure to run from 0 to 1, with higher values indicating higher levels of worry. See the appendix for more details on question wording.

16. All of these differences, between the Terror Threat and Good Times conditions within each grouping, are statistically significant according to t-tests.

17. The audiovisual studies were done in 2004 and 2005, while the newspaper versions were done in 2006 and 2007, when worry about terrorism had waned a bit. One of the downsides to taking out the control in the newspaper studies is that we cannot identify whether mean worry about terrorism was lower in these later studies.

18. We confirmed this with an analysis. We ran a regression on worry and included as independent variables the Terror Threat condition, the version of the treatment, the interaction between the two, and a country dummy. If the audiovisual treatment was

more effective, the interaction term would be significant and positive. The interaction term was not significant in the model. Results are available in Web Supplement A, Table 2.a.

19. We consider factor loadings over .5 as moderate to highly significant, which is consistent with textbook treatments of factor analysis of which we are familiar. For example, Hair, Anderson, Tatham, and Black (1998, 111) define a factor loading of .5 or above as "practically significant."

20. We should note that if we only look at the U.S. studies, only two factors emerge, one in which the anxiety and anger emotions load highly and one in which the positive emotions load highly. Both of these are significantly higher in the Terror Threat condition compared to the Good Times condition.

21. We again ran an analysis to test for this and it can be found in Web Supplement A, Table 2.c.

22. Note that Bartels did a study (1999) of the bias present in panel studies conducted by the ANES. Looking at the 1992/1994/1996 ANES panel study, he found a slightly different demographic profile than subjects from cross-sectional studies in the same year. However, he did not find that this led to many significant biases in inferences. In a review of twelve studies, he only found significant biases with respect to turnout and campaign interest.

23. Most potential proxies in the ANES time-series studies either directly reference existing political figures and parties or do not capture worry about future threats. For example, one question asks whether the Bush administration has made the United States more or less secure against foreign enemies. In addition to tying threat perceptions to the administration, this measure is also problematic in that it does not really tap into prospective concerns about future threats. An individual can think the administration has made the United States more secure and be worried or not worried about future threats. Another measure asks which party is better able to handle the terror threat. Again, this measure does not capture existing concern with the terror threat.

Chapter 3

1. The Ad Council's thirty- and sixty-second spots are available at their Web site: http://www.adcouncil.org/default.aspx?id=141.

2. FBI data on anti-Islamic hate incidents is found at http://www.fbi.gov/ucr/hc2005/abouthc.htm (accessed October 16, 2007).

3. The latter two questions, in 2002, were only asked of a subgroup of the sample. See the appendix for full statements of all question wordings for all measures in the chapter.

4. Comparing only those individuals who responded to the questions in both 2000 and 2002, respectively, we find means levels on these dichotomous variables, coded so that *distrust* is the higher value, to be .419 and .426 for question 1; .282 and .248 for question 2; and, .304 and .268 for question 3. Two-tailed difference of proportions tests fail to reach statistical significance at $p = .75$, $p = .24$, and $p = .21$, respectively.

5. For all analyses of changes in predicted probabilities reported in this chapter (and those that follow), we use CLARIFY (King, Tomz, and Wittenberg 2000; Tomz, Wittenberg, and King 2001). All other variables are held constant at their means, except the dichotomous independent variables are set at the modal value (in the case of the ANES data, these are female and white).

6. Difference of means tests, comparing only respondents who answer each question in both waves of the survey, are significant for Neighbor Trust 3 (higher values on these variables indicate greater trust) at $p = .007$ and for Neighbor Trust 4 at $p = .06$. The mean response to Neighbor Trust 2 does not shift at all across the years. The mean response to Neighbor Trust 1 shifts slightly away from distrust, but the difference is not significant at $p \leq .10$, two-tailed.

7. Ideology and education were asked in the 2002 wave but not in 2004; we therefore use the 2002 measures for these variables in any analysis of the 2004 ANES data in which we include these controls.

8. Again, we include the same basket of controls in each analysis. The dependent variables are difference measures created by subtracting one's response in 2000 from his or her response in 2004.

9. It is not clear that greater affect toward these groups is linked to perceptions of threat itself. Davis (2007) finds little evidence that concern about another terrorist attack on U.S. soil translated into warmer feelings toward Latinos and Blacks among white Americans, though he does find that terrorist threat leads to warmer feelings toward Latinos among Blacks and toward Blacks among Latinos. In analyses not reported here, we examined feelings toward Blacks, Latinos, and Asians among white respondents to the ANES 2000/2002/2004 panel survey. We used the same control variables as in our other analyses of these data reported in this chapter. Our analyses complement the work by Davis, in that we find no statistically significant relationships between terror threat and feelings toward these groups in either year, nor with respect to change in these attitudes before and after 2001. As a near exception, in the analysis predicting change in attitudes toward Latinos from 2000 to 2004, the coefficient on the Terror Threat variable is *negative* and close to statistical significance ($p = .148$, two-tailed; the coefficient is also negative in the 2000 to 2002 analysis and the p-value is $p = .255$ in this case).

10. Some of the ideas presented here and earlier versions of U.S. experimental analyses appear in an earlier working paper coauthored with Jennifer Ramos (Merolla, Ramos, and Zechmeister 2007).

11. We created these measures using principal components factor analysis. The unidimensional solution is supported by the fact that, in each case (US05ns and US05s), only a single factor with an eigenvalue over 1.0 emerged.

12. Overall, respondents to our study in Mexico tended to leave few questions unanswered, but these two batteries were an exception to that rule. Just over one-quarter of the respondents declined to answer each childrearing and word-choice question. Nonresponses can be a sign of ambivalence, in particular in response to difficult questions (Brehm and Alvarez 2002). We imagine that these questions were particularly difficult to our subjects in Mexico, who likely were less familiar with the language of experimental studies like ours. Given our sense that these nonresponses may have indicated ambivalence, we chose to recode missing data for all six predisposition questions to the mid-point between the two options (coded as "1" if authoritarian and "0" otherwise); thus, nonresponses are recoded to 0.5.

13. To create the predispositions variable, we add together responses to all six questions, and divide by six, so that our combined scale runs from 0 to 1. The Cronbach's alpha statistic provides a measure of the internal consistency of a scale. The closer the statistic is to 1.0, the higher the reliability of the scale. The Cronbach's alpha

for this measure (.68) is somewhat higher than the score achieved by the two different sets of questions, child-rearing and word choice, on their own (.62 and .61, respectively).

14. We do acknowledge the importance of Altemeyer's work in the development of the RWA scale and we further acknowledge that our use of the reduced form means that we may not be tapping exactly the same underlying tendencies that are captured by the full scale.

15. We examined the reliability of the scale for each study and found a Cronbach's alpha coefficient of .87 for US05ns, .85 for US05s, and .66 for MEX06s. We further examined whether factor analysis supported the assumption that these variables capture a single underlying dimension of expressed authoritarian attitudes. We ran principal factor analysis for each of the three cases. In the two U.S. cases this analysis yielded only one factor with an eigenvalue over 1.0. More specifically, in the case of the US05 student study, Factor 1 had an eigenvalue of 4.27 and Factor 2 had an eigenvalue of 0.82. In the case of the US05 nonstudent study these values were 4.65 and .88, respectively. For the Mexico study, the analysis yielded two factors with eigenvalues over 1.0 (the eigenvalues on factors 1, 2, and 3 are 2.08, 1.42, and .35). As a robustness check on our coding decision, we rotated and scored these two factors in analyses not shown here. When considered as dependent variables in place of the single additive measure, the results were nearly identical for the two factors.

16. We further include several control variables, in order to isolate the effects of threat and authoritarian predispositions. One concern with measures of authoritarianism is that they may not be politically neutral. For example, Stenner (2005) criticizes the RWA scale for being unable to distinguish between authoritarianism and conservatism. While we are using a reduced form of the scale, we still include Political Ideology as a control variable in order to ensure that we are isolating the effect of authoritarian predispositions, independent of political dispositions, on attitudes. Political Ideology is a seven-point measure, coded so that higher values mean the respondent is more conservative. Second, while the random assignment technique we employ is designed to attempt an even distribution of subject types across our conditions, poststudy diagnostics revealed that, in the U.S. nonstudent study, subjects were unevenly distributed by education and political sophistication. In the Mexico study, subjects were somewhat unevenly distributed by political interest, ideology, and partisanship. We include these measures in our analyses in order to rule out any confounding effect that these measures may have on authoritarian attitudes.

17. In calculating these predicted values (and those for the remaining figures in this chapter), all other variables are held constant at their mean values.

18. Our results further differ from Hetherington and Weiler's work showing that certain threats result in less tolerant attitudes primarily among those predisposed in nonauthoritarian ways (Hetherington and Weiler 2009). It should be kept in mind, though, that there are key differences in the nature of our data and threat treatment.

19. While subjects chose an array of groups, the most common group identified was fascists (44.1%). The other groups that had a high number of mentions were PRD supporters (20%) and Communists (11%).

20. The Cronbach's alpha scale reliability coefficient is .89.

Chapter 4

1. Some parts of this chapter also appear in Merolla and Zechmeister (forthcoming).

2. In an analysis of Bush's first twenty speeches during the election, Oxley and Gangl (2007) found that in 90% of them Bush focused on specific actions he took in the war on terror and in other policy domains (while 80% characterized Kerry as a weak and indecisive leader). The comparable percentage for Kerry was 55%.

3. We refer to only one opponent here (in keeping with the empirical analyses that follow); theoretically, however, we assume individuals will downgrade evaluations of all relevant challengers.

4. "Vice President's Remarks at a Town Hall Meeting in Minnesota, August 6, 2004," http://www.whitehouse.gov/news/releases/2004/08/20040806-15.html (accessed Aug. 24, 2004).

5. A question on Kerry was not included in the ANES panel study.

6. Including partisanship measures in our multiple variable analyses also allows us to control for the fact that Democrats are overrepresented in all of the samples drawn for our U.S. experiments.

7. If the inclusion of interaction terms passes an f-test, then we run models that include the partisan interactions and report the results in the text or in footnotes.

8. Details on the coding can be found in the appendix.

9. Using principal components factors analysis, in 2004 we find a single factor with an eigenvalue over 1. In 2006 we find two factors with an eigenvalue over 1. See the appendix for details on question wording. While the factor analysis found that economic and security issues loaded on a single dimension, we acknowledge that there may be distinct priming effects for the two issue measures. We estimated the 2004 and 2006 results separating the measures for economic and security issues. We do not find any significant effects for the interaction between either issue and the terror threat measure in 2004 or 2006. Meanwhile, the results for an increased weight of leadership in times of terror threat remain the same. Thus, we retain the measures outlined in the text.

10. We attempted to estimate the model with interactions between the conditions and partisanship as well for 2004, but that model had difficulty converging given high collinearity among the many interaction terms. We also tried to run the analysis separately for different groups of partisans and ran into similar problems. Our results for the leadership variable and its interactions hold across models that drop the issue interactions. Finally, we do not include female in the model for 2004 or interest and ideology for 2006 because they were highly insignificant and the pattern of results remains the same.

11. One finding that may look odd in the 2004 results is the negative effect for *Terror Threat*, as a predictor of vote choice. However, recall that because of the interaction terms this is the effect among those who see no difference in leadership, are pure Independents, and who are in the middle on issues.

13. These were generated using the CLARIFY software package in Stata. Party Identification and Issues were set at their mean value.

13. At the level where Bush receives the maximum edge on Kerry (when the Leadership Gap variable is 2.75 or higher), there is no overlap in the confidence intervals, suggesting that the effect of leadership is highly divergent across conditions at this point.

14. There is no overlap in the confidence intervals for the two groups from the value of .75 on Leadership Gap until the end value of 3.

15. Given concerns with collinearity, we ran a separate model for each trait. The results are in Web Supplement A, tables A4.c through 4.f.

16. As the analysis demonstrates, the pattern of effects at each level of terror threat is not perfectly linear, so we use the dummy variables instead of the ordinal scale.

17. We do not include issue measures due to the fact that this significantly reduced our total number of observations. We instead use the variable, *Ideology*, as a proxy for issues.

18. As we mentioned earlier, Berinsky (2009) also finds support for these arguments with respect to feelings toward Bush in a comparison of the weight of leadership on evaluations of Bush in 2000, 2002, and 2004.

Chapter 5

1. Small parts of this chapter are abstracted from a previously published article, coauthored with Jennifer Ramos (Merolla, Ramos, and Zechmeister 2007).

2. We borrow the term "glass floor" from work by Awamleh and Gardner (1999) on charisma and leadership in the world of business.

3. Also at the level of the individual himself, studies have argued that perceptions of charisma can be affected by the nature of the leader's performance in office (e.g., Shamir and Howell 1999).

4. Research has demonstrated its validity across contexts (Bass and Avolio 1993, 1995; see also table 1 in Antonakis, Avolio, and Sivasubramaniam 2003).

5. These were drawn specifically from the batteries related to Attributed Charisma, Idealized Influence, and Inspirational Motivation.

6. We used a smaller set of five questions that loaded highly on a charisma factor analyzed in a study of the 2004 U.S. presidential election (Merolla, Ramos, and Zechmeister 2007). We used the questions with the following trigger words: pride, respect, moral and ethical, goes beyond self-interest, and vision. Questions containing the first three trigger words were asked only to half the sample, while the whole sample evaluated both leaders with respect to the last two trigger words.

7. To validate this variable, we analyzed the scale reliability of the charisma statements for each study in which we included charisma questions, and for each political leader referenced within those studies. The Perceptions of Charisma variables show very good reliability across the studies. The Cronbach's alpha for each scale generated from the experiment-based data was as follows, by candidate and study: Bush04 .929; Kerry04 .943; Bush05 .939; Calderón .914; AMLO .879. For the CIDE-CSES study, the alphas for each scale are as follows: Calderón five-question version .941; Calderón two-question version .892; AMLO five-question version .942; and, AMLO two-question version .893. These diagnostics give us further confidence that these traits tap a single underlying dimension.

8. Within the 2006 CIDE-CSES Mexico survey, the basic measure we use as a proxy for perceptions of the economy is a question that asks respondents to evaluate whether the economy these days is better or worse. Higher values on the five-point scale represent worse evaluations of the economy.

9. The team's campaign ads compared López Obrador to Venezuelan President

Hugo Chávez and explicitly labeled the Mexican leftist candidate a risky and dangerous choice.

10. The public security indicator was coded as "1" if respondents mentioned a public security issue, such as insecurity, political assassinations, drug trafficking, violence, kidnappings, and guerrilla conflict, as the most important problem facing Mexico.

11. Including partisanship measures in our multiple variable analyses also allows us to control for the fact that Democrats are overrepresented in all of our samples in the United States, and Panistas are overrepresented in the student sample in Mexico.

12. For each analysis in this chapter, we test for whether the inclusion of interaction terms between the experimental conditions and partisanship passes an f-test at $p \leq .10$. If we find this to be the case, we run models that include the partisan interactions and report the results in the text or in footnotes. If we say that the effects of the treatments are the same across different partisan groups, this means that the p-value on the f-test was higher than .10.

13. It is important to note that, lacking a nonrecursive model, we cannot say with certainty that perceptions of threat are not endogenous to evaluations of charisma. Nonetheless, we believe they likely are. Theory strongly supports the notion that perceptions of threat influence perceptions of charisma and vice-versa; any correlation we find between the two variables, then, is likely due to two-way causation. The advantage of our experiments is that they provide strong support for the assertion that threat elevates perceptions of charisma.

14. The inclusion of interaction terms complicates the interpretation of the results. The slope and standard errors on the treatment dummy variables are the effect when the political information scale is at 0. Though the coefficients on the interaction terms are not all that meaningful, the p-values do tell us if there is support for a moderating relationship between the two variables (Kam and Franzese 2007). If we look at the table of results (table 5.1), we find support for a moderating relationship between the Terror Threat condition and political information. However, it does not appear that there is a moderating relationship between the Economic Threat condition and political information.

15. We found evidence of partisan interactions enhancing both models but present results for the simpler models since the direction of the effects was similar across partisan groups in almost every case. For example, with respect to Calderón, the economy measure led to negative and significant effects for all groups (the exception is that it was negative but insignificant among PRD supporters), but the effects were more pronounced among PRI supporters. The election measure had a significant negative effect on Calderón's charisma for all partisan groups, but the effects were much stronger among PRI supporters and those who did not identify with one of the three major parties. Meanwhile, the public security measure only had a significant effect for PRI supporters (though the sign was positive across groups). We do not have a clear explanation for why the effect would be higher for PRI supporters (as opposed to PAN supporters), but these results are consistent with our general finding that party identification does not condition the effects of crisis in predictable manners. Turning to López Obrador, we again found no effect of the economic measure and a positive effect for the election measure across all partisan groups, with the effect greatest among those who did not identify with one of the three major parties. The only unexpected

result was that PRD supporters gave López Obrador a boost if they were concerned with public security.

16. These variables were only asked of half the sample, so the number of observations is much lower in these models.

17. For an excellent discussion of the steps involved in establishing a mediating relationship, see MacKinnon, Fairchild, and Fritz 2007. Note that most all the mediating effects we detect are *partial*, in that the insertion of charisma in the model only partly accounts for the relationship between threat and the outcome variable (as seen by the fact that the coefficient on threat decreases in size when charisma is added to the model but does not drop to 0). All of the analyses without charisma in the model can be found in Web Supplement A.

18. As noted in table 5.2 we use OLS analysis; however, we should also note that the results are consistent if ordered probit is used rather than OLS.

19. The remaining variable in the model, Female, is held constant at its mode (female).

20. As the table shows, the Terror Threat and Status Quo variables are statistically significant in the expected direction, and with the effect more pronounced for the former. The fact that respondents in the Status Quo group are less likely to blame Bush than those in the Good Times (baseline) condition makes sense, given that subjects entered the lab with some moderate level of concern about terrorist attacks likely resulting from the information environment surrounding the 2004 election.

21. For example, a Republican in the Terror Threat condition who perceives Bush to have minimal levels of charisma assigns an amount of blame equal to about 4.2 units; in contrast, a Democrat in the Terror Threat condition who perceives Bush as highly charismatic assigns only about 3 units of blame. Of course, not many Democrats are predisposed to view Bush as highly charismatic; yet, in our sample, about 15% of Democrats gave Bush ratings of four or over on the charisma scale.

22. Evaluating either the models with Charisma or those without (see our Web Supplement A, table 5d), this is the only dependent variable for which the coefficient on the Terror Threat variable is statistically significant.

23. The conditions for a mediating relationship are met. See Web Supplement A, table 5.d, for results without Charisma in the model.

24. These first differences were computed using CLARIFY, assuming an individual is in the Terror Threat condition, has an independent or other partisan affiliation, and has mean levels of education and political sophistication. For all models in the chapter in which we do not use OLS, we generate first differences using CLARIFY. We set control variables to the mean, if they are ordinal or quantitative, and dummy variables to the mode.

25. For the remaining dependent variables—Homeland Security, Environment, and Economy—the effect of moving from minimum to maximum perceptions of Bush's charisma in the Terror Threat condition (for an Independent with mean levels of education and political sophistication) is to increase the likelihood of the outcome by 45, 55, and 58 percentage points, respectively.

26. Our analyses do not support the existence of a mediating relationship for Charisma in the case of the Environment, Economy, Homeland Security, or Iraq given that the relationship between Terror Threat and these dependent variables is not significant with or without Charisma in the model. In the latter two cases, the introduction

of Charisma into the model does decrease both the coefficient on Terror Threat but the *p*-value in both models is out of the range of statistical significance.

27. To check our assumption that these acts tap a similar construct related to Self-Sacrifice, we performed principal factors analysis on the set of four responses (yes/no to each act). The analysis produced a single factor with an eigenvalue over 1.0 (the Cronbach's α for the four items is .78).

28. While we use OLS, we also ran these analyses with ordered probit and the results were consistent.

29. This result is conditional upon whether we examine the level or the likelihood (via order probit) of sacrificial behavior; in other analyses (Merolla, Ramos, and Zechmeister 2007), we examine the likelihood of self-sacrifice. We find support for our argument across all partisan groups. We do not have an explanation for this difference across the two results and, instead, conclude that the effect for Republicans is quite robust while the effect detected via ordered probit for non-Republicans is tenuous. Clearly more research is warranted.

30. The conditions for a mediating relationship are met. See Web Supplement A, table 5.e, for the model without charisma.

31. As in our other analyses of these data in this chapter, we control for partisanship, political sophistication, and education. We tested whether the effects of the Terror Threat, Economic Threat, and Status Quo conditions were conditional upon political sophistication; block f-tests showed that the interactions were not significant at $p \leq .10$ for any of the six cases.

32. Once again, the conditions for a mediating relationship are met. See Web Supplement A, table A5.e for analyses without charisma.

33. We replicated these analyses, without the Bush Charisma variable (because the questions were not asked) using data from the US05s study (see Web Supplement A, Table A5.f). Here we also find positive coefficients on the Terror Threat variable for the case of the Self-Sacrifice–Iraq and Self-Sacrifice–Homeland variables; in the case of the former analysis, the Terror Threat condition is statistically significant. Again, we do not find a similar statistically reliable effect for the Economic Threat variable on either of these two dependent variables; in fact, Economic Threat is a statistically significant but negative predictor of sacrifice for homeland security. We do not find any significant effects for the Terror Threat condition for three of the other dependent variables of Self-Sacrifice. The exception is Self-Sacrifice-Environment in which case, for reasons we admittedly cannot explain, the Terror Threat variable is positive and statistically significant.

34. This question appears on the *Learning Democracy 2000* survey, created by Roderic Ai Camp and executed in Mexico and the United States.

35. The first three questions were from a survey, Global Views 2004: Mexican Public Opinion and Foreign Policy, jointly sponsored by CIDE/CMAI/ and the CCFR. We added the fourth option.

36. Because the Strong Executive variable is dichotomous, we use probit analysis and, because the Presidential Powers variable has five categories, we use OLS analysis. We also ran the latter analyses with ordered probit and the results are consistent.

37. It is interesting to note that the coefficients on the PAN partisanship variable are positive and statistically significant in both cases; those who identify with the partisanship of the candidate who had been officially declared the next executive are

more likely to prefer that the institutional balance work in his favor. In contrast, those whose loyalties lie with the partisanship of the second-place candidate are more likely to prefer the exact opposite. Of course, it is also the case that the PAN is right-leaning and the PRD is left-leaning and thus we cannot be certain whether these partisan effects are driven by ideology and/or partisan bias given the outcome of the election.

38. The mediating role is supported by the fact that the required conditions are met.

Chapter 6

1. According to a 2006 poll, Bush earned his lowest ratings since the beginning of his presidency on foreign policy, Iraq, and the economy. Two-thirds of those polled had little faith he could successfully conclude the war and also saw the country as worse off than when his presidency began. See Adam Nagourney and Megan Thee, "Bush's Public Approval at New Low Point," *New York Times*, May 9, 2006, http://www.nytimes.com/2006/05/09/washington/09cnd-poll.htm?ex=1182052800&en=6b91d bf3a00de61f&ei=5070.

2. The Pew Research Center for the People and the Press, "Foreign Policy Attitudes Now Driven by 9/11 and Iraq," August 18, 2004, http://people-press.org/reports/display.php3?ReportID=222.

3. Gallup Poll, 2007, "Terrorism in the United States," http://www.galluppoll.com/content/default.aspx?ci=4909 (accessed August 4, 2007).

4. The Pew Research Center's full report is accessible on the web at http://people-press.org/reports/display.php3?ReportID=267.

5. Barry Hughes (1978) was one of the first scholars to recognize that internationalism may have two dimensions. Mandelbaum and Schneider (1979) argue that there are three foreign policy "outlooks": liberal internationalism, conservative internationalism, and noninternationalism (see also Holsti 1979).

6. Likely because of this fact, no existing surveys of Mexicans include questions on preferences toward unilateral foreign policy actions by the Mexican government.

7. For instance, Knopf (1998) showed that social protest had a positive effect on U.S. security cooperation, helping the United States to enter into strategic arms talks with the Soviet Union during the Cold War.

8. Please see the appendix for more details on question wording and coding.

9. We include controls for the following measures in all of the survey data analyses: party identification, education, income, and gender, as these variables have been shown to be important in the expression of foreign policy opinions. Full coding information on these measures can be found in the appendix. Since the dependent variable is dichotomous, we use probit analysis.

10. First differences for this analysis and subsequent analyses with dichotomous dependent variables were calculated using CLARIFY statistical software; see Tomz, Wittenberg, and King (2003). For the Mexico surveys, education and income were set to their mean values, female was set to its maximum value, and PAN, PRI, and PRD were set to their minimum values. For the U.S. surveys, ideology, education, and income were set to their mean values, while female was set to its maximum value.

11. This is a departure from our typical multivariate analyses, made possible by the fact that we did not find any significant differences in demographic and political predisposition measures across the Good Times and Terror Threat conditions for the Mexico and U.S. student study (US07s) and so we can directly compare across the two

conditions (recall there was no control group in these two studies). We included such measures when earlier analyzing these data since there were significant differences in some demographic and political predisposition measures when the Economic Threat condition was included in the sample.

12. Specifically, we found that anxiety and anger loaded on a single factor. The rotated factor loadings were around .70 for variables indicating whether the respondent feels "afraid" (.78) and "scared" (.76), as well as feelings of being "upset" (.77) and "hostile" (.65).

13. These differences are close to significant, $p = .11$ (one-tailed) for the negative emotion factor, and are significant for the positive emotion factor, $p = .00$ (one-tailed).

14. The mean negative emotion factor for those in the Terror Threat condition in 2006 is $-.01$, while the mean for those in the Terror Threat condition in 2007 is .22, and these differences are statistically significant at $p = .085$ (one-tailed). The comparable values for the positive emotion factor are .254 in 2006 and .039 in 2007, and these differences are statistically significant, $p = .07$ (one-tailed).

15. Since these emotion questions were asked toward the end of our survey, we believe the emergence of the positive factor reflects the use of our outlined coping strategies by some subjects, who were already feeling more proud and strong by the time they answered the emotions battery.

16. For the U.S. survey data, both immigration measures are based on three-point scales and OLS estimates are used. We also estimated models with ordinal values using a more appropriate ordered probit estimation technique. The results were nearly identical and thus we chose to use the easily accessible OLS results.

17. As noted in the text, we also examined preferences over taxation for homeland security in chapter 5; our analyses there, for consistency with other analyses in that chapter, also included party identification. The results are similar, as can be seen in the Web appendix.

18. See, for example, http://news.bbc.co.uk/2/hi/middle_east/3756650.stm.

Conclusion

1. Economist David Henderson, who contributes a series of articles under the title "The War Time Economist" on http://www.antiwar.com, pointed this out.

2. "Giuliani to Run for President of 9/11," *The Onion*, February 21, 2007, http://www.theonion.com/content/news/giuliani_to_run_for_president_of_9 (accessed November 21, 2007).

3. A number of studies demonstrate that the effect of war costs (typically, casualties) is conditional upon other factors, for example on politicians' stances on the war (Gartner, Segura, and Barratt 2004) and the public's expectations of success (Gelpi, Feaver, and Reifler 2005/6); but see Berinsky (2007).

4. Simon Romero, "In Chávez Territory, Signs of Dissent," *New York Times*, November 30, 2007, http://www.nytimes.com/2007/11/30/world/americas/30venez.html (accessed November 30, 2007).

5. Another contributing factor was clearly the fact that public opinion had already turned against the war in Iraq; a sense that the Al Qaeda attack was in retribution for Spain's participation in this conflict may have also helped turn opinion against the incumbent administration. Not surprisingly, almost immediately after taking office, the new administration began to talk about withdrawing Spanish forces from Iraq.

6. For a more detailed study than we offer here of elite engineering in the face of terrorist threat, see the unpublished dissertation work by Gabriel Rubin, MIT. Rubin distinguishes between "executive response" and "executive threat-shaping" and examines how constraints imposed by the public and "political constellations" shape the executive's ability to pass legislation on civil liberties in times of terrorist crises.

7. See, for example, work by Pyszczynski, Solomon, and Greenberg (2002).

References

Abramson, P. R., J. H. Aldrich, and D. W. Rohde. 2002. *Change and continuity in the 2000 elections*. Washington, D.C.: Congressional Quarterly Press.

Achen, C. H. 1992. Social psychology, demographic variables, and linear regression: Breaking the iron triangle in voting research. *Political Behavior* 14:195–211.

Adorno, T. W., E. Frenkel-Brunswik, D. J. Levinson, and R. N. Sanford. 1950. *The authoritarian personality*. New York: Harper and Row.

Aldrich, J. H., J. L. Sullivan, and E. Borgida. 1989. Foreign affairs and issue voting: Do presidential candidates 'waltz before a blind audience'?" *American Political Science Review* 83:123–41.

Aldrich, J. H., P. Gronke, and J. D. Grynaviski. 2003 (updated version). Policy, personality, and presidential performance. Paper originally delivered at the Annual Meeting of the Midwest Political Science Association, Palmer House Hotel, Chicago, April 15–18, 1999.

Allison, G. 2004. *Nuclear terrorism: The ultimate preventable catastrophe*. New York: Times Books.

Almond, G. 1950. *The American people and foreign policy*. New York: Praeger.

Altemeyer, B. 1981. *Right-wing authoritarianism*. Winnipeg, Canada: Univ. of Manitoba Press.

———. 1988. *Enemies of freedom*. San Francisco: Jossey-Bass.

———. 1996. *The authoritarian specter*. Cambridge: Harvard Univ. Press.

Alvarez, R. M. 1997. *Information and elections*. Ann Arbor: Univ. of Michigan Press.

Anderson, C. J. 2000. Economic voting and political context. *Electoral Studies* 19:151–70.

Ansolabehere, S., S. Iyengar, and A. Simon. 1999. Replicating experiments using aggregate and survey data: The case of negative advertising and turnout. *American Political Science Review* 93:901–9.

Antonakis, J., B. J. Avolio, and N. Sivasubramaniam. 2003. Context and leadership: An examination of the nine-factor full-range leadership theory using the Multifactor Leadership Questionnaire. *Leadership Quarterly* 14 (3): 261–95.

Arian, A. 1989. A people apart: Coping with national security problems in Israel. *Journal of Conflict Resolution* 33 (4): 605–31.

Avolio, B. J., D. A. Waldman, and W. O. Einstein. 1988. Transformational leadership in a management game simulation. *Group and Organizational Studies* 13 (1): 59–80.

Awamleh, R., and W. L. Gardner. 1999. Perceptions of leader charisma and effectiveness: The effects of vision content, delivery and organizational performance. *Leadership Quarterly* 10 (3): 345–73.

Babbie, E., and L. Benaquisto. 2002. *Fundamentals of social research.* 1st Canadian ed. Scarborough, ON: Nelson Education Ltd.

Bartels, L. M. 1999. Panel effects in the American national election studies. *Political Analysis* 8 (1): 1–20.

———. 2002. Beyond the running tally: Partisan bias in political perceptions. *Political Behavior* 24 (2): 117–50.

Bass, B. M. 1985. *Leadership and performance beyond expectations.* New York: Free Press.

Bass, B. M., and B. J. Avolio. 1993. Transformational leadership: A response to critiques. In *Leadership theory and research: Perspectives and directions*, ed. M. M. Chemers and R. Ayman, 49–80. New York: Academic Press.

———, eds. 1994. *Improving organizational effectiveness through transformational leadership.* Thousand Oaks, CA: Sage Publications.

———. 1995. *Manual for the Multifactor Leadership Questionnaire: Rater form (5x short).* Palo Alto, CA: Mind Garden.

Bean, C., and A. Mughan. 1989. Leadership effects in parliamentary elections in Australia and Britain. *American Political Science Review* 83 (4): 1165–79.

Behling, O., and J. M. McFillen. 1996. A syncretical model of charismatic/transformational leadership. *Group and Organization Management* 21 (2): 163–91.

Berinsky, A. J. 2007. Assuming the costs of war: Events, elites, and American public support for military conflict. *Journal of Politics* 69 (4): 975–97.

———. 2009. *America at war: Public opinion during war time, from World War II to Iraq.* Chicago: Univ. of Chicago Press.

Blais, A., E. Gidengil, R. Nadeau, and N. Nevitte. 2001. Measuring party identification: Britain, Canada and the United States. *Political Behavior* 23:5–22.

Bligh, M. C., J. C. Kohles, and J. R. Meindl. 2004. Charisma under crisis: Presidential leadership, rhetoric, and media responses before and after the September 11th terrorist attacks. *Leadership Quarterly* 15 (2): 211–39.

Bligh, M. C., J. C. Kohles, and R. Pillai. 2005. Crisis and charisma in the California recall election. *Leadership* 1 (3): 323–52.

Bowen, G. L. 1989. Presidential action and public opinion about U.S. Nicaraguan policy: Limits to the "Rally Round the Flag" syndrome. *PS: Political Science and Politics* 22 (4): 793–800.

Brader, T. 2005. Striking a responsive chord: How political ads motivate and persuade voters by appealing to emotions. *American Journal of Political Science* 49:388–405.

———. 2006. *Campaigning for hearts and minds.* Chicago: Univ. of Chicago Press.

Brehm, J., and M. R. Alvarez. 2002. *Hard choices, easy answers: Values, information, and American public opinion.* Princeton, N.J.: Princeton Univ. Press.

Brehm, J., and W. Rahn. 1997. Individual-level evidence for the causes and consequences of social capital. *American Journal of Political Science* 41 (3): 999–1023.

Brody, R. 1991. *Assessing the president: The media, elite opinion, and public support.* Stanford, CA: Stanford Univ. Press.

Brophy-Baermann, B., and J. A. C. Conybeare. 1994. Retaliating against terrorism: Rational expectations and the optimality of rules versus discretion. *American Journal of Political Science* 38:196–210.

Bryman, A. 1992. *Charisma and leadership in organizations.* London: Sage Publications.

Byman, D. L., M. C. Waxman, and E. Larson. 1999. *Air power as a coercive instrument.* Santa Monica, CA: Rand.

Callaghan, K. J., and S. Virtanen. 1993. Revised models of the 'Rally Phenomenon': The case of the Carter presidency. *Journal of Politics* 55 (3): 756–64.

Campbell, A., P. E. Converse, W. E. Miller, and D. E. Stokes. 1960. *The American voter.* New York: Wiley.

Campbell, D. T., and J. C. Stanley. 1963. *Experimental and quasi-experimental designs for research.* Chicago: Rand McNally.

Caspary, W. R. 1970. The mood theory: A study of public opinion and foreign policy. *American Political Science Review* 64:536–47.

Chanley, V. A. 1999. U.S. public views of international involvement from 1964 to 1993: Time-series analyses of general and militant internationalism. *Journal of Conflict Resolution* 43 (1): 23–44.

———. 2002. Trust in government in the aftermath of 9/11: Determinants and consequences. *Political Psychology* 23 (3): 469

Charters, D. A., ed. 1994. *The deadly sins of terrorism: Its effect on democracy and civil liberty in six countries.* Westport, CT: Greenwood Press.

Cheibub, J. A., and A. Przeworski. 1999. Democracy, elections, and accountability for economic outcomes. Chapter 7 of *Democracy, accountability, and representation,* ed. A. Przeworski, S. C. Stokes, and B. Manin. New York: Cambridge Univ. Press.

Choi, Y., and R. R. Mai-Dalton. 1998. On the leadership function of self-sacrifice. *Leadership Quarterly* 9 (4): 475–501.

Chittick, W. O., and K. R. Billingsley. 1989. The structure of elite foreign policy beliefs. *Western Political Quarterly* 42 (2): 201–24.

Chittick, W., O., K. R. Billingsley, and R. Travis. 1990. Persistence and change in elite and mass attitudes toward U.S. foreign policy. *Political Psychology* 11 (2): 385–401.

———. 1995. A three-dimensional model of American foreign policy beliefs. *International Studies Quarterly* 39:313–31.

Cialdini, R., S. L. Brown, B. P. Lewis, C. Luce, and S. L. Neuberg. 1997. Reinterpreting the empathy-altruism relationship: When one into one equals oneness. *Journal of Personality and Social Psychology* 73 (3): 481–94.

Citrin, J., and D. P. Green. 1986. Presidential leadership and the resurgence of trust in government. *British Journal of Political Science* 16 (4): 431–53.

Cohen, W. A. 1992. The potential revolution in leadership. *Business Forum* 17 (1): 37–39.

Conger, J. A., and R. N. Kanungo. 1987. Toward a behavioral theory of charismatic leadership in organizational settings. *Academy of Management Review* 12 (4): 637–47.

———, eds. 1988. *Charismatic leadership: The elusive factor in organizational effectiveness.* San Francisco: Jossey-Bass.

Conger, J. A., R. N. Kanungo, and S. T. Menon. 2000. Charismatic leadership and follower effects. *Journal of Organizational Behavior* 21 (7): 747–67.

Conniff, M. L., ed. 1999. *Populism in Latin America.* Tuscaloosa: Univ. of Alabama Press.

Converse, P. E. 1964. The nature of belief systems in mass publics. In *Ideology and Discontent,* ed. D. Apter, 206–221. New York: Free Press.

Crenshaw, M. 2003. Terrorism and international violence. In *Handbook of War Studies II,* ed. Manus I. Minlarsky, 3–24. Ann Arbor: Univ. of Michigan Press.

Crouse, T. 1973. *The boys on the bus.* New York: Random House.

Davies, J. C. 1954. Charisma in the 1952 campaign. *American Political Science Review* 48 (4): 1083–1102.

Davis, D. W. 2007. *Negative liberty: Public opinion and the terrorist attacks on America.* New York: Russell Sage Foundation.

Davis, D. W., and B. D. Silver. 2004a. Civil liberties vs. security: Public opinion in the context of the terrorist attacks on America. *American Journal of Political Science* 48 (1): 28–46.

———. 2004b. The threat of terrorism, presidential approval, and the 2004 election. Paper delivered at the annual meeting of the American Political Science Association, Chicago, September 2–5, 2004.

Delli Carpini, M. X., and S. Keeter. 1996. *What Americans know about politics and why it matters.* New Haven: Yale Univ. Press.

Doty, R. M., B. E. Peterson, and D. G. Winter. 1991. Threat and authoritarianism in the United States, 1978–1987. *Journal of Personality and Social Psychology* 61 (4): 629–40.

Downs, A. 1957. *An economic theory of democracy.* New York: Harper and Row.

Druckman, J. N. 2001. The implications of framing effects for citizen competence. *Political Behavior* 23:225–56.

———. 2004. Political preference formation: Competition, deliberation, and the (ir)relevance of framing effects. *American Political Science Review* 98:671–86.

Druckman, J. N., and K. R. Nelson. 2003. Framing and deliberation: How citizens' conversations limit elite influence. *American Journal of Political Science* 47 (4): 729–45.

Duckitt, J., and K. Fisher. 2003. The impact of social threat on worldview and ideological attitudes. *Political Psychology* 24 (1): 199–222.

Easton, D. 1965. *A systems analysis of political life.* New York: John Wiley and Son.

Eisenstadt, S. N, ed. 1968. *Max Weber: On charisma and institution building.* Chicago: Univ. of Chicago Press.

Eisenstadt, T. A., and A. Poiré. 2006. Explaining the credibility gap in Mexico's 2006 presidential election, despite strong (albeit perfectable) electoral institutions, *Working Paper,* American University, Center for North American Studies. Last accessed February 15, 2007 at http://american.edu/ia/cnas/pdfs/workingpaper4_elections.pdf.

Emrich, C. G., H. H. Brower, J. M. Feldman, and H. Garland. 2001. Images in words: Presidential rhetoric, charisma, and greatness. *Administrative Science Quarterly* 46 (3): 527–57.

Enders, W., T. Sandler, and J. Cauley. 1990. UN conventions, technology, and retaliation in the fight against terrorism: An econometric evaluation. *Terrorism and Political Violence* 2:83–105.

Evangelista, M. 1995. The paradox of state strength: Transnational relations, domestic structures, and security policy in Russia and the Soviet Union. *International Organization* 49:1–38.

Feldman, S., and K. Stenner. 1997. Perceived threat and authoritarianism. *Political Psychology* 18 (4): 741–70.

Fisher, J. L. 1984. *Power of the presidency.* New York: Free Press.

Fisher, L. 1995. *Presidential war power.* Lawrence: University Press of Kansas.

Fiorina, M. P. 1981. *Retrospective voting in American national elections.* New Haven, CT: Yale Univ. Press.

Friedland, N., and A. Merari. 1985. The psychological impact of terrorism: A double-edged sword. *Political Psychology* 6 (4): 591–604.

Friedrich, Carl J. 1961. Political leadership and the problem of charismatic power. *Journal of Politics* 23 (1): 3–24.

Fromm, E. 1941. *Escape from freedom.* New York: Rinehart and Company.

Funk, C. 1997. Implications of political expertise in candidate trait evaluations. *Political Research Quarterly* 50 (3): 675–97.

———. 1999. Bringing the candidate into models of candidate evaluation. *Journal of Politics* 61 (3): 700–720.

Gartner, S. S., G. M. Segura, and B. A. Barratt. 2004. War casualties, policy positions, and the fate of legislators. *Political Research Quarterly* 57 (3): 467–77.

Geer, J. G., and J. H. Geer. 2003. Remembering attack ads: An experimental investigation of radio. *Political Behavior* 25 (1): 69–95.

Gelpi, C., P. D. Feaver, and J. Reifler. 2005/6. Success matters: Casualty sensitivity and the war in Iraq. *International Security* 30 (3): 7-46.

Gibson, J. L. 2006. Enigmas of intolerance: Fifty years after Stouffer's communism conformity and civil liberties. *Perspectives on Politics* 4 (1): 21–34.

———. 2007. Political intolerance in the context of democratic theory. Chapter 17 in *The Oxford Handbook of Political Behavior,* ed. R. J. Dalton and H.-D. Klingemann, 323–41. Oxford: Oxford Univ. Press.

Gilens, M. 1995. Racial attitudes and opposition to welfare. *Journal of Politics* 57 (4): 994–1014.

Glaser, J., and P. Salovey. 1998. Affect in electoral politics. *Personality and Social Psychology Review* 2:156–72.

Glass, D. P. 1985. Evaluating presidential candidates: Who focuses on their personal attributes? *Public Opinion Quarterly* 49 (4): 517–34.

Gomez, B. T., and J. M. Wilson. 2001. Political sophistication and economic voting in the American electorate: A theory of heterogeneous attribution. *American Journal of Political Science* 4:899–914.

Gordon, C., and A. Arian. 2001. Threat and decision making. *Journal of Conflict Resolution* 45:197–215.

Gordon, S. B., and G. M. Segura. 1997. Cross-national variation in the political sophistication of individuals: Capability or choice? *Journal of Politics* 59 (1): 126–47.

Gosnell, H. F. 1927. *Getting out the vote: An experiment in the stimulation of voting.* Chicago: Univ. of Chicago Press.

Gowa, J. 1994. *Allies, adversaries, and international trade*. Princeton, N.J.: Princeton Univ. Press.

Greenberg, J., T. Pyszczynski, S. Solomon, A. Rosenblatt, M. Veeder, S. Kirkland, and D. Lyon. 1990. Evidence for terror management theory II: The effects of mortality salience on reactions to those who threaten or bolster the cultural worldview. *Journal of Personality and Social Psychology* 58 (2): 308–18.

Grieco, J. M. 1988. Anarchy and the limits of cooperation: A realist critique of the newest liberal institutionalism. *International Organization* 42:485–508.

Hair, J. F., R. E. Anderson, R. L Tatham, and W. C. Black. 1998. *Multivariate data analysis with readings*. Englewood Cliffs, N.J.: Prentice-Hall.

Hanushek, E. A., and J. E. Jackson. 1977. *Statistical methods for social scientists*. New York: Academic Press.

Hawkins, K. 2003. Populism in Venezuela: The rise of Chavismo. *Third World Quarterly* 24 (6): 1137–60.

Herrmann, R. K., and P. E. Tetlock. 1999. Mass public decisions to go to war: A cognitive-interactionist framework. *American Political Science Review* 93:553–72.

Herrmann, R. K., J. F. Voss, Tonya Y. E. Schooler, and J. Ciarrochi. 1997. Images in international relations: An experimental test of cognitive schemata. *International Studies Quarterly* 41 (3): 403–33

Hetherington, M. J. 1998. The political relevance of political trust. *American Political Science Review* 92 (4): 791–808.

Hetherington, M. J., and M. Nelson. 2003. Anatomy of a rally effect: George W. Bush and the war on terrorism. *PS: Political Science and Politics* 36:37–42.

Hetherington, M. J., and J. Weiler. 2009. *Authoritarianism and polarization in American politics*. New York: Cambridge University Press.

Holsti, O. R. 1979. The three-headed eagle: The United States and system change. *International Studies Quarterly* 23:339–59.

———. 1992. Public opinion and foreign policy: Challenges to the Almond-Lippmann Consensus Mershon Series: Research programs and debates. *International Studies Quarterly* 36 (4): 439–46.

———. 1996. *Public opinion and American foreign policy*. Ann Arbor: Univ. of Michigan Press.

Holsti, O. R., and J. N. Rosenau. 1984. *American leadership in world affairs: Vietnam and the breakdown of consensus*. Boston: Allen and Unwin.

House, R., and J. M. Howell. 1992. Personality and charisma. *Leadership Quarterly* 3 (2): 81–108.

House, R. J., W. D. Spangler, and J. Woycke. 1991. Personality and charisma in the U.S. presidency: A psychological theory of leader effectiveness. *Administrative Science Quarterly* 36 (3): 364–96.

Huddy, L., S. Feldman, and G. Marcus. 2007. Going to war: Anger, knowledge, partisanship, and the media. Paper presented at the annual meeting of the International Society of Political Psychology, Portland, Oregon, July 4–7, 2007.

Huddy, L., S. Feldman, C. Taber, and G. Lahav. 2005. Threat, anxiety, and support of antiterrorism policies. *American Journal of Political Science* 49 (3): 593–608.

Huddy, L., and A. H. Gunnthorsdottir. 2000. The persuasive effects of emotive visual imagery. *Political Psychology* 21:745–78.

Huddy, L., N. Khatib, and T. Capelos. 2002. The polls—trends: Reactions to the terrorist attacks of September 11, 2001. *Public Opinion Quarterly* 66 (3): 418–50.

Hughes, B. 1978. *The domestic context of American foreign policy*. San Francisco: W. H. Freeman.

Hunt, J. G., K. B. Boal, and G. E. Dodge. 1999. The effects of visionary and crisis-responsive charisma on followers: An experimental examination of two kinds of charismatic leadership. *Leadership Quarterly* 10 (3): 423–48.

Jackman, R. W. 1987. Political institutions and voter turnout in the industrial democracies. *American Political Science Review* 81 (2): 405–24.

Jackman, R. W., and R. A. Miller. 1995. Voter turnout in the industrial democracies during the 1980s. *Comparative Political Studies* 27 (4): 467–92.

Jentleson, B., and R. L. Britton. 1998. Still pretty prudent: Post–Cold War American public opinion on the use of military force. *Journal of Conflict Resolution* 42:395–417.

Jentleson, B. W. 1992. The pretty prudent public: Post post-Vietnam American opinion on the use of military force. *International Studies Quarterly* 36 (1): 49–73.

Jervis, R. 1982. Security regimes. *International Organization* 36:357–78.

Jorgenson, D. O. 1975. Economic threat and authoritarianism in television programs: 1950–1974. *Psychological Reports* 37:1153–54.

Kahn, K. F., and P. J. Kenney. 1997. A model of candidate evaluations in Senate elections: The impact of campaign intensity. *Journal of Politics* 59 (4): 1173–1205.

Kahneman, D., and A. Tversky. 1979. Prospect theory: An analysis of decision under risk. *Econometrica* 47 (2): 263–92.

———. 1981. The framing of decisions and the psychology of choice. *Science* 211: 453–58.

Kam, C. D. 2005. Who toes the party line? Cues, values, and individual differences. *Political Behavior* 27 (2): 163–82.

Kam, C. D., and R. J. Franzese Jr. 2007. *Modeling and interpreting interaction hypotheses in regression analysis*. Ann Arbor: Univ. of Michigan Press.

Kam, C. D., and D. R. Kinder. 2007. Terror and ethnocentrism: Foundations of American support for the war on terrorism. *Journal of Politics* 69 (2): 320–38.

Kam, C. D., and J. M. Ramos. 2008. Joining and leaving the rally: Understanding the surge and decline in presidential approval following 9/11. *Public Opinion Quarterly* 72 (Winter): 619–50.

Kam, C. D., J. R. Wilking, and E. Zechmeister. 2007. Beyond the "narrow data base": Another convenience sample for experimental research. *Political Behavior* 29 (4): 415–40.

Khan, Z. R. 1976. Leadership, parties and politics in Bangladesh. *Western Political Quarterly* 29 (1): 102–25.

Kinder, D. R. 1986. Presidential character revisited. In *Political cognition: The 19th Annual Carnegie Symposium on Cognition*, ed. R. R. Lau and D. O. Sears. Hillsdale, NJ: Lawrence Erlbaum Associates.

Kinder, D. R., and D. R. Kiewiet. 1981. Sociotropic politics: The American case. *British Journal of Political Science* 11 (2): 129–62.

Kinder, D. R., and T. R. Palfrey. 1993. Preface. In *Experimental foundations of political science*, ed. Kinder and Palfrey. Ann Arbor: Univ. of Michigan Press.

King, G., M. Tomz, and J. Wittenberg. 2000. Making the most of statistical analyses:

Improving interpretation and presentation. *American Journal of Political Science* 44 (2): 347–61.

Kirkpatrick, S. A., and E. A. Locke. 1996. Direct and indirect effects of three core charismatic leadership components on performance and attitudes. *Journal of Applied Psychology* 81 (1): 36–51.

Klesner, J. L. 2007. The 2006 Mexican elections: Manifestation of a divided society? *PS: Political Science and Politics* (January): 27–32.

Knopf, J. W. 1998. Domestic sources of preferences for arms cooperation: The impact of protest. *Journal of Peace Research* 35:677–95.

Krause, G. A. 1997. Voters, information heterogeneity, and the dynamics of aggregate economic expectations. *American Journal of Political Science* 41 (4): 1170–1200.

Kushner Gadarian, Shana. 2008. The fire next time: How terrorism news shapes foreign policy attitudes. Working Paper, Princeton University.

Landau, M. J., S. Solomon, J. Greenberg, F. Cohen, T. Pyszczynski, J. Arndt, C. H. Miller, D. M. Ogilvie, and A. Cook. 2004. Deliver us from evil: The effects of mortality salience and reminders of 9/11 on support for President George W. Bush. *Personality and Social Psychology Bulletin* 30 (9): 1136–50.

Laquer, W. 1999. *The new terrorism: Fanaticism and the arms of mass destruction.* London: Oxford Univ. Press.

Lau, R. R., and D. P. Redlawsk. 1997. Voting correctly. *American Political Science Review* 91 (3): 585–98.

Lavine, H., D. Burgess, M. Snyder, J. Transue, J. L. Sullivan, B. Haney, and S. H. Wagner. 1996. Threat, authoritarianism, and voting: An investigation of personality and persuasion. *Personality and Social Psychology Bulletin* 25 (3): 337–47.

Lavine, H., M. Lodge, and K. Freitas. 2005. Threat, authoritarianism, and selective exposure to information. *Political Psychology* 26 (2): 219–44.

Lavine, H., M. Lodge, J. Polichak, and C. Taber. 2002. Explicating the black box through experimentation: Studies of authoritarianism and threat. *Political Analysis* 10 (4): 343–61.

Lazarus, R. S. 1991a. Progress on a cognitive-motivational-relational theory of emotion. *American Psychologist* 46 (8): 819–34.

———. 1991b. *Emotion and adaptation.* New York: Oxford Univ. Press.

Lesser, I. O. 1999. Countering the new terrorism: Implications for strategy. In *Countering the new terrorism*, ed. I. O. Lesser, B. Hoffman, J. Arquilla, D. Ronfeldt, and M. Zanini. Santa Monica, CA: Rand.

Levi, M., and L. Stoker. 2000. Political trust and trustworthiness. *Annual Review of Political Science* 3:475–507.

Lupia, A., and M. D. McCubbins. 1998. *The democratic dilemma: Can citizens learn what they need to know?* New York: Cambridge Univ. Press.

MacKinnon, D. P., A. J. Fairchild, and M. S. Fritz. 2007. Mediation analysis. *Annual Review of Psychology* 58:593–614.

MacKuen, M. 1983. Political drama, economic conditions, and the dynamics of presidential popularity. *American Journal of Political Science* 27:165–92.

Madsen, D., and P. G. Snow. 1991. *The charismatic bond: Political behavior in times of crisis.* Cambridge: Harvard Univ. Press.

Maggiotto, M. A., and E. R. Wittkopf. 1981. American public attitudes toward foreign policy. *International Studies Quarterly* 25:601–31.

Mandelbaum, M., and W. Schneider. 1979. The new internationalisms: Public opinion and American foreign policy. In *Eagle entangled: U.S. foreign policy in a complex world,* ed. K. A. Oye, D. Rothschild, and R. J. Lieber. New York: Longman.

Marcus, G. E., W. R. Neuman, and M. MacKuen. 2000. *Affective intelligence and political judgment.* Chicago: Univ. of Chicago Press.

Markus, G. B. 1982. Political attitudes during an election year: A report on the 1980 NES panel study. *American Political Science Review* 76:538–60.

Mayer, W. G. 1992. *The changing American mind: How and why American public opinion changed between 1960 and 1980.* Ann Arbor: Univ. of Michigan Press.

McCann, S. J. H. 1997. Threatening times, "strong" presidential popular vote winners, and the victory margin, 1824–1964. *Journal of Personality and Social Psychology* 73 (1): 160–70.

McCurley, C., and J. J. Mondak. 1995. Inspected by #1184063113: The influence of incumbents' competence and integrity in U.S. House elections. *American Journal of Political Science* 39 (4): 864–85.

McClosky, H. 1964. Consensus and ideology in American politics. *American Political Science Review* 58:361–82.

McDermott, R. 2002. Experimental methods in political science. *Annual Review of Political Science* 5:31–61.

Mendelsohn, M. 1996. The media and interpersonal communications: The priming of issues, leaders, and party identification. *Journal of Politics* 58 (1): 112–25.

Merolla, J. L., J. M. Ramos, and E. J. Zechmeister. 2006. Authoritarian attitudes under crisis conditions. Paper presented at the annual meeting of the International Society of Political Psychology, July 12–15, Barcelona, Spain.

Merolla, J. L., J. M. Ramos, and E. J. Zechmeister. 2007. Crisis, charisma, and consequences: Evidence from the 2004 U.S. presidential election. *Journal of Politics* 69 (1): 30–42.

Merolla, J. L., and E. J. Zechmeister. Forthcoming. Terrorist threat, leadership, and vote choice: Evidence from three examinations. *Political Behavior.*

Miller, A. H., and W. E. Miller. 1976. Ideology in the 1972 election: Myth or reality—a rejoinder. *American Political Science Review* 70 (3): 832–49.

Miller, A. H., Martin P. Wattenberg, and O. Malanchuk. 1986. Schematic assessments of presidential candidates. *American Political Science Review* 80 (2): 521–40.

Miller, J., and J. Krosnick. 2000. News media impact on the ingredients of presidential evaluations: Politically knowledgeable citizens are guided by a trusted source. *American Journal of Political Science* 44:301–15.

Miller, W. E. 1991. Party identification, realignment, and party voting: Back to the basics. *American Political Science Review* 85 (2): 557–68.

Miller, W. E., and J. M. Shanks. 1996. *The new American voter.* Cambridge: Harvard Univ. Press.

Mook, D. G. 1983. In defense of external invalidity. *American Psychologist* 38:379–87.

Morgenstern, S., and E. Zechmeister. 2001. Better the devil you know than the saint you don't? Risk propensity and vote choice in Mexico. *Journal of Politics* 63 (1): 93–119.

Morgenthau, H. 1948. *Politics among nations: The struggle for power and peace.* New York: Alfred A. Knopf.

Morin, R., and D. Balz. 2004. Bush retains a slim lead in poll. *Washington Post,* http://

www.washingtonpost.com/ac2/wp-dyn/A42984-2004Oct18?language=printer (accessed January 4, 2005).

Morton, R., and K. Williams. 2006. *Experimental political science and the study of causality.* Unpublished manuscript. New York Univ.

Moskalenko, S., C. McCauley, and P. Rozin. 2006. Group identification under conditions of threat: College students' attachment to country, family, ethnicity, religion, and university before and after September 11, 2001. *Political Psychology* 27 (1): 77–97.

Mueller, J. E. 1970. Presidential popularity from Truman to Johnson. *American Political Science Review* 64 (1): 18–34.

———. 1971. Trends in popular support for the wars in Korea and Vietnam. *American Political Science Review* 65 (2): 358–75.

———. 1973. *War, presidents, and public opinion.* New York: John Wiley.

———. 1979. Public expectations of war during the Cold War. *American Journal of Political Science* 23:301–29.

———. 2006. *Overblown: How politicians and the terrorism industry inflate national security threats, and why we believe them.* New York: Free Press.

Mutz, D. C. 1992. Mass media and the depoliticization of personal experience. *American Journal of Political Science* 36 (2): 483–508.

Nagourney, A., and J. Elder. 2006. New poll finds mixed support for wiretaps. *New York Times.* http://www.nytimes.com/2006/01/27/politics/27poll.html (accessed January 31, 2006).

Nelson, T. E., Rosalee A. Clawson, and Z. M. Oxley. 1997. Media framing of a civil liberties conflict and its effect on tolerance. *American Political Science Review* 91 (3): 567–83.

Nelson, T. E., and Z. M. Oxley. 1999. Issue framing effects on belief importance and opinion. *Journal of Politics* 61 (4): 1040–67.

Nichols, D. K. 1994. *The myth of the modern presidency.* University Park: Penn State Press.

Nie, N. H., S. Verba, and J. R. Petrocik. 1976. *The changing American voter.* Cambridge: Harvard Univ. Press.

Nincic, M. 1992. *Democracy and foreign policy: The fallacy of political realism.* New York: Columbia Univ. Press.

Nyhan, B., and J. Reifler. 2006. Why are political misperceptions so difficult to correct? Paper presented at annual meeting of the American Political Science Association, Philadelphia, September 1.

O'Donnell, G. A. 1996. Illusions about consolidation. *Journal of New Democracy* 7 (2): 34–51.

———. 1998. Horizontal accountability in new democracies. *Journal of Democracy* 9 (3): 112–26.

Oxley, Z., and A. Gangl. 2007. Appealing to women: The 2004 U.S. presidential election. Paper presented at the annual meeting of the International Society of Political Psychology, Portland, Oregon, July 4–7, 2007.

Page, B. I., and R. A. Brody. 1972. Policy voting and the electoral process: The Vietnam issue. *American Political Science Review* 66 (3): 979–88.

Page, B. I., and R. Y. Shapiro. 1988. Foreign policy and the rational public. *Journal of Conflict Resolution* 32: 211–47.

———. 1992. *The rational public: Fifty years of opinion trends.* Chicago: Univ. of Chicago Press.

Petrocik, J. R. 1974. An analysis of intransitivities in the index of party identification. *Political Methodology* 1 (3): 31–47.

———. 1996. Issue ownership in presidential elections, with a 1980 case study. *American Journal of Political Science* 40 (3): 825–50.

Pillai, R. 1996. Crisis and the emergence of charismatic leadership in groups: An experimental investigation. *Journal of Applied Social Psychology* 26 (2): 543–62.

Pillai, R, J. C. Kohles, and M. C. Bligh. 2007. Through thick and thin: Follower constructions of presidential leadership amidst crises, 2001-2005. In *Follower-centered perspectives on leadership: A tribute to the memory of James R. Meindl*, ed. B. Shamir, R. Pillai, M. C. Bligh, and M. Uhl-Bien, 135–65. Greenwich, CT: Information Age Publishing.

Pillai, R., and J. R. Meindl. 1998. Context and charisma: A "meso" level examination of the relationship of organic structure, collectivism, and crisis to charismatic leadership. *Journal of Management* 24 (5): 643–64.

Pillai, R., and E. A. Williams. 1998. Does leadership matter in the political arena? Voter perceptions of candidates' transformational and charismatic leadership and the 1996 US presidential vote. *Leadership Quarterly* 9 (3): 397–416.

Pillai, R., E. A. Williams, K.B. Lowe, and D. I. Jung. 2003. Personality, transformational leadership, trust, and the 2000 US presidential vote. *Leadership Quarterly* 14 (2): 161–92.

Pomper, G. 1972. From confusion to clarity: Issues and American voters, 1956–1968. *American Political Science Review* 66:415–28

Powell, G. B., Jr. 1986. American voter turnout in comparative perspective. *American Political Science Review* 80:17–43.

Powell, G. B., Jr., and G. D. Whitten. 1993. A cross-national analysis of economic voting: Taking account of the political context. *American Journal of Political Science* 37:391–414.

Putnam, R. 2002. *Democracies in flux: The evolution of social capital in contemporary society.* New York: Oxford Univ. Press.

Przeworski, A., M. E. Alvarez, J. A. Cheibub, and F. Limongi. 2000. *Democracy and development: Political institutions and well-being in the world, 1950-1990.* New York: Cambridge Univ. Press.

Pyszczynski, T. A., S. Solomon, and J. Greenberg. 2002. *In the wake of 9/11: The psychology of terror.* Washington, D.C.: American Psychological Association.

Radcliff, B. 1992. The welfare state, turnout, and the economy: A comparative analysis. *American Political Science Review* 86 (2): 444–54.

Rahn, W. M., J. H. Aldrich, E. Borgida, and J. L. Sullivan. 1990. A social-cognitive model of candidate appraisal. In *Information and Democratic Processes*, ed. J. Ferejohn and J. Kuklinski. Urbana: Univ. of Illinois Press.

Ramakrishnan, K., and T. Wong. 2008. Immigration policies go local: The varying responses of local governments to undocumented immigration. Working Paper for the Chief Justice Earl Warren Institute on Race, Ethnicity, and Diversity.

Rehnquist, W. H. 1998. *All the laws but one: Civil liberties in wartime.* New York: Vintage Books.

Rickert, E. J. 1998. Authoritarianism and economic threat: Implications for political behavior. *Political Psychology* 19 (4): 707–20.

Riker, W. H. 1982. *Liberalism against populism: A confrontation between the theory of democracy and the theory of social choice*. San Francisco: W. H. Freeman.

Roberts, K. 2000. Populism and democracy in Latin America. Paper prepared for presentation at the Carter Center's Conference on *Challenges to Democracy*. http://www.cartercenter.org/documents/nondatabase/Roberts.pdf (accessed April 30, 2007).

Roberts, K, and M. Arce. 1998. Neoliberalism and lower-class voting behavior in Peru. *Comparative Political Studies* 31 (2): 217–46.

Roberts, K. M. 1995. Neoliberalism and the transformation of populism in Latin America: The Peruvian case. *World Politics* 48 (1): 82–116.

Rogers, M. Brooke, R. Amlot, G. J. Rubin, S. Wessely, and K. Krieger. 2007. Mediating the social and psychological impacts of terrorist attacks: The role of risk perception and communication. *International Review of Psychiatry* 19 (3): 279–88.

Rokeach, M. 1960. *The open and closed mind: Investigations into the nature of belief systems and personality Systems*. New York: Basic Books.

Roth, A. E. 1988. Laboratory experimentation in economics: A methodology overview. *Economic Journal* 393:974–1031.

Russet, B. 1990. *Controlling the sword*. Cambridge: Harvard Univ. Press.

Sales, S. M. 1972. Economic threat as a determinant of conversion rates in authoritarian and nonauthoritarian churches. *Journal of Personality and Social Psychology* 23 (3): 420–28.

———. 1973. Threat as a factor in authoritarianism: An analysis of archival data. *Journal of Personality and Social Psychology* 23 (3): 44–57.

Sales, S. M., and K. E. Friend. 1973. Success and failure as determinants of level of authoritarianism. *Behavioral Science* 18:163–72.

Sandler, T. 2003. Collective action and transnational terrorism. *World Economy* 26: 779–802.

———. 2005. Collective versus unilateral responses to terrorism. *Public Choice* 124:75–93.

Sandler, T., and H. E. Lapan. 1988. The calculus of dissent: An analysis of terrorists' choice of targets. *Synthese* 76:245–61.

Schlenger, W. E., Juesta M. Caddell, L. Ebert, B. K. Jordan, K. M. Rourke, D. Wilson, L. Thalji, M. Dennis, J. A. Fairbank, and R. A. Kulka. 2002. Psychological reactions to terrorist attacks. *JAMA* 288 (5): 581–88.

Schudson, M. 1998. *The good citizen: A history of American civic life*. New York: Free Press.

Schuster, M. A., B. D. Stein, L. H. Jaycox, R. L. Collins, G. N. Marshall, M. N. Elliot, A. J. Zhou, D. E. Kanouse, J. L. Morrison, and S. H. Berry. 2001. A national survey of stress reactions after the September 11, 2001, terrorist attacks. *New England Journal of Medicine* 345:1507–12.

Schweller, R. L. 1997. New realist research on alliances: Refining, not refuting, Walt's balancing proposition. *American Political Science Review* 91 (4): 927–30.

Sears, D. 1986. College sophomores in the laboratory: Influences of a narrow data base on social psychology's view of human nature. *Journal of Personality and Social Psychology* 86:515–30.

Shamir, B. 1994. Ideological position, leaders' charisma, and voting preferences: Personal vs. partisan elections. *Political Behavior* 16 (2): 265–87.

Shamir, B., and J. M. Howell. 1999. Organizational and contextual influences on the emergence and effectiveness of charismatic leadership. *Leadership Quarterly* 10 (2): 257–83.

Shamir, B., E. Zakay, E. Breinin, and M. Popper. 1998. Correlates of charismatic leader behavior in military units: Subordinates' attitudes, unit of characteristics, and superiors' appraisals of leader performance. *Academy of Management Journal* 41 (4): 387–409.

Shaw, D. R., and B. H. Sparrow. 1999. From the inner ring out: News congruence, cue-taking, and campaign coverage. *Political Research Quarterly* 52 (2): 323–51.

Skocpol, T. 2002. Will 9/11 and the war on terror revitalize American civil democracy? *American Political Science Association* 35:537–40.

Smith, T 1987. That which we call Welfare by any other name would smell sweeter: An analysis of the impact of question wording on response patterns. *Public Opinion Quarterly* 51 (1): 75–83.

Sniderman, P. M., R. A. Brody, and P. E. Tetlock. 1991. *Reasoning and choice: Explorations in political psychology.* New York: Cambridge Univ. Press.

Spinrad, W. 1991. Charisma: A blighted concept and an alternate formula. *Political Science Quarterly* 106 (2): 295–311.

Stenner, K. 2005. *The authoritarian dynamic.* New York: Cambridge Univ. Press.

Stewart, M. C., and H. D. Clarke. 1992. The (un)importance of party leaders: Leader images and party choice in the 1987 British election. *Journal of Politics* 54 (2): 447–70.

Stone, G. R. 2004. *Perilous times: Free speech in wartime from the Sedition Acts in 1798 to the war on terrorism.* New York: W. W. Norton.

Stouffer, S. 1955. *Communism, conformity, and civil liberties.* New York: Doubleday.

Sullivan, J. L., J. E. Piereson, and G. E. Marcus. 1978. Ideological constraint in the mass public: A methodological critique and some new findings. *American Journal of Political Science* 22:233–49.

———. 1982. *Political Tolerance and American Democracy.* Chicago: Univ. of Chicago Press.

Tejeda, M. J., T. A. Scandura, and R. Pillai. 2001. The MLQ revisited: Psychometric properties and recommendations. *Leadership Quarterly* 12 (1): 31–52.

Tomz, M., J. Wittenberg, and G. King. 2001. CLARIFY: Software for interpreting and presenting statistical results. Version 2.0. Cambridge: Harvard Univ.

Traugott, M., T. Brader, D. Coral, R. Curtin, D. Featherman, R. Groves, M. Hill, J. Jackson, T. Juster, R. Kahn, C. Kennedy, D. Kinder, B. Pennell, M. Shapiro, M. Tessler, D. Weir, and R. Willis. 2002. How Americans responded: A study of public reactions to 9/11/01. *Political Science and Politics* 35:511–16.

Valentino, N. A., V. L. Hutchings, K. Gregorowicz, E. W. Groenendyk, and T. Brader. 2006. Election night's alright for fighting: The participatory impact of negative emotions. Paper presented at the annual meeting of the American Political Science Association, Philadelphia, August 31–September 3.

Walt, S. M. 1987. *The origins of alliances.* Ithaca: Cornell Univ. Press.

Waltz, K. N. 1979. *Theory of international politics.* New York: McGraw-Hill.

Watson, D., L. A. Clark, and A. Tellegen. 1988. Development and validation of brief measures of positive and negative affect: The PANAS scales. *Journal of Personality and Social Psychology* 54:1063–70.

Weber, M. 1922. *Wirtschaft und Gesellschaft*. Tubingen: J.C.B. Mohr.

———. 1947. *The theory of social and economic organization*. Translated by A. M. Henderson and T. Parsons. New York: Oxford Univ. Press.

Weyland, K. 2001. Will Chavez lose his luster? *Foreign Affairs* 80 (6): 73–88.

———. 2002. *The politics of fragile reforms in market democracies. Argentina, Brazil, Peru, and Venezuela*. Princeton, NJ: Princeton Univ. Press.

———. 2003. Economic voting reconsidered: Crisis and charisma in the election of Hugo Chavez. *Comparative Political Studies* 36:822–48.

Willer, R. 2004. The effects of government-issued terror warnings on presidential approval ratings. *Current Research in Social Psychology* 10 (1): 1–12.

Willner, A. R. 1984. *The spellbinders: Charismatic political leadership*. New Haven: Yale Univ. Press.

Wittkopf, E. R. 1986. On the foreign policy beliefs of the American people: A critique and some evidence. *International Studies Quarterly* 30:425–45.

Zaller, J. 1992. *The nature and origins of mass opinion*. New York: Cambridge Univ. Press.

Index